A Geography of Heritage

Power, Culture and Economy

BRIAN GRAHAM
Professor of Human Geography, University of Ulster,
Coleraine, Northern Ireland

G. J. ASHWORTH
Professor of Heritage Management and Urban Tourism,
University of Groningen, The Netherlands

J. E. TUNBRIDGE
Associate Professor of Geography,
Carleton University, Ottawa, Canada

A member of the Hodder Headline Group
LONDON
Distributed in the United States of America by
Oxford University Press Inc., New York

First published in Great Britain in 2000
This impression reprinted in 2004 by
Arnold, a member of the Hodder Headline Group,
338 Euston Road, London NW1 3BH

http://www.arnoldpublishers.com

Distributed in the United States of America by
Oxford University Press Inc.,
198 Madison Avenue, New York, NY10016

© 2000 Brian Graham, G. J. Ashworth and J. E. Tunbridge

British Library Cataloguing in Publication Data
A catalogue record for this book is available from the British Library

Library of Congress Cataloging in Publication Data
A catalog record for this book is available from the Library of Congress

ISBN 0 340 67779 1 (hb)
ISBN 0 340 67778 3 (pb)

3 4 5 6 7 8 9 10

Typeset by Saxon Graphics Ltd, Derby
Printed and bound in India by Replika Press Pvt. Ltd.

What do you think about this book? Or any other Arnold title?
Please send your comments to feedback.arnold@hodder.co.uk

Contents

Part III: The economic uses of heritage

Part IV: Heritage and scale

Acknowledgements

Despite our shared general agreement on the nature of geography and heritage, the book still embraces a variety of perspectives and concerns because we do not necessarily subscribe to a common political agenda, nor are we fully in agreement on the importance of the 'cultural turn' in geography. In addition, the divergent educational cultures in the United Kingdom, The Netherlands and Canada have led to different priorities and demands being placed on the authors as the book has evolved. In many ways, however, the difficulties which we have encountered in writing the book faithfully mirror the complexities of heritage itself. It is not an agreed enterprise. Thus while our varying perspectives and priorities have certainly complicated the process of writing the book, they have allowed us to approach the study of this contested field of enquiry from several angles, which, we hope, is precisely what the heterogeneous nature of a geography of heritage requires.

We would like to express our deep gratitude to Kilian McDaid and Nigel McDowell of the University of Ulster at Coleraine for their invaluable help in preparing the figures. We must also thank Laura McKelvie, formerly Geography Editor at Arnold, for commissioning the book and being so supportive in its early stages. Her successor, Luciana O'Flaherty, who has shown great patience as several deadlines came and went, has maintained that faith in the project.

Introduction: heritage and geography

The central aim of this book is to trace and explain the relationships between heritage and geography. The first is an idea that is being increasingly loaded with so many different connotations as to be in danger of losing all meaning; the second is a discipline, which, while noted for its wide-ranging and eclectic interests and absence of agreed content, maintains some form of common focus around its interest in space and place. Our first task in a book which contains both terms so prominently in the title, is to state what we mean and thus to establish some delimitation of the phenomenon and of our particular approach to it.

What is heritage?

Until only a few decades ago, the word heritage was commonly used only to describe an inheritance that an individual received in the will of a deceased ancestor or bequeathed when dead to descendants. The range of meanings attached to this formerly precise legal term has recently undergone a quantum expansion to include almost any sort of intergenerational exchange or relationship, welcome or not, between societies as well as individuals. In North America, and increasingly also in Europe, support for artistic performances and productivity, whether of the past or present, is justified in terms of them being actual or potential heritage. The current social behaviour of individuals is explained and excused in terms of their group or individual heritage. Poor economic performances of industries, countries or even whole continents are blamed upon a heritage of capitalist exploitation, slavery or colonialism. Official heritage agencies and ministries around the world have assumed responsibility for a wide range of contemporary cultural, sporting, or media activities regarded as constituting a national heritage. A growing commercial heritage industry is commodifying pasts into heritage products and experiences for sale as part of a modern consumption of entertainment. The adjective, 'heritage', is not only being applied to the provision of goods and services that come from or relate to a past in some way, however vaguely, but is increasingly being use to convey a feeling of generalized quality, continuity or simply familiarity and well-being. What can we make of a term now used to cover such a range of occurrences?

First, let us be clear what we do not mean. Although the three terms, the past, history and heritage, have elided in practice into interchangeable synonyms, they are clearly separated in our arguments. The past, all that has ever happened, is not our direct concern: indeed the debate concerning the existence of the past as an objective reality is not a precondition for the creation of heritage. The attempts of successive presents to relate and explain selected aspects of a past is the concern of the historical disciplines, while the collection, preservation and documentation of the records and physical remains of the past is a task for archivists and antiquarians. If these concerns, however, focus upon the ways in which we use the past now, or upon the attempts of a present to project aspects of itself into an imagined future, then we are engaged with heritage. The concept of time has remained central: heritage is a view from the present, either backward to a past or forward to a future. In both cases, the viewpoint cannot be other than now, the perspective is blurred and indistinct and shaped by current concerns and predispositions, while the field of vision is restricted to a highly selective view of a small fraction of possible pasts or envisaged futures. None of these conditions are in themselves significant as rendering heritage less accurate, less real or less important than other ways of treating the past, or considering the future. Simply, it is different.

The straightforward definition of heritage as the contemporary use of the past has the advantage of side-stepping some contentious issues, while improving the focus upon others. The present needs of people form the key defining element in our definition. We are not concerned, therefore, with whether one piece of heritage is historically more correct, intrinsically authentic, innately valuable or qualitatively more worthy than another. If people in the present are the creators of heritage, and not merely passive receivers or transmitters of it, then the present creates the heritage it requires and manages it for a range of contemporary purposes. Like many other aspects of modern society, this can be done well or badly, for the benefit, or at the cost, of few or many. It is the focus on present use that prompts the key questions addressed in this book.

In this respect, perhaps the easiest way to conceptualize our interpretation of heritage is through the idea of representation. Hall (1997) argues that culture is essentially concerned with the production and exchange of meaning and their real, practical effects. 'It is by our use of things, and what we say, think and feel about them – how we represent them – that we give them a meaning' (Hall 1997, p. 3). Although he is writing specifically of language as one of the media through which meaning is transmitted, heritage can be regarded as analogous. Like language, it is one of the mechanisms by which meaning is produced and reproduced. Hall proposes a 'cultural circuit',

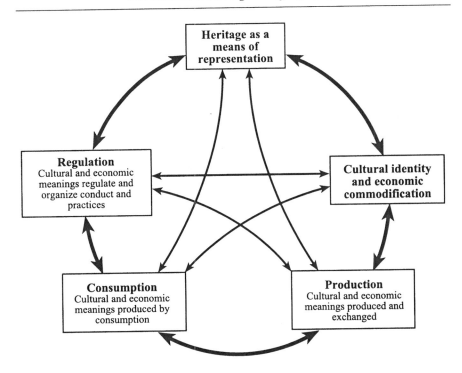

Figure I.1   A circuit of heritage
Source: Adapted from Hall (1997, p. 1)

which can be extended to include heritage. In terms of language, meaning is marked out by identity, and is being produced and exchanged through social interaction in a variety of media; it is also being produced through consumption. Finally, meanings also regulate and organize our conduct and practices by helping set rules, norms and conventions (Figure I.1). If language is a 'signifying practice', then so too is heritage.

> It is us – in society, within human culture – who make things mean, who signify. Meanings, consequently, will always change, from one culture or period to another.
>
> (Hall 1997, p. 61)

But the synonymity is not precise because heritage also exists as an economic commodity, which may overlap, conflict with or even deny its cultural role. It is capable of being interpreted differently within any one culture at any one time, as well as between cultures and through time. Heritage fulfils several inherently opposing uses and carries conflicting meanings simultaneously. It is this intrinsic dissonance, or lack of agreement as to what constitutes a heritage defined by meaning, which, paradoxically, acts as the cement to this book's arguments.

What is a geography of heritage?

A principal aim of this book is to integrate the study of heritage into the wider realm of contemporary cultural and economic geography. Despite the close analogy between the conceptualization of heritage and that, for example, of landscape, hitherto the geographical debate on heritage has remained uneasily poised between being an addendum to tourism studies and forming an isolated, self-sustaining if micro-scale theme within the discipline. Heritage, cultural and economic geography and tourism literature commonly proceed on parallel tracks, rarely overlapping despite their shared concerns. In seeking to locate heritage in the wider geographical realm and its contestation, the book seeks to redress this curious division of labour. We can identify three dimensions along which heritage and geography intersect.

In the first instance, heritage is inherently a spatial phenomenon. All heritage occurs somewhere and the relationship between a heritage object, building, association or idea and its place may be important in a number of ways. These concerns reoccur in various guises throughout the book but can be summarized here.

- Location: if heritage occurs somewhere then the traditional geographical questions of 'where?' and 'why is it there?' are relevant. Although all heritage is someone's heritage, and thus inseparable from people, even if constructed from non-human elements, not all heritage is bound to specific places. Much is, however, and thus sites, points and locations can contribute to heritage or even, in themselves, be someone's heritage.
- Distribution: similarly once space is involved, then some places will have more or less, or simply different heritage. Furthermore, heritage can be moved across space, one often potent source of disagreement and conflict as to its meaning.
- Scale: an intrinsic attribute of places is that they exist within a hierarchy of spatial scales. Places therefore have a heritage at local, regional, national, continental and international scales, while, in turn, a particular heritage artefact can function at a variety of scales.

Second, heritage is of fundamental importance to the interests of contemporary cultural and historical geography, which focus on signification, representation and the crucial issue of identity. Places are distinguished from each other by many attributes that contribute to their identity and to the identification of individuals and groups within them. Heritage is one of these attributes. The sense, or more usually senses, of place is both an input and an output of the process of heritage creation. Geography is concerned with the ways in which the past is remembered and represented in both formal or official senses and within popular forms, and the implications which these have for the present and for ideas and constructs of belonging.

The stories and places of contemporary heritage are often the most overt examples of the contemporary politics of the past, but other historical forms, including the writing of . . . geography, need to consider the implications of the ways in which the past is retold. Much of the stimulus for this critical reflection . . . comes from challenges to local, national, or global historical narratives, which have excluded or marginalised women, the working class, minority ethnic groups, indigenous people or the histories and cultures of the non-Western world.

(Nash and Graham 1999, p. 2)

Thus instead of simply attempting to uncover or reconstruct the geographies of the past, the study of heritage, like that of geography itself, involves acknowledging the ways in which interpretations are context bound and power laden. Moreover, the conceptualization of heritage as meaning rather than artefact inevitably ensures that it is a field of social conflict and tension, carrying differing and incompatible meanings simultaneously.

Finally, as we have explained above, heritage is both a cultural and an economic good and is commodified as such. This multiple use and consumption occurs with virtually all heritage and is a potent source of conflict between the various interest groups involved. In so far as geography is concerned with issues of regional development and regeneration, urban planning and tourism, heritage constitutes a prime element in these processes and a principal component of the various strategies of policy implementation. Consequently, the economic commodification of heritage is one factor among many in evaluating the success or otherwise of spatially oriented development policies. Customarily, however, the geographical literature has been more concerned – if it is interested at all – with the cultural connotations of heritage. It is one of the functions of this book to attempt an integration of these dual and often inherently conflicting cultural and economic roles.

The themes and structure of the book

Our discussion of this integration of the cultural and economic domains and of geography and heritage is organized through three distinct themes:

- the plurality of use and consumption of heritage as, simultaneously, a multi-sold cultural and economic resource;
- the conflicts and tensions that arise from this multiple construction of heritage with its connotations of who decides what is heritage?
- the interaction of the production and consumption of heritage with an array of geographical scales and identities, the question here being – whose heritage is it?

The book itself is divided into four rather unequal parts.

The single chapter in Part I provides the conceptual introduction to the book and establishes the issues which we pursue in subsequent discussion. It briefly addresses the origins, and provides a general outline of the uses of heritage. We explain how contestation – conceptualized as dissonance – is an intrinsic quality of heritage, but demonstrate that it also stems from its multiple uses and roles and the variety of scales implicated in the definition and meaning of heritage.

Part II deals with heritage and the cultural realm, examining its social and political uses and contestation. Linked by the underlying theme of dissonance (*see* Chapter 1), the four chapters deal primarily with the relationships between heritage and identity. The social and political uses of heritage are so complexly interlinked that they are considered together here because they cannot effectively be separated. Chapter 2 sets out the general relationships between heritage, power and identity and establishes the many axes along which the meanings of heritage are defined. In Chapter 3, we concentrate on modernist depictions of identity in which the primary axis of contestation is defined by nationalism. The relationships between heritage, modernity and national identity are explored, as are their enduring significance, post-Cold War Central and Eastern Europe providing a key example. Chapter 4, in contrast, examines the role of heritage in more fragmented postmodern conceptions of the world, defined by multiple feelings of belonging and an apparent diminution in the importance of identity as bounded by place. We argue, however, that both place and nationalism retain an enduring significance. Finally, Chapter 5 addresses the evidence for multicultural societies, drawing on a number of examples and discussing the potential for dissonance which exists within them.

In Part III, the emphasis switches to the economic uses of heritage, the broad dichotomy between the cultural and economic uses of heritage constituting a potent source of contestation. Economic connotations have often been added later to artefacts first endowed with cultural meaning. In addition, because heritage is multi-sold and multi-consumed, any example, whether building, art object or landscape, carries with it an array of conflicting cultural and economic motivations and messages. Heritage has also emerged as a primary economic good in tourism, now the world's largest service industry. Nevertheless, this economic dimension has received far less research attention than the cultural realm, shown, for example, by the absence in the literature of an economic conceptualization of heritage.

The two chapters in Part III attempt to redress this imbalance, one which has to be considered to make sense of the scale and management issues discussed in Part IV. In Chapter 6, the ambiguous relationship between heritage and economics is explored, first through a study of the economics of heritage and secondly, by a consideration of the role of heritage in economics. Chapter 7 focuses specifically on the role of heritage in economic development strategies at a variety of scales, concluding with a set of illustrative case studies.

Finally, Part IV deals at some length with the question of heritage and scale. The four chapters included here continue the analysis of the relationships between people, heritage and places but the focus is changed so that place – in the sense of spatial scale – rather than function becomes the central variable. In addition, we examine the implications of the complex cultural and economic constructions and meanings of heritage for this multiplicity of layerings of scale, which range from the global to the local. This basic geographical characteristic has implications for identity and identification. Places at different scales may have different identities, which may be mutually reinforcing, irrelevant or contradictory. Heritage plays a distinctive role at each of these scales, while people may identify, with varying strength of conviction, with one or more such scales. Part IV successively examines the national, local, continental and global connotations of heritage and further explores how places at various scales acquire identities and the ways in which people identify with places at those scales. Central to this discussion is the importance of the role of heritage management. Thus the key questions posed include:

- those of motive – at which scale is heritage needed and who has this requirement?
- those of management – at which scale is heritage created and managed by institutions and related instruments?

This interpretation of heritage and scale concludes a book, which, in its making and through its themes, demonstrates the vibrancy and relevance of the study of heritage to contemporary cultural, political and economic geography. As Heffernan (1997, p. 2) argues in his justification for the present importance of historical geography:

> Traditional disciplinary allegiances, like traditional political ideologies and economic structures, are collapsing into a more fluid (and potentially liberating) kaleidoscope of reformulations, reconfigurations and deconstructions. In these circumstances, the intellectual necessity of a hybrid disciplinary arena in which spaces, places, environments and landscapes are considered and analysed historically, not as an exercise in antiquarianism, but as a commentary with direct bearing on the contemporary scene, becomes all the more urgent.

We do not analyse heritage through an historical methodology, but we share Heffernan's concern about the necessity of more fully understanding the interaction of the past and present. Heritage is about the political and economic structures of the present using the past as a resource, but as that present becomes markedly more diverse and heterogeneous, heritage itself becomes ever more complex and malleable, not so much in its physical extent as in the conflicting meanings which are piled upon it.

PART

I

The context

1

The uses and abuses of heritage

Introduction

This chapter establishes the context for the debate. It first considers the origins of heritage as defined by using the past as a resource for the present. We show how this way of thinking about the past emerged at the same time as the codification of nationalism into the nation-state. Second, we begin our explanation of the functions and uses of heritage, which can be subdivided between the cultural – or socio-political – and the economic. Finally, in examining the issue of 'whose heritage?', we begin to consider the reasons for the contested nature of heritage.

The origins of heritage

Heritage, or a concern for the past, emerged from the raft of ideas and ideologies which loosely constitute what we have come to know as modernity. The 'modern' is usually divided into the early modern of the sixteenth and seventeenth centuries, the modern eighteenth and nineteenth centuries, and the (post)modern twentieth century. The modern era, as traditionally defined, often necessarily reflects a Eurocentric perspective on the world. The European eighteenth and nineteenth centuries are seen as being the apogee of modernism as the secular culture conceived in the Renaissance ultimately evolved into the eighteenth-century Enlightenment, the Age of Reason with its belief in an individual's ability to think and act for oneself. The concept of the European territorial state was shaped within such a mindset, the French Revolution being a defining catalyst in this process. Like the Renaissance before it, we can see the Enlightenment being framed by its particular rendition of the past, one in which the values and traditions of European Christianity were depicted as the principal reactionary forces in

European society. In turn, the modern era is defined by the emergence of the 'one-out-of-many' meta-narrative of nationalism as 'the ideology of belong-ingness' (Hall 1995, p. 185) and principal force of legitimation in the processes of state formation. For Woolf (1996, pp. 25–6):

> National identity is an abstract concept that sums up the collective expression of a subjective, individual sense of belonging to a socio-political unit: the nation state. Nationalist rhetoric assumes not only that individuals form part of a nation (through language, blood, choice, residence, or some other criterion), but that they identify with the terri-torial unit of the nation state.

Hobsbawm (1990), for example, regards nationalism as pre-eminently the product of triumphant bourgeois liberalism in the period *ca.* 1830–1880, although other commentators place its origins rather earlier. Colley (1992) locates the making of a Britishness vested in recurrent Protestant wars, com-mercial success and imperial conquest to the eighteenth century, while Hastings (1997) argues for an even earlier medieval origin of both nationalism and nations. Although it is often argued that nationalism received its biggest boost from the French Revolution, its crystallization as the driving social and political force of nineteenth- and early twentieth-century Europe stems from a succes-sion of previous 'revolutions' that transformed societies in Europe – and North America – between the sixteenth and eighteenth centuries. In parts of Europe, the cumulative effect was to replace the medieval power structures of church and nobility with a recognizably capitalist and secular élite. Nevertheless, as Davies (1996, p. 821) argues, irrespective of the precise relationship between nationalism and modernization, 'it is indisputable that the modernizing process expanded the role of nationalism beyond all previous limits'.

In this conceptualization of a political state that is also the homeland of a single, homogeneous people, heritage is a primary instrument in the 'discov-ery' or creation and subsequent nurturing of a national identity. Nationalism, and a representation of the past designated as 'national heritage', developed synchronously as the 'nation' was asserted over communities defined by other spatial scales or social relationships. The nation-state required national heritage for a variety of reasons. It supported the consolidation of this national identification, while absorbing or neutralizing potentially competing heritages of social-cultural groups or regions. Again, a national heritage helped combat the claims of other nations upon the nation's territory or peo-ple, while furthering claims upon nationals in territories elsewhere. Small wonder then that the fostering of national heritage has long been a major responsibility of governments and that the provision of many aspects of her-itage has become in most countries a near-monopoly of national govern-ments. (We return to these issues in Chapters 3 and 8, which consider the creation and content of national heritage.)

In turn, the Age of Reason spawned its antithesis in a nineteenth-century Romanticism, that emphasized the irrational and the deification of nature.

Familiar in literature from the works of a panoply of writers and poets, including Goethe, Shelley and Wordsworth, these ideas informed the work of the 'prophets of wilderness' as Schama (1995, p. 7) calls the nineteenth-century founding fathers of modern environmentalism. Among others, Henry David Thoreau, George Perkins Marsh and John Muir were responsible for the representation of the American West as a 'wilderness . . . awaiting discovery . . . an antidote for the poisons of industrial society'. Schama (1995, p. 61) argues, however, that:

> [l]andscapes are culture before they are nature; constructs of the imagination projected onto wood and water and rock . . . But it should also be acknowledged that once a certain idea of landscape, a myth, a vision, establishes itself in an actual place, it has a peculiar way of muddling categories, of making metaphors more real than their referents; of becoming, in fact, part of the scenery.

Indeed, that idea of landscape became institutionalized in the later nineteenth century through the creation of the United States's national parks. The first, the 'strange unearthly topography' of the Yosemite Valley, was established by an Act of Congress in 1864, testimony, as Schama (1995, p. 7) observes, that the 'wilderness . . . does not locate itself, does not name itself'. National parks were originally identified with natural environmental heritage and commonly prompted or paralleled the development of a system of national historic parks or sites to conserve places of cultural significance. It became apparent early on, however, that the two realms could not be separated satisfactorily. Thus national park agencies in the wider world of European settlement have been instrumental in the creation of cultural heritage, not least through establishing the hegemony of Eurocentric imagings of place at the expense, for example, of the landscape representations particular to the cultures of the indigenous peoples.

Equally, it is salutary to remember that the desire to preserve large parts of the existing built environment is both recent and historically aberrant. While it is possible to cite odd cases from settlement history of the deliberate preservation of particular buildings – usually for symbolic reasons – these remain exceptions to the general trend that what we now possess has survived through chance, neglect and lack of motive to redevelop, rather than the deliberate act of preservation, an idea that dates only to the late eighteenth and nineteenth centuries. Religious buildings are something of an exception to this generalization as they were commonly continuously maintained, if not actually self-consciously preserved, as we would understand that term. In terms of the cultural past, the Romantic concomitant to wilderness was a renewed fascination with the medieval world, which had been marginalized both by Renaissance and Enlightenment thinkers. Although 'Gothic' was used in the eighteenth century to denote the barbarous and uncouth, it has since become synonymous with the architecture of Northern Europe's great medieval cathedrals, which were one of the cardinal enthusiasms of the

Romantics who conflated a hatred of industrial civilization with a vision of a rationalist and even ideal Middle Ages. John Ruskin's minutely detailed descriptions of the cathedrals at Rouen, Amiens and Bourges were among the principal inspirations of Marcel Proust's rendering of the past recreated through memory in *A la Recherche du Temps Perdue*. Besides Ruskin, the key figures – largely anti-modernist Romantics – included A. W. N. Pugin and William Morris in Britain, together with the Frenchmen, Eugène Viollet-le-Duc and Prosper Mérimée.

Thus the will to conserve was the obsession of a passionate, educated and generally influential minority and the social, educational and political characteristics of heritage producers have changed little since the nineteenth century. The initiative for the identification and conservation of heritage was by no means always governmental, but was frequently triggered by the concerns of private citizens for the protection of a past legacy perceived to be disappearing under the weight of nineteenth-century urbanization and industrialization. In some major cases the initiative began and remained with voluntary organizations, which succeeded in winning governmental favour and the necessary legislative protection for their activities. Among these, by far the most successful and best known are the British National Trusts, founded in 1895 (England, Wales and Northern Ireland) and 1931 (Scotland), which in

Figure 1.1 The restored medieval cité of Carcassonne, Aude, France, which once guarded the routeway separating the Montagne Noire in the north and the Corbières massif to the south

Figure 1.2 Carcassonne's fortified Porte d'Aude demonstrates Viollet-le-Duc's style of restoration

conserving natural and cultural heritage have become the biggest private landowners, pillars of national culture in their own right and increasingly potent agents of geographical change (Tunbridge 1981).

In the nineteenth century, the idea that some buildings and even cityscapes should not be replaced when physical or functional obsolescence dictated was thus a novel one. Rather, because they contained transferable values, whether architectural/aesthetic, social or moral, particular buildings and townscapes should be preserved (and even 'restored') back to some previous condition (Ashworth 1998). Then as now, the extent of restoration permitted and the definition of 'true' values was the subject of bitter debate and controversy. Hewison (1987) defines preservation as the maintenance of an object, building or landscape in a condition defined by its historic context and in such a way that it can be studied with a view to revealing its original meaning. In so far as it is possible to achieve such an aim, which invokes notions of an objective and value-free history, the careful preservation of archaeological sites or monuments provides the best example. The only rebuilding done is that necessary to preserve the stability of the structure – which may well be a ruin. In contrast, conservation may involve preservation but also restoration of the physical fabric. Much European heritage of apparently medieval origin owes its present appearance to nineteenth-century tastes in restoration.

To paraphrase Ruskin, however, every instance of restoration must lie in the sense that authenticity is unattainable, all heritage being created in and by the present. Extensively restored during the nineteenth century, the contemporary appearance of the *cité* of Carcassonne in south-west France, often described as among Europe's finest medieval towns, owes more to the energetic Viollet-le-Duc's imaging of the Middle Ages than to any 'reality' grounded in academic study of medieval urbanization (Figures 1.1 and 1.2). As Henry James somewhat pretentiously observed of the *cité*, while entirely missing the point:

> One vivid challenge, at any rate, it flings down before you; it calls upon you to make up your mind on the subject of restoration. For myself, I have no hesitation; I prefer in every case the ruined, however ruined, to the reconstructed, however splendid. What is left is more precious than what is added: the one is history, the other is fiction; and I like the former the better of the two – it is so much more romantic.
>
> (James 1884, p. 144)

None the less, the search for authenticity and spirituality took the artist, Paul Gaugin, for example, first to the margins of Europe at Pont-Aven in Brittany, and then to Tahiti. In his evocation of the West of Ireland, the poet, W.B. Yeats, is perhaps 'the supreme example of an artist setting out to construct a deliberate, symbolic landscape allegory of identity, impressing himself on a landscape like a "phase of history"' (cited in Duffy 1997, p. 66).

The celebration of the romantic was paralleled by the processes through which cultures of non-European people were appropriated:

> so called "pre-modern" non-European cultures were both desired and denigrated as "primitive". European discourses of gender and the "primitive" were intermeshed in complex ways, gender on the one hand, structuring these asymmetrical power relations and imaginative geographies of primitivism, and on the other deployed to reinforce European superiority. European discourses of modern and gendered domesticity were central to the ways in which Europeans defined themselves as "modern" in contrast to the "primitivism" of non-European people, and set the privatised, patriarchal, bourgeois nuclear family and culturally specific concepts of reason, individual freedom, citizenship and the nation state as global registers of modernity, and narratives of "progress" as a universal target of development.
>
> (Nash 1999, p. 22)

In sum, nineteenth-century conceptualizations of heritage emerged in the ethos of a singular and totalized modernity, in which it was assumed that to be modern was to be European, and that to be European or to espouse European values (even in the United States) was to be at the pinnacle of cultural achievement and social evolution. The acquisition of the adjective, 'modern', for itself by Europe was an integral part of imperialism and the pinnacle of heritage was to become the European metropolitan cores of the imperial empires.

The functions and uses of heritage

If its origins lie in the tastes and values of a nineteenth-century educated élite, the wider conceptualization of heritage raises many of the same issues that attend the debate on the role of the past and the meaning of place. To reiterate, heritage is that part of the past which we select in the present for contemporary purposes, be they economic, cultural, political or social. The worth attributed to these artefacts rests less in their intrinsic merit than in a complex array of contemporary values, demands and even moralities. As such, heritage can be visualized as a resource but simultaneously, several times so. Clearly, it is an economic resource, one exploited everywhere as a primary component of strategies to promote tourism, economic development and rural and urban regeneration. But heritage also helps define the meanings of culture and power and is a political resource; and it thus possesses a crucial socio-political function. Consequently, it is accompanied by an often bewildering array of identifications and potential conflicts, not least when heritage places and objects are involved in issues of legitimization of power structures.

The social and political uses of heritage

Heritage is a knowledge, a cultural product and a political resource. In Livingstone's terms (1992), the nature of such knowledge is always negotiated, set as it is within specific social and intellectual circumstances. Thus our concern is partly with questions such as why a particular interpretation of heritage is promoted, whose interests are advanced or retarded, and in what kind of *milieu* was it conceived and communicated. If heritage knowledge is situated in particular social and intellectual circumstances, it is time-specific and thus its meaning(s) can be altered as texts are re-read in changing times, circumstances and constructs of place and scale. Consequently, it is inevitable that such knowledges are also fields of contestation.

As Lowenthal (1985, 1996) has argued, this suggests that the past in general, and its interpretation as history or heritage in particular, confers social benefits as well as costs. He notes four traits of the past (which can be taken as synonymous with heritage in this respect) as helping make it beneficial to a people. First, its antiquity conveys the respect and status of antecedence, but, more important perhaps, underpins the idea of continuity and its essentially modernist ethos of progressive, evolutionary social development. Second, societies create emblematic landscapes in which certain artefacts acquire cultural status because they fulfil the need to connect the present to the past in an unbroken trajectory. Third, the past provides a sense of termination in the sense that what happened in it has ended, while, finally, it offers a sequence, allowing us to locate our lives in what we see as a continuity of events.

Although Lowenthal's analysis is couched largely in social terms and pays little attention to the past as an economic resource, it is helpful in identifying the cultural – or more specifically socio-political – functions and uses of heritage. Building on these traits, which can help make the past beneficial to people, Lowenthal sees it as providing familiarity and guidance, enrichment and escape but, more potently perhaps in the context of this book's discussion, we can concentrate on the functions of validation (or legitimation) and identity. The latter can be visualized as a multi-faceted phenomenon that embraces a range of human attributes, including language, religion, ethnicity, nationalism and shared interpretations of the past (Guibernau 1996), and constructs these into discourses of inclusion and exclusion – who qualifies and who does not. This form of definition refers therefore to the processes, categories and knowledges through which communities are defined as such, and the ways in which they are rendered specific and differentiated (Donald and Rattansi 1992). Central to the entire concept of identity is the idea of the Other, groups – both internal and external to a state – with competing, and often conflicting, beliefs, values and aspirations. The attributes of Otherness are thus fundamental to representations of identity, which are constructed in counter-distinction to them. As Douglas (1997, pp. 151–2) argues:

the function of identity lies in providing the basis for making choices and facilitating relationships with others while positively reinforcing these choices . . . In emphasizing sameness, group membership provides the basis for supportive social interaction, coherence and consensus. As identity is expressed and experienced through communal membership, awareness will develop of the Other . . . Recognition of Otherness will help reinforce self-identity, but may also lead to distrust, avoidance, exclusion and distancing from groups so-defined.

According to Lowenthal, the past validates the present by conveying an idea of timeless values and unbroken lineages and through restoring lost or subverted values. Thus, for example, there are archetypal national landscapes, which draw heavily on geographical imagery, memory and myth (Gruffudd 1995). Continuously being transformed, these encapsulate distinct home places of 'imagined communities' (Anderson 1991; *see* Chapter 2), comprising people who are bound by cultural – and more explicitly political – networks, all set within a territorial framework that is defined through whichever traditions are currently acceptable, as much as by its geographical boundary. Such national traditions are narratives that are invented and imposed on space, their legitimacy couched in terms of their relationship to particular representations of the past.

Implicit within such ideas is the sense of belonging to place that is fundamental to identity, itself a heavily contested concept and a theme pursued here in subsequent chapters. Lowenthal sees the past as being integral both to individual and communal representations of identity and its connotations of providing human existence with meaning, purpose and value. Such is the importance of this process that a people cut off from their past through migration or even by its destruction – deliberate or accidental – in war, often recreate it, or even 'recreate' what could or should have been there but never actually was. European cities, for instance, contain numerous examples of painstakingly reconstructed buildings that replace earlier urban fabric destroyed in World War II (Ashworth 1991a).

Inevitably, therefore, the past as rendered through heritage also promotes the burdens of history, the atrocities, errors and crimes of the past which are called upon to legitimate the atrocities of the present. Indeed, as we explore later in the book, atrocity can become heritage. Lowenthal also comments that the past can be a burden in the sense that it often involves a dispiriting and negative rejection of the present. Thus the past can constrain the present, one of the persistent themes of the heritage debate being the role of the degenerative representations of nostalgic pastiche, and their intimations of a bucolic and somehow better past that so often characterize the commercial heritage industry.

The economic uses of heritage

As Sack (1992) states, heritage places are places of consumption and are
arranged and managed to encourage consumption; such consumption can
create places but is also place altering. 'Landscapes of consumption . . .
tend to consume their own contexts', not least because of the 'homogenizing effect on places and cultures' of tourism (Sack 1992, pp. 158–9).
Moreover, preservation and restoration freezes artefacts in time whereas
previously they had been constantly changing. Heritage – variously defined
– is the most important single resource for international tourism. That market is highly segmented but although heritage will be consumed at different
levels by different types of tourist, that consumption is generally superficial
for culture is rapidly consumed. Tourism is an industry with substantial
externalities in that its costs are visited upon those who are not involved in
tourism consumption. The same also applies to the transport industries
upon which tourism depends. Thus tourism is parasitic upon culture, to
which it may contribute nothing. If taken to the extreme, the economic
commodification of the past will so trivialize it that arguably it can result in
the destruction of the heritage resource which is its *raison d'être*. Thus
major European heritage sites such as the Norman monastery of Mont St
Michel (Figure 1.3) or Carcassonne may be seen simultaneously by different observers as either successful and profitable providers of satisfying heritage experiences, or little more than stage-sets for mock medieval displays
and inappropriate economic exchange, infested with tawdry souvenir
shops and cafés. Around them are arrayed the car parks that compound
their trivialization.

Tourism producers operate both in the public and private sectors. They
may be development agencies charged with regional regeneration and
employment creation, or they can be private sector firms concerned
almost entirely with their own profit margins. Whichever, tourism producers impose what may well be relatively unconstrained costs on heritage
resources. In turn, the relationship between costs and benefits is very
indirect. It may well be that the capital from tourism flows back to heritage
resources only indirectly (if at all). It follows, therefore, that heritage
tourism planning and management has enthusiastically embraced the idea
of sustainable development. Notoriously difficult to define, this concept is
usually operationalized through concepts such as parsimony and reuse
of resource inputs, output equities, intergenerational equities, environmental or perceptual carrying capacity, and the internalizing of negative
externalities (*see* Chapters 6 and 7). In sum, sustainability requires that
contemporary development must address the demands of the present
without compromising the ability of future generations to meet their own
requirements.

If heritage is regarded as a resource, sustainability in this context has three
basic conditions. First the rates of use of renewable heritage resources must

Figure 1.3 The dramatically sited Gothic monastery of Mont St Michel, Manche, is the most visited historic monument in France after Versailles

not exceed their rates of generation: in one sense, all heritage resources are renewable because they can be continuously reinterpreted. Their physical fabric, however, is a finite resource, one factor promoting the immense widening of what might be called the heritage portfolio. Second, the rates of use of non-renewable physical heritage resources should not exceed the rate at which sustainable renewable substitutes are developed (for example, the substitution of irreplaceable sites or artefacts with replicas). Finally, the rates of pollution emission associated with heritage tourism should not exceed the assimilative capacity of the environment. Heritage management is thus implicated in the belated recognition that the growth in personal mobility in the western world cannot be sustained indefinitely. Nevertheless, sustainability remains an exceptionally difficult issue, and not only because of the inherent vagueness of the concept. It is about values and rights over resources, the primacy of the economic over the cultural (and vice-versa), public and private and, finally, about individual profit and communal rights.

The duality of heritage

To summarize, therefore, heritage can be visualized as a duality – a resource of economic and cultural capital. This is less a dialectic than a continuous tension, these broad domains generally being in conflict with each other. To put it succinctly, heritage can be visualized as a commodity, moreover one that is simultaneously multi-sold in many segmented market places. The relics and events of the past are thus raw materials which are commodified for contemporary consumption (Ashworth 1991b). The two heritage domains are linked by their shared dependence on the conservation of past artefacts and the meanings with which these are endowed; it is the latter which generally constitute the broad arena of contestation. Within both domains, however, we can detect both 'high' and 'low' constructions of heritage, a dichotomy which enriches and complicates the extent of contestation. The economic commodification of heritage embraces, on one hand, the consumption of culture through art and museums and the largely élitist landscapes protected by agencies such as the United Kingdom's several National Trusts – theatres for the re-enactment of the past in Hewison's terms (1987) – and, on the other, commercial theme-park heritage, largely a pastiche with no higher purpose than popular entertainment. 'High' heritage, in contrast, is generally accorded an educational role in addition to its function as superior entertainment. The cultural commodification of heritage embraces state-sponsored allegories of identity expressed through an iconography that is congruent with processes of legitimation of structures of power, but also more localized renditions of identity, which in their appeal to the popular and resistance to the centre, may be subversive of state power. Tension and conflict are thus inherent qualities of heritage, whatever its form.

Contestation: whose heritage?

The axes of contestation

It is quite inevitable given this range of different uses of heritage, and its importance to so many people for such different reasons, that it has emerged as a major arena of conflict and contestation. In the first instance, the primary contestation lies within heritage itself because of these distinct and often incompatible uses. Heritage is multi-sold and multi-consumed. Urry (1990, 1995) points to the exceptional levels of contestation that result when socially or politically invoked memories, embedded in place, are consumed as tourism commodities. Brett (1996) concurs, regarding heritage as part of the entire cultural logic of late capitalism (post-Fordism), which demands the commodification of everything. Drawing on Baudrillard, he argues that the subsequent piling of representation upon representation could preclude the rediscovery of any absolute level of the real, which, in turn, also renders illusion impossible. Culture disintegrates into pure image without referent, content, or effects, creating a mental landscape in which everything is pastiche (Urry 1995), and combined with its resonances of nostalgia, one that is inimical to the modernist belief in the future. In essence, however, there are élitist connotations to this argument, which depends on the assumption that people are unthinking dupes when interacting with tourism commodities. Consequently, Brett argues that trivialization of heritage is not necessarily the issue. Instead, we must view some heritage, at least, as a contemporary form of popular culture, which should offer representations that are 'based on a sense of self and community that is neither contrived or shallow' (Brett 1996, p. 35). (Much heritage, of course, is distinctly unpopular.) Whatever, the point here concerns the tourism commodification of heritage, and the wide range of potential conflicts that emanate from the commercialization of what can be sacred objects. The tensions arising from the multi-selling and multi-consumption of heritage form a recurring theme that emerges at almost every stage of the arguments in this book. As discussed below, it has been conceptualized largely through the notion of dissonance, the discordance or lack of agreement and consistency as to the meaning of heritage (Tunbridge and Ashworth 1996).

Second, as Cosgrove (1993) argues, the cultural realm involves all those conscious and unconscious processes whereby people dwell in nature, give meaning to their lives and communicate that meaning to themselves, each other and to outsiders. Thus culture is signification and Cosgrove believes that there is no way out of the hermeneutic circle of signification and interpretation; consequently, 'cultures cannot be seen as uniform but rather are constantly reproduced and contested' (1993, p. 6), not least in the realm of social power. Control of the media of representation – of which heritage is one – is vital in determining the trajectory of such contestation in which cultural hegemony is the goal. Albeit historically transient, this can be defined as the attempt by a powerful social group to determine the limits of meaning for everyone else by universalizing its own cultural truths. Reality is rarely so simple, however, as one dominant élite imposing its values on a subordinate group through heritage. There are usually many ideas communicated with varying success to others who may, or equally may not, receive the messages as intended.

Heritage dissonance

The most sustained attempt to conceptualize this contestation of heritage and its repercussions is to be found in Tunbridge and Ashworth's examination of what they term dissonance (1996). To reiterate, this condition refers to the discordance or lack of agreement and consistency as to the meaning of heritage. For two sets of reasons, this appears to be intrinsic to the very nature of heritage and should not be regarded as an unforeseen or unfortunate by-product. First, dissonance is implicit in the market segmentation attending heritage – essentially place products which are multi-sold and multi-interpreted by tourist and 'domestic' consumers alike; that landscapes of tourism consumption are simultaneously people's sacred places is one of the principal causes of heritage contestation on a global scale. Second, dissonance arises because of the zero-sum characteristics of heritage, all of which belongs to someone and logically, therefore, not to someone else. The creation of any heritage actively or potentially disinherits or excludes those who do not subscribe to, or are embraced within, the terms of meaning defining that heritage. This quality of heritage is exacerbated because it is often implicated in the same zero-sum definitions of power and territoriality that attend the nation-state and its allegories of exclusivity. In this sense, dissonance can be regarded as destructive but, paradoxically, it is also a condition of the construction of pluralist, multicultural societies based on inclusiveness and variable-sum conceptualizations of power. Whether through indifference, acceptance of difference or, preferably, mutuality (or parity) of esteem, dissonance can be turned round in constructive imaginings of identity that depend on the very lack of consistency embodied in the term.

The intrinsic dissonance of heritage, accentuated by its expanding meanings and uses and by the fundamentally more complex constructions of identity in the modern world, is the primary cause of its contestation. Because of its ubiquity, heritage cannot be examined without addressing the implied questions – who decides what is heritage, and whose heritage is it? More simply put, can the past be 'owned' and, if so, who 'owns' it, what do we mean by 'own', and who reconciles conflicting claims to such ownership? These issues constitute yet another theme that permeates the entire content of this book and, at this stage, it is sufficient to frame a general response in terms of the myriad axes of differentiation that characterize contemporary society – notably ideology, class, gender and ethnicity (*see* Chapter 2).

In terms of ideology, a useful distinction can be found in Hardy's distinction (1988) between heritage as a conservative force that supports and reinforces dominant patterns of power, and a radical force that challenges and attempts to subvert existing structures of power. It follows that once a subversive heritage succeeds to power, it quickly loses its revolutionary intent and becomes a conservative force in itself. A Marxist critique would explain this in terms of popular consciousness being moulded to suit the needs of the dominant class and its ideology. Ideas such as Bourdieu's concept of dominant ideology (1977) have been adapted to the heritage debate. This assumes that a ruling élite upon assuming power must capture 'cultural capital' – the 'accumulated cultural productivity of society and also the criteria of taste for the selection and valuation of such products' (Ashworth 1994, p. 20) – if it is to legitimate its exercise of power. It has to be remembered, however, that because the medium is the message, the same heritage artefacts support different ideologies; the object remains but its messages change. Again, constructions of heritage are commonly framed within conventional stereotypes of gender. There is little critical literature referring to this dimension but national heritages, for example, are commonly rendered in terms of war and its ethos of (masculine) glory and sacrifice, while women are relegated to a domestic role – the keepers of the hearth.

Despite the development of multicultural societies, the content of heritage is also likely to reflect dominant ethnicities. The prevailing themes of English heritage, for example, whether exemplified in the pastoral nostalgia largely created in the early nineteenth century, or in the late twentieth-century exploitation of the country's decayed industrial fabric (mines, canals, warehouses etc.), have little space for the heritage of the many European and non-European minority groups who live in the country. Again, no European heritage – still heavily informed by the fabric of Christianity despite the avowedly secular nature of contemporary European society – has yet found a way to accommodate the traditional enemy of Islam, although there has been substantial immigration of Islamic peoples into most Western European states. Even Spain and Portugal, historically the part of Western Europe most heavily influenced by Islamic culture, evolved an iconography of Christian victory and Arab subjugation. Moreover, most European societies are loathe to acknowledge the cultural identities of their former colonial subjects. Indeed the heritage of the former colonies themselves may largely remain that of the metropolitan powers; it can often not be torn down or even reinterpreted, the key factor in the former colonial world being that 'ideology is manifestly constrained by practicality' (Western 1985, p. 356).

Conclusion

These issues of contestation are addressed at every point throughout the remainder of the book, because they are intrinsic to the uses and abuses of heritage. This forms part of the socialization process, one mechanism of social reproduction, with all the tensions implied in such a role. It is notable in this regard that heritage is widely held to have an educative role and that the young are among its most commonplace consumers. Heritage is implicated in all society's divisions, carrying its multiple and conflicting messages at a variety of scales. And yet, simultaneously, it is a crucial product in the world's largest service industry, international tourism.

We are all too aware that we have created a complex matrix of potential interaction. To state that the past is contested and that heritage is the instrument of that contest is simple. To trace the nature, consequences and management of such conflicts within the socio-political and economic domains, and within and between spatial entities at various scales, is inevitably complex. It is perhaps worth stating before we commence the detailed discussion of the long inventory of difficulties, issues and conflicts addressed in the subsequent chapters, that most heritage, most of the time, and for most people is harmoniously experienced, non-dissonant and an essential enrichment of their lives. It is the minority of cases that raise the very serious issues upon which we now embark.

P A R T

II

Heritage and the cultural realm:
its social and political uses

|2|
Heritage, power and identity

Introduction

In this chapter, we begin our investigation of the political and social uses of heritage and their role in the construction, elaboration and reproduction of identities. The debate builds upon the relationships between heritage and the ideas of legitimation, cultural capital and dominant ideology briefly examined in Chapter 1, but is sited within geography's wider concerns with the meaning and representation of place. This latter debate has been heavily informed by the contested concept of identity and its relationship to constructions of place. Again geographers are much exercised with landscape and the dichotomy between its interpretation as a physical entity or, alternatively, as a symbolic, socially constructed representation derived from interpretations of words and images. Heritage can also be viewed in these latter terms, not least because – as we have seen in the previous chapter – it is fundamental to constructs of identity. Moreover, landscapes and other empirical manifestations of the heritage complex are in themselves unlikely to be 'real' or 'authentic', and may even have been purpose-made or purpose-built, while we have argued that meaning is more fundamental than artefact in defining the content of heritage. Hence it must be emphasized that we are concerned with the interplay between knowledges of heritage in the context of politics and power, but also with their physical manifestation in built environments. Inevitably, too, the study of heritage must address the questions as to why certain knowledges are privileged while others are suppressed.

The key and universal question that underpins this debate is: whose heritage? There are two facets to this issue (Tunbridge 1994): what is identified as heritage, and how is it interpreted? In either case, selection is involved and, consequently, dissonance will occur. As that selection and its accompanying discord will reflect wider power relationships in society, the chapter begins with a discussion of two analogies to heritage, landscape and museology, both of which help underline the ways in which social phenomena are mediated through a mesh of conflicting and contested identities. If any one achieves hegemony, it is only a transient form of power, nationalism being the principal example discussed in this chapter. In pursuing the issue of 'whose heritage?' we then consider the linkages between heritage, power and the creation of collective memory. But the choice of heritage will also reflect the other dimensions of difference and contestation in societies. Thus the second half of the chapter examines the ways in which heritage is constructed through the perspectives of class, gender and sexuality, ethnicity and 'race'.

Analogies to heritage: landscape and museology

Although heritage is largely symbolic in its representation of identity and landscape, that in itself does not deny the politics of representation that underlies any formation of heritage, no matter how apparently benign this may be. Consequently, we are concerned with the innumerable ways in which heritage is implicated in the interplay between power and identity, the primary reason why we have not separated out its political and social uses. This politics of representation is shaped by, but also helps mould, the mechanisms of heritage interpretation. These can depend strongly on the visual senses and some critics (for example, Urry 1990; Brett 1996) argue that heritage is inevitably distorted because its predominant emphasis on visualization results in an artefactual history in which a whole variety of social experiences – war, hunger, disease, exploitation (they neglect fellowship, charity and love) – may be ignored. None the less, the geographical array of heritage also invokes far more than visual representation, a perspective which can be further explored through the analogies of landscape and museology. Both are implicated in heritage although they do not define its content.

Landscape

To geographers, 'landscape' has meant different things at different times in different places. Paul Vidal de la Blache, and, somewhat later, Carl Sauer believed that landscape was indicative of a harmony between human life and the *milieu* in which it was lived (Cosgrove 1984). Baker (1984) has shown that Vidalian ideas, such as *genre de vie*, *milieu* and *personnalité*, were crucial to the emergence of the *Annales* school of French *géohistoire*, and its concerted attempt to map and explain the complex reality of human life by reference to local and regional studies. It became a tenet of *géohistoire*, particularly as interpreted by Fernand Braudel, that any social reality must be referred to the space, place or region within which it existed. The basis of *géohistoire* was provided by the *pays*, literally an area with its own identity derived, not only from divisions of physical geography, but also from ethnic and linguistic divisions imposed on a region by its history.

Larger generalizations could emerge only gradually from a series of detailed and exact case studies of various *pays*.

Contemporary cultural geographers, however, regard landscapes less as places shaped by lived experience than as largely symbolic entities. Thus they can be interpreted as texts that interact with social, economic and political institutions and can be regarded as signifying practices 'that are read, not passively, but, as it were, rewritten as they are read' (Barnes and Duncan 1992, p. 5). Similarly, the heritage complex of the European city has been likened to a text that can be read in different ways, even though it may be difficult to determine which identities are being shaped by which communications (Ashworth 1998). Nevertheless:

> A symbolic or iconographic approach to landscape recognises explicitly that there is a politics to representation. Landscape representations are situated: the view comes from somewhere, and both the organisation of landscapes on the ground, and in their representations, are and have been often tied to particular relationships of power between people.
>
> (Seymour 1999, p. 194)

To Duncan (1990, p. 17), landscape is 'as an ordered assemblage of objects, a text [which] acts as a signifying system through which a social system is communicated, reproduced, experienced and explored'. The fundamentally Marxian ethos of this statement sets landscape firmly within the essentially modernist domain of legitimation, cultural capital and dominant ideology discussed in Chapter 1. Perhaps the most developed exemplar of this approach is Cosgrove's study (1993) of the fifteenth- and sixteenth-century Venetian Republic and the construction of its Palladian landscape by a dominant urban merchant class. He argues that the visual scene and its various representations are regarded as key elements in the complex individual and social processes, whereby people continuously transform the natural world into cultural realms of meaning and lived experience. These realms are historically, socially and geographically specific, as is our reading of them, separated by time, space and language from their origins. Cultural landscapes, therefore, are 'signifiers of the culture of those who have made them' (Cosgrove 1993, p. 8) and, in urban cultures, powerful groups will attempt to determine the limits of meaning for everyone else by universalizing their own cultural truths through traditions, texts, monuments, pictures and landscapes.

It has already been observed that other commentators see landscape somewhat differently as a polyvocal text, rewritten as it is read, albeit more commonplace as something to be viewed. But whichever the perspective, it is more than a straightforward hegemonic relationship of some form. For Daniels (1993), landscape is a highly complex discourse in which a whole range of economic, political, social and cultural issues is encoded and negotiated. This works along two separate dimensions. First, we have a complexity of images and a polyvisuality of interpretation that reflects an array of social differences. Landscape interconnects with a series of interacting and constantly mutating aspects of identity, which include: nationalism, gender, sexuality, 'race', class, and colonialism/postcolonialism. Second, a single landscape can be viewed simultaneously in a variety of ways, emphasizing how hegemonic interpretations are always open to subversion. Thus Cosgrove's analysis of landscape as power has been criticized as being unduly narrow, not least because it fails to address issues such as gender, sexuality and 'race' (Rose 1993; Seymour 1999).

Museology

If landscape, as a form of representation that parallels – and indeed may constitute – heritage, is inevitably an arena of contestation, so too is museology. Museums 'present imaginative geographies of communities, regions, nations and human history on a global scale' (Nash 1999, pp. 27–8). They themselves are the product of specific historical circumstances, while

> both the institutional framework within which [they] operate, and the information they disseminate, are not neutral or natural, but are the product of very particular social conditions and have a definite social and political role beyond that of simply telling people about the past (or present).
>
> (Merriman 1991, p. 3)

As the 'places [in] which the processes of modernization . . . symbolized the idea of modernity', modernist museums reproduced ideas of order and progress, 'with their roots firmly placed in industrialization and urbanization' (Walsh 1992, pp. 29 and 31). They produced linear narratives, which largely froze time, and were inaccessible to questioning or criticism. Moreover, like representations of landscape, traditional museology elided particular knowledges while emphasizing others through the same mirrors of gender, class, 'race' and nationalism. Thus in their display of certain forms of knowledge as cultural capital, museums are clearly far from being neutral but, like all texts, they also have the capability of being read differently from the intentions of those selecting the messages (Shurmer-Smith and Hannam 1994). The so-called 'new museology', in contrast, seeks to embrace contestation and make a virtue, both in its interpretations and through the physical lay-out of museum buildings, of the postmodern fragmentation of meaning. For Ennen (1997), in her discussion of the paradoxically consciously postmodern museum in the Dutch city of Groningen, authenticity does not exist, the 'realities' of the museum being shaped by the users' experiences and interpretations. Again the Tower Museum in Northern Ireland's divided Derry/Londonderry presents a representation of the walled city that can equally be understood by Catholics and Protestants, although it cannot offer any resolution to their differences. It is the user – the consumer – who defines and chooses the interpretation.

McLean (1998) argues, however, that many museums were founded for precisely the opposite purpose of conveying a sense of national pride to a country's citizens, a function which they still retain, for the advent of the postmodern does not in itself deny the continuing importance of a national dimension to identity. Rather that remains as one of the intersecting and often antagonistic discourses within a multiply constructed or fragmented and fissured conceptualization of identity. In exploring the contemporary nature of museums, McLean uses a circuit of culture model (Du Gay *et al.* 1997). With its five stages – representation, production, consumption, regulation and identity – this is very similar to that shown in Figure I.1. Representation refers to the process of producing meaning, not directly from an object but from the way in which its representation is created through classification and display. 'In particular, classifications impose a rationality upon the objects that will reflect wider epistemologies' (Tunbridge and Ashworth 1996, p. 37). Production describes the processes involved in producing the artefact being represented, notably the culture of the organization itself, and the designers who encode artefacts with symbolic forms. Cultural consumption in postmodernist thought is the diversity of meanings out of which identities are constructed – we become what we consume through appropriation or resistance. Regulation refers to the idea that an artefact is simultaneously in the public and private domain. For example, it is subject to national policies on preservation and conservation, while its consumption may be a function of the personal. And so to identities, which increasingly are polyvocal. The complexities of the 'new museology', the array of actors involved and the numerous stages in the process underscore the problems of privileging or suppressing particular identities, and of the needs to challenge and confront past accounts that were more likely to be sited within a particular conceptualization of the national.

The implications for heritage

Three conclusions arise from the analogies of landscape and museology as they might illuminate the relationships between heritage, power and identity:

- both are characterized by a complexity of images and a polyvocality of interpretation reflective of a wide array of social differences;
- none the less, the images portrayed are selected by someone, thereby raising issues of privileging or suppressing particular viewpoints;
- however, a single landscape or museum display can be viewed simultaneously in a variety of ways, which means that ostensibly hegemonic interpretations are open to subversion.

It is these points which inform the discussion in Part II, leading ultimately to the relationship between heritage and multiculturalism.

Heritage, power and collective memory

The notion of a privileged interpretation of heritage suggests its appropriation as the recognized inheritance of a particular social group. This act of empowerment inevitably carries the corollary that all heritage necessitates disinheritance of some sort for some people in some circumstances. Heritage disinheritance exists on a spectrum, ranging from a purely hypothetical or potential condition to violent, deliberate disinheritance associated with human atrocity towards the disinherited (*see* Chapter 3). One potent example, now often being redressed, is provided by the marginalization of indigenous people's heritages by the former colonial powers. Since it was not in imperial interests to legitimate pre-colonial identities, the indigenous built heritage tended to be depicted as a pre-modern curiosity where, as in Morocco, it was visibly substantial (Abu-Lughod 1980), or peripheralized where it was not (as in much of sub-Saharan Africa). Meanwhile other dimensions of native heritage became the stuff of ethnographic museums and cultural tourism. Postcolonial re-evaluations recognize indigenous heritage in ostensibly natural landscapes and built environments, while seeking to insert the missing figures into the historical record and adding resistance to, or simply difference of emphasis from, the colonial order. The postapartheid heritage adjustment of South Africa (*see* Chapters 5 and 10) is a particularly critical illustration of such processes, the commemoration of non-white deaths in the Anglo-Boer War of 1899–1900 (like those of the US Civil War) being just one noteworthy case of 're-inheritance' by those traditionally written out of the script of history.

An interesting variant of these processes is deliberate self-inheritance, whereby, to varying degrees, a population challenges or denies its own heritage as changing circumstances destroy its relevance or utility. This can come about through sudden and drastic imposed ideological changes, as occurred in Eastern Europe during the early phase of the Cold War in the 1950s, and again after the collapse of Communism at the end of the 1980s. Alternatively, as in the debate on republicanism in contemporary Australia, deliberate self-disinheritance can reflect changing political circumstances, conflated in this particular case by calls to redress Aboriginal disinheritance and a self-inflicted questioning of the legitimacy of settler heritage.

These linked ideas of appropriation and disinheritance emphasize that the nature and shaping of heritage is intimately related to the exercise of power, heritage being part of the process of defining criteria of social inclusion and – by extension – social exclusion. What counts as heritage, and whose heritages are valued, is thus an arena of intense contestation. Simultaneously, however, heritage is consumed in both official and popular terms and there may well be a disjunction between them. If heritage has sometimes been conceptualized in terms of dominant or hegemonic ideas, it may well prove an inefficient means of conveying these. We explore this point further through the relationship between heritage and memory.

The embodiment of public memory in landscape provides an apparently robust example of the ways in which representations of place are intimately related to the creation and reinforcement of official constructions of identity and power and to the whole question of empowerment (Schama 1995). These mythical worlds become literal (Agnew 1996), even though they may bear little relationship to the places in which most people who subscribe to the mythology actually live. Memory can be outer- or inner-directed but, whichever, it too is a social construct. Thus Samuel (1994) regards memory, not as timeless tradition, but as being transformed from generation to generation through, for example, the contrived nature of heritage, defined, not as artefacts and traditions inherited from the past, but by the contested modern meanings that are attached to these objects. Like heritage, with which it overlaps in complex ways, the meaning and function of memory is defined by the present, its connections with history and place vested in emblematic landscapes and places of meaning that encapsulate public history and official symbolism. Socially invoked memories are seen as being authoritative and able to speak for a place.

Thus to Samuel (1994, p. x):

> memory, so far from being merely a passive receptacle or storage system, an image bank of the past, is rather an active shaping force; that it is dynamic – what it contrives . . . to forget is as important as what it remembers . . . Memory is historically conditioned . . . so far from being handed down in the "timeless" form of tradition it is progressively altered from generation to generation . . . Like history, memory is inherently revisionist and never more chameleon than when it appears to stay the same.

Following Pierre Nora (1989), Johnson (1999a and b) suggests that real environments of memory have been replaced by sites or places of memory in these discourses of inheritance. Monuments such as Paris's Arc de Triomphe, or Berlin's Brandenburg Gate, act as fixed points in ceremonial urban landscapes and incorporate a 'sense of collective identity' (Harvey 1989, p. 85). In this sense, monuments can be visualized as politically charged and deliberately physical manifestations of ideology imposed on the landscape (Shurmer-Smith and Hannam 1994). In a study of the role played by public monuments in shaping popular narratives of Irish nationalism and statebuilding, Johnson (1995a, p. 63) believes that statues act 'as circuits of memory where individual elements can be jettisoned from popular consciousness', an interpretation which points to the role of heritage in privileging and empowering an élitist narrative of place. Conversely, in another study of memorialization in the Scottish Highlands, Withers (1995, p. 340), who warns that 'we should not talk of *one* collective memory', agrees that sites of memory are important in giving places identity, but that it is a popular and local memory rather than a public, dominant and élite memory contesting matters of local rather than national identity.

We can illustrate this point through the varying attitudes in Ireland to landscapes of remembrance of the dead of the World Wars. Heffernan (1995) argues that the war memorials and cemeteries of World War I's Western Front in north-east France – muted, serene, peaceful and intensely moving – convey no real sense of sacrifice to the nation-state. Instead, they are immortal, sacred landscapes – essentially apolitical. In Northern Ireland, however, Unionists regard them as symbolic of Ulster's embattled past, thereby fulfilling some part of the need for an outer-directed memory. The slaughter of the 36th (Ulster) Division on 1 July 1916, the opening day of the Battle of the Somme, is central to Unionist mythology as the debt that Britain owes. Thus, while the Somme Heritage Centre, opened in 1994 near Newtownards, County Down, is predicated 'upon the moral necessity of remembering the dead', there is a clear tension between this role and the simultaneous renditions of the events which it records in competing political discourses. In the Unionist state of Northern Ireland, Ulster's sacrifice for Britain became the leitmotif of loyalty while, in the then Irish Free State (later Republic of Ireland) and nationalist North, public remembrance of Irish deaths in the Great War became little more than a peripheral embarrassment (Leonard 1996).

The carnage of the Somme and the other battlegrounds of the Western Front can also be read, however, as a memory of shared loss, the sacrifice of the 'sons of Ulster' matched, for example, by that of the mainly Catholic 16th

Figure 2.1 Mill Road Military Cemetery, on the 1916 Somme battlefield near Thiepval in north-east France, contains the graves of some of the Irish soldiers killed during the opening offensive on 1 July 1916

(Irish) Division around Messines in the several Battles of Ypres (Figure 2.1). Indeed the 16th (Irish) Division also fought at the Somme, where its role is commemorated by a monument in the village of Guillemont. Thus Remembrance Day, long regarded as a Unionist ceremony, was much more widely observed in 1998, particularly in the Irish Republic, when, in the wake of the Good Friday Belfast Peace Agreement, it was seen as a symbol of reconciliation. In particular, the presence of the Irish President, Mary McAleese and Queen Elizabeth at the opening of the Irish Peace Park at Messines (Mesen) in November 1998 was widely interpreted as a potent symbol of a renegotiated relationship between Britain and Ireland and one which marked the first formal recognition by the Irish state of its war dead. The 30 m high monument, built in the form of an Irish round tower, stands in memory of 50 000 Irish dead and in honour of 250 000 Irish people who served in the British forces in World War I. Similarly, the Ulster Tower, located near Thiepval in the heart of the 1916 Somme battlefield, and built as the memorial to the 36th Division, can become an inner-directed mnemonic symbol of the mutual suffering of Protestants and Catholics alike and thus again a focus of reconciliation (Graham 1994a). Its small visitor centre points to this role with a display that invokes the Irish rather than strictly Ulster involvement on the Western Front (Figure 2.2).

Both the Irish monuments at Messines and Thiepval are essentially unofficial heritage in that although state recognized, they are administered by private organizations – respectively the Journey of Reconciliation Trust and the Somme Association. This distinction between official (in the sense of state-sponsored) and unofficial renditions of memory is a recurring theme in the framing and interpretation of heritage. In Ireland, for example, it may well be the case that unofficial forms of heritage are far more effective in the shaping and reproduction of popular memory than are monuments laden with state ideology. In contemporary Belfast, popular territorial landscapes of fear are marked and reinforced by flags, murals, painted kerb-stones and graffiti, and claimed by marching (Figure 2.3). These cultural signifiers embody memory, wall-murals, for example, often entrenching existing structures and beliefs rather than advocating any potential transformation toward a new Ulster (Jarman 1992; Bryson and McCartney 1994). 'Freedom Corner' in Protestant east Belfast and 'Free Derry Corner' in the city's Catholic Bogside do not seek consensus but merely echo the mutual incomprehension of the question: whose freedom? To Longley (1991, p. 37), such symbols are an inner-directed mnemonic, a rhetoric of memory that tries to place the past beyond argument. If this is so, then the messages of the murals can be interpreted as one means by which paramilitary organizations establish and maintain power over the inhabitants of the residential areas which they control.

We explore this fragmentation of meaning of memory and heritage further in Chapter 4, but return here to the import of Johnson's conclusions that heritage privileges and empowers an élitist narrative of place. These are rather similar to the ideas encapsulated in Ashworth's argument (1994) that dominant ideologies create specific place identities, which reinforce support for

Figure 2.2   The Ulster Tower on the 1916 Somme battlefield near Thiepval. Built in 1921 to commemorate the dead of the 36th (Ulster) Division, who were largely raised from the ranks of the Ulster Volunteer Force, it can now be read as a symbol of reconciliation which helps commemorate all the Irish dead of the Great War

Figure 2.3   Unofficial heritage: part of the wall-mural at East Belfast's Freedom Corner

particular state structures and related political ideologies. Drawing upon Bourdieu's concept of 'cultural capital' (*see* Chapter 1), he contends that upon assuming power, each governmental regime must capture this capital, including heritage, through political structures, education, socialization and media representations. In this reading, heritage remains central to assumptions that evocations of official collective memory can underpin the quintessential modernist constructs of nationalism and legitimacy.

It is, however, the fragmented and inconsistent nature of the interrelationships between memory and heritage, and the dichotomy between official and unofficial representations and even forms, which substantially undermines the notion that heritage does provide the state with legitimacy, even though, somewhat paradoxically, this clearly remains one of its continuing sociopolitical functions. Any attempt to exploit heritage as a particular manifestation of power is likely to be subverted by the contradictory messages transmitted and received. Accordingly, as Foucault argues:

> we should not be deceived into thinking that . . . heritage is an acquisition, a possession that grows and solidifies; rather it is an unstable assemblage of faults, fissures and heterogeneous layers that threaten the fragile inheritor from within or underneath.

(cited in Matless 1992, p. 51)

This desire to capture the fragmented is the antithesis of the ordered world of historical continuity vested in the nexus of modernity and the nation-state (Philo 1992). Further, it again underscores the futility of the debate concerning the authenticity of heritage referred to in Chapter 1 (see, for example, Hewison 1987).

Heritage and identity

Alongside this complex role in the validation of power structures, heritage is also deeply implicated in the construction and legitimation of collective constructs of identity, such as class, gender, ethnicity and nationalism. This suggests that the past in general and its interpretation as history – or heritage – confers certain social benefits as well as costs. As we noted in Chapter 1, Lowenthal (1985) defines four traits of the past (which can be taken as being synonymous with heritage in this context) as conferring benefits on a people. These are: antiquity; the connection of the present to the past; a sense of termination; and the idea of a sequence. To take Ireland as an example of these traits, the nationalism which evolved in the later nineteenth century to underpin the growing political movement seeking Home Rule and later independence from Britain, created a vision of Ireland that essentially eschewed time in seeking continuity to a distant age prior to the 'book of invasions' that Anglophobic Irish history all too often became. The imagery accompanying this narrative was of a predominantly rural Ireland, its true cultural heartland defined by the landscapes and way of life of the wild, western Atlantic fringes – those furthermost removed from the anglicizing influences that had multiplied after the twelfth century. Iconic sites of continuity in this heritage mythology included Celtic monasteries of the first millennium AD, Iron Age hill-forts and megalithic tombs. There was no place for urban heritage, towns being dismissed as an alien – and particularly English – innovation (Graham 1994b, 1997).

While Lowenthal (1985) sees the past and its reconstitution as heritage providing familiarity, guidance, enrichment and escape, the traits which he identifies also fulfil the function of validating and legitimating a people's present sense of sameness. He argues that the past validates present attitudes and actions by affirming their resemblance to past ones, to the previous usage which we term tradition. In turn, this is employed to sanction contemporary actions and policies. In this way, the past validates the present through the idea of timeless values and lineages, and by restoring what are held to be lost or subverted values. Explicit here too is the sense of belonging to place that is so fundamental to identity, a topic which we pursue in subsequent chapters. Inevitably, the past as rendered through heritage also promotes the burdens of history, the atrocities, errors and crimes of the past, which are called upon to legitimate the atrocities of the present. (Indeed, as we explore in Chapter 4, atrocity can become heritage.) Lowenthal also comments that the past can be a burden in the sense that it often involves a dispiriting and negative rejection of the present.

The benefits of the past and heritage are, moreover, counter-balanced by its costs, largely derived from the privileging of one social group's viewpoint at the expense of those of other groups and peoples. That this is so reflects the dynamic importance of the past and particular appropriations of heritage in the construction of identities. Acting as one means of representing the past, heritage provides meaning to human existence by conveying the ideas of timeless values and unbroken lineages that underpin identity. As we have seen in Chapter 1, representations of heritage are also defined in relation to traditions and values ascribed to the Other. It is generally the case that such 'universal' traditions and values are modern inventions (Donald and Rattansi 1992), part and parcel of the modernist construction of identities. Although Said's (1978) construct of Otherness has been tremendously influential in cultural studies generally, Rose (1994) cautions against its bi-polar nature and assumption of a hegemonic ideology and a counter-hegemonic opposition. Instead, she argues for a hybridity of culture and a multiplicity of alternative visions of places. Massey (1994) also disputes the assumption that places are bounded and enclosed spaces defined through opposition to an Other who is outside. The point is not to deny the role of Otherness but to emphasize its complexity, a point to which we return in Chapter 4.

Despite these qualifications, the notion of Otherness is fundamental to representations of identity, which are constructed in counter-distinction to them. In this context, heritage can be regarded as one form of the media used to convey identity messages. As we explored in Chapter 1, it is part of the production and exchange of meanings. 'It is by our use of things, and what we say, think and feel about them – how we represent them – that we give them a meaning' (Hall 1997, p. 3). We give objects significance by the ways in which we use them or integrate them into everyday life, but also by how we represent them. Heritage plays a central and crucial role in the construction of the symbolic domains at the very heart of social life. The key point, however, is that the meshing of heritage and identity is also implicated in the patterns and conflicts of privileging and exclusion, of marginalization and resistance that result from the fracturing of societies along the axes of class, gender, ethnicity and nationalism, which remain fundamental to the question, whose heritage?

Heritage and class

Human society has always tended to internal division, even where superficially homogeneous in its cultural characteristics. This is particularly apparent in the complex urban-focused societies, increasingly the human norm since the Industrial Revolution, in which social class is the most obvious basis of division. In the late twentieth century, however, as our understanding of human differentiation has become markedly more nuanced, other formerly suppressed axes of division such as gender, sexual orientation and physical ability have emerged. These intersect with class in complex ways and also with a further axis of differentiation constituted by cultural distinctiveness, one often mixed with perceptions of 'race' and widely referred to as ethnicity. From the perspective of this book, the significance of all social groups, whatever the basis and credibility of their distinction, lies in their capacity to generate a distinctive heritage or, at least, the claim upon one. As the expression of this heritage in competition with others commonly becomes a means of legitimating a group's presence and claim upon status and resources, it has accordingly become an intrinsic part of larger processes of social competition and reproduction.

Heritage is largely consumed by the middle classes. As Merriman (1991) observes, the expansion in the range of heritage presentations has not been accompanied by any matching expansion in the range of people visiting them. 'Time and time again surveys show that individuals of above average income and affluence are represented far out of all proportion to their numbers in the population as a whole' (Merriman 1991, p. 2). More widely, social class has been implicated in the process of heritage awareness and designation from the beginnings of organized historic preservation and heritage awareness. Recognition of the relics of the past as heritage almost invariably began at the instigation of a social élite and commonly designated the grand and spectacular, including the buildings and artefacts most closely identified with that self-same élite. In terms of legitimation, such heritage could be interpreted as one means of perpetuating élitist control and power, if not always with conscious intent. Thus with their portfolios of 'power' houses and landed estates, paternalistic institutions such as the various UK National Trusts – the English version was described by Hewison (1987, p. 55) as a 'self-perpetuating oligarchy' – stand accused of being conservation agencies run by and to showcase the inheritance of an élite (Dwyer and Hodge 1996; Larkham and Barrett 1998). It has also been argued that the Trusts place the inalienability of property above the rights of ordinary people (Tunbridge 1981). Conversely the unspectacular, commonplace and less durable artefacts of humbler citizens are (in so far as they survive at all) much later and more tentative claimants to inclusion in the heritage portfolio, to which they might be admitted under the rubric of the 'vernacular'.

The initial widening of the range of heritage representations beyond the artefacts of past and present élites was largely driven by commerialization. By the 1970s, for example, it was widely appreciated that the artefacts of the Industrial Revolution constituted an invaluable and saleable heritage. Although industrial archaeology, then of recent origin, had also originally emphasized the spectacular, it rapidly became more vernacular in focus. This broadening of the heritage field, however, accentuated the issue of class and prompted attention to the heritage of the industrial workforce and, inevitably, to the social justice issues thereby implied (Alfrey and Putnam

1992; Goodall 1993). The exploitation of industrial heritage was pioneered in the United Kingdom, not surprisingly since it possessed Europe's largest pre-twentieth-century resource base, by then in terminal economic decline. However, failed or exhausted coal mines and the like could be repackaged as tourism heritage, given a fertile climate of national nostalgia for a greater past. The proliferation of industrial museums and heritage sites in Britain during the 1980s prompted much critical comment. Hewison (1987, p. 9), for one, argued that: 'Instead of manufacturing goods, we are manufacturing heritage, a commodity which nobody seems able to define, but which everyone is eager to sell.' He criticized heritage products for being fantasies of a world that never was, their very preservation involving a reassertion of past social values, while hastening contemporary decline by stifling the culture of the present.

Nevertheless, the growth of the heritage industry did provide economic opportunities to many depressed industrial areas. Perhaps the best example is provided by Ironbridge Gorge in Shropshire, one of England's earliest industrial regions, developed as an assemblage of museums and linked industrial sites to become an UNESCO World Heritage Site and sold as the 'birth-place of the Industrial Revolution'. Chatterly Whitfield Colliery in Stoke-on-Trent, the largest and most complete nineteenth-century coal mine in Britain, is described as the 'Stonehenge of the coal industry'. Numerous British cities have sought to remarket their declined nineteenth-century industrial areas: the textile mills of Bradford, Leeds and Manchester, the potteries of Stoke, the docks of Plymouth, Newcastle and especially Liverpool have all been cleaned up and re-packaged as heritage. Such developments have attracted widespread criticism and controversy, particularly with respect to the class implications of such heritage, the manner in which its proponents chose to engage with these, and the gearing of whole localities to tourism consumption, arguably reproducing contemporary forms of exploitation and entrepreneurship from the relics of nineteenth-century capitalism and its social relationships (Lumley 1988).

The recognition of industrial heritage has diffused globally. It has been extensively developed in continental Europe and the United States. The classic US manifestation is provided by Lowell, Massachusetts, the archetypal nineteenth-century transatlantic industrial town (Ashworth and Tunbridge 1990; Figure 2.4). Local initiative succeeded in generating Congressional pressure for the US National Parks Service to create a then-novel urban industrial National Historical Park in Lowell. Established in 1978, this has remained the model for other American industrial heritage aspirants. Considerable attention is given to class and gender in Lowell's interpretation. Its original workers were New England farm girls, attracted by secure and profitable working conditions in which class exploitation was abnormally inconspicuous; only when cheap immigrant labour became abundant did Lowell slip into the more familiar class polarization of industrial enterprise.

Figure 2.4   Lowell, MA.: restored textile mill in adaptive reuse, including National Parks Service headquarters, retailing and office facilities

Heritage, gender and sexuality

By comparison with the ubiquity of class in the heritage debate, other axes of social differentiation, most notably gender, still appear as more marginal and tentative dimensions. It has been argued that modernity – and consequently its heritage – has largely been conceptualized in masculine, middle-class, urban and eurocentric terms (Melosh 1994). To Nash (1999, p. 20), for example, modernity was:

> dependent on the construction of the inferiority and difference of women, other races and the working classes, all defined as pre-modern, primitive and still located in the immanent world of nature.

In particular, the essentially masculine gendering of modernity led to the equation of women – especially rural women – with the authentic and premodern. This depended on the equation of the modern with 'a male-directed logic of rationalization, objectification and developmental progress', while, according to Felski (1994, p. 149), feminine qualities were equated with 'artificiality and decadence, irrationality and desire'. In contrast, romanticism 'sought to demonstrate women's greater continuity with organic processes and natural rhythms of pre-industrial society', pre-modern woman 'located within the household and intimate web of familial relations', being more 'closely linked to nature through her reproductive capacity' (Felski 1994, p. 146). Nash (1999, p. 21) argues that:

this version of femininity could be denigrated as of limited value and a constraint on progress, or romantically celebrated as an antidote to the superficiality and meaningless nature of modern life.

Whichever, the key point is that both viewpoints are gendered constructions, which privilege masculine authority. Hitherto, women have been largely invisible and misrepresented in the archives of history and it can be argued that the artefacts of the past endowed with contemporary meanings as heritage have been largely selected from a perspective of 'heritage masculinization' (Edensor and Kothari 1994). For example, with the remarkable exception of Queen Victoria, women are essentially missing figures in monumental representations of noteworthy past lives throughout the former British Empire. Even the lives of 'militant' women, who transcended the domestic web of social relations, have been endowed with masculine readings. As Warner (1981, p. 256) shows, nineteenth-century France saw a literal contest for the possession of Joan of Arc, between the Church to which she was the personification of virtue, and the secular politicians who saw her as the symbol of republican France, 'a species of Marianne, spirit of the republic'.

None the less, there is some evidence that Lowenthal's (1996, pp. 48–9) claim that heritage 'is traditionally a man's world', 'men having . . . monopolized the transmission of history' is now less appropriate as women challenge the patriarchal and unrepresentative nature of so many representations of culture. Women, for example, are often prominent, and frequently dominant, in conservationist movements, as in Savannah, Georgia, where they have acted as the critical catalyst in the city's conservation movement since the 1950s (Ashworth and Tunbridge 1990). In general terms, however, heritage has yet to monumentalize the victimization of women by men, while questions of gender-differentiated consumption patterns in the representations sold by heritage tourism have received little attention (Squire 1994).

Homosexuality and disability have also acquired distinct profiles in recent heritage recognition. Amsterdam, for example, has a homosexual monument and an associated tourism trail. The Stonewall memorial in New York to a 1969 riot over police action against a homosexual bar (Henry 1994) could be interpreted in these or in larger human rights terms, its contentious status being reflected and magnified by its enforced removal from public space to a university campus. The Franklin D. Roosevelt Memorial in Washington, D.C. illustrates the problem of group identification with a heritage of disabled achievement: while many argued that Roosevelt should be portrayed in a wheelchair, others (who might well have included the subject himself) contended the issue to be irrelevant to his national stature. In the Canadian capital, Ottawa, however, achievement overcoming disability is conspicuously honoured in the memorial to Terry Fox, a one-legged transnational runner.

Heritage and ethnicity

Ethnicity is arguably the most fundamental basis of perceived distinction between human groups. Although usage of the term is elastic and often vague, an ethnic group can be defined as a socially distinct community of people who share a common history and culture and often language and religion as well (Sillitoe and White 1992). While 'ethnicity' is very often used simply as a synonym for 'race', this definition points to a more flexible interpretation. Poole (1997, pp. 131–2) identifies three basic strands to ethnicity:

> the activity segregation which gives rise to the socially distinct community; the myth or actuality of a common perceived historical and cultural origin distinguishing the group from others; the delimitation of the group by key social or cultural markers such as language and religion.

As he observes, ethnic identity is not an attribute which is simply present or absent, because people may have it to varying degrees. As it can also change over time, ethnic identity is a feeling 'subject to ebb and flow' (Poole 1997, p. 133).

The power of attachment to ethnic identity underlines the importance of ethnic heritage, as the vehicle of transmission and legitimation of that identity through time. That individuals vary in their sensitivity to ethnicity and motivation by its heritage does not detract from its overall significance in this respect. The most stridently chauvinistic proclamations of heritage and savage attacks on that of others have been defined in ethnic terms. Two vivid illustrations were Nazi Germany's attempt to obliterate Jewish heritage, and the mutual heritage destructions by Croats, Serbs and Muslims during the wars in the former Yugoslavia during the 1990s. The extension of this conflict into Kosovo (1998–9) effectively demonstrates the interplay between the linguistic and religious components of ethnic identity, the majority population being Albanian-speaking and Muslim. This conflict further illustrates the importance of shifts of population and heritage claims as, irrespective of its later substantial ethnic displacement, the Serb Orthodox minority which controlled Kosovo until 1999 regarded the province as the historic Serb heartland to be held at all costs.

Thus, despite its questionable and sometimes unsavoury resonances, indeed in part because of them, ethnicity is of cardinal importance as a basis for social conflict. That the groups in question may be arbitrarily defined by their mutual perceptions does not significantly alter the reality that human competition and aggression for resources and status is very often defined and justified primarily in ethnic terms. Ethnicity may coincide with the other dimensions to social differentiation. One example is the deep-seated class racial divide between most Europeans and Africans in South Africa (although both broad groups are ethnically composite). More often, however, human diversity is reflected in ethnic identities which cut across other differentiating criteria. Where this occurs, it is commonplace, although not invariably so, for ethnicity to take precedence over class or gender in the individual's sense of identification. The widespread ethnic precedence in human identity requires us to look more closely at the interaction between heritage and the main cultural components of ethnicity, namely language, religion and 'race'. The importance of ethnicity is most eloquently demonstrated by the priority now being accorded in major democracies to programmes of multiculturalism, as the basis for redefining society in the presence of growing ethnic diversity (*see* Chapter 5).

Language

The linguistic demarcation of ethnic and indeed national identity is particularly characteristic of Europe, language being the principal delineating factor in the creation of nation-states. The exceptions to the general pattern – states speaking the multinational languages such as English, French and German or including minor languages such as Welsh, Frisian and Breton – disturb but do not negate the general pattern. Rather than fostering multilingual national identities, the existence of numerous and indeed multiplying linguistic minorities tends to foster resentment of their presence among elements of the majority (Williams 1998). Switzerland, although not entirely free of linguistic conflict, is the prime exception, by virtue of the strong local autonomy that exists within its four-language confederation. Belgium, conversely, labouring ineffectively to reconcile two main language groups, is closer to the European norm of national identity defined, or – in this case – effectively denied, by its divisions. The country's politics are dominated by the almost absolute language barrier, further exacerbated by economic variations, between the more prosperous Flemish north (about 60 per cent of the population) and the relatively poorer Walloon south. If the intractable bitterness of this division is regrettable, it has not spilled over into overt violence, indicative perhaps of the import of Zetterholm's optimistic conclusion (1994, p. 65):

> There is nothing inevitable about strife or political conflict between different cultural or ethnic groups living within a common social and political framework. There are many examples of peaceful and tolerant co-existence and interaction between different groups within multicultural communities.

None the less, twentieth-century Europe has seen far more strident appeals to linguistic identity. The most infamous, because ultimately it precipitated World War II, was Hitler's demand for a *Grossdeutschland*, which used language, compounded by Nazi theories of 'race', to justify the absorption, first of Austria and then of the territories occupied by German linguistic minorities throughout *Mitteleuropa*. While Germany's defeat muted the appeal of linguistic identity, the end of the Cold War has led to an often aggressive re-emergence of this factor in parts of Central and Eastern Europe, expressed, for example, in the antagonism to Hungarian minorities living in Romania and Slovakia.

Language-based identity, and its fragmentation both between and within states, is by no means confined to Europe. In Africa, a particularly serious problem of misalignment exists between state boundaries and ethnic patterns defined chiefly (though not entirely) by language. The colonial powers, which created these boundaries, partitioned the continent and its tribal ethnic groups with little or no regard for the chiaroscuro of local patterns of that very attribute deemed so critical to identity formation in Europe. This is one among the many causes of the ethnic politics, which led to the genocidal horrors of 1994, when in Rwanda, alone, perhaps one million people, mostly from the country's Tutsi minority, were massacred. Ethnic tensions continue to cause war and continuing instability in Central Africa today, most notably in the Congo. In the Americas, although in excess of 40 states and dependent territories share just five superimposed European languages, these too can have sensitive identity conflicts, for example, between English and Spanish within the US Southwest and, above all, between English and French within Canada. In the latter case, every election campaign in the province of Québec is overshadowed by the tension created by the avowed intent of the governing Parti Québecois to seek national independence for the province through yet another referendum, expressly on the basis of the French linguistic identity of most of its inhabitants.

Heritage is, of course, central to the transmission of these identities, language becoming ingrained in the very built environment. Hitler glorified a linguistic German identity through reference to German mythology and cultural achievement expressed in heroic artistic and architectural heritage representations, many of which still exist as profoundly dissonant heritage. Moreover, the complex and often violent vicissitudes of history have routinely resulted in shifts of population and/or heritage, which aggravate these rivalries and resentments. This is classically the case in Europe, as exemplified by the flight of German-speakers from what is now Poland and Czechia after World War II, and renewed migration from Transylvania and elsewhere since the end of the Cold War. Ostensibly, the German language has been eradicated from the townscapes and landscapes of most of these lost territories, but enough traces of German business signs, church engravings and gravestone inscriptions survive from Bohemia to the Kaliningrad region of Russia to sustain contemporary German tourist interest in – and identification with – the heritage of these regions (Figures 2.5 and 2.6).

Although such linguistic population/heritage mislocations around the world can sponsor irredentist claims to lost territory, they can also be resolved by gradual, undramatic unravellings and reweavings from past to present. In Québec, for example, these mislocations are witnessed by the evolution of compound placenames. Among dozens of examples which reveal areas of linguistic flux, the prefix of St Pierre-de-Wakefield

Figure 2.5 Kaliningrad, Russia (formerly Königsberg, East Prussia): inner-city commercial building burnt out in 1945. A German sign, Kreuz Apotheke, is still visible over the nearest doorway

Figure 2.6 A former inn in the Sudetenland, Bohemia, Czechia. A German *Gasthof* sign is still visible after more than 50 years

represents the addition of a French (and Catholic) identity to what was originally an English-speaking settlement. Through time the English suffix is likely to fade from use. In Québec City, however, these gentle transitions of identity may have a sharper edge, especially as the multicultural dimension to its designation as a World Heritage Site may be threatened by the political imperative of separatists to disavow the city's British heritage (*see* Chapter 11).

Religion

Globally, religion, either alone or in association with language, frequently forms the basis of ethnic identity and influences the ways in which this spills over into nationalism. The Catholic/Orthodox/Muslim schism of the former Yugoslavia, and the ways in which language and religion combine in Polish identity, provide two European examples. More widely, Christianity has been locked in conflict with Islam since the seventh century, a rivalry that has now become transmuted into the struggle between the West and a resurgent, militant version of Islam and its transnational network of terrorist groups. In part, this struggle represents the resistance of Islam to secularization, which means that in an Islamic state still defined by its religious beliefs, these latter can compete with nationalism because they perform most of its functions (Gellner 1997). In Asia, states such as Pakistan, created at the cost of enormous bloodshed during the 1947 partition of British India, and Malaysia reflect the interaction of religion with other modes of identity. Traditional Irish nationalism was framed by its entirely Catholic ethos, one reason why Protestants, especially those in Northern Ireland, lost any real sense of Irishness after the partition of Ireland in 1921 (Graham 1998a; Graham and Shirlow 1998). In Québec, religion traditionally meshed with language in defining the distinct Québecois identity. As is also the case in Ireland, its significance is now muted and it is a largely secular Québec which is restive within contemporary Canada. However, the monolithic nature of religions should not be overstated for they too are fractured into multiple, historically-based allegiances that are often the causes of conflict. The tensions in the Middle East between Iran, Iraq and Saudi Arabia owe much to the fractured relationships between rival Islamic sects. Divisions within Christianity likewise provide a basis for conflicting identities.

Religion can constitute the most powerful foundation to the social and political uses of heritage. Jerusalem, for example, stands testimony to the centuries-old power of religious iconography in human value systems and identities. It also sustains the idea of religion as the principal basis of conflicting heritages, representing as it does a site sacred to, and fiercely contested by, three major world religions – Judaism, Christianity and Islam – which ironically share a common geographical origin. Jerusalem is the archetypal 'holy city', a place which symbolizes in itself a theological idea and thus

Figure 2.7   The magnificent Romanesque cathedral of St James, wrapped in its eighteenth-century Baroque facade, dominates the holy city of Santiago de Compostela,
Galicia, Spain

acquires an array of monuments and buildings of profound heritage signifi-
cance to that religion's adherents. Other holy cities like Rome may be highly
multifunctional and even 'multiheritage' places, while others, such as the
Galician pilgrimage centre of Santiago de Compostela in north-west Spain, or
Lourdes in south-west France, may possess a relatively greater 'holy' focus
(Figure 2.7). All the major world religions have sacred cities, either in their
entirety or with respect to particular shrines. For Muslims, these include
Mecca, and regional centres such as Qom and Isfahan in Iran; for Sikhs,
Amritsar; for Hindus, Varanasi (Singh 1997); and for Buddhists, Kandy or
Lhasa. Even recently-founded sects have their holy places as in the Mormon
'capital' of Salt Lake City, Utah. While their heritage significance varies
immensely, holy cities are often among the most sensitive illustrations of the
wider issues of heritage contestation and management addressed in this book.
They can be the epicentres of revolution (Iran) or, as in Lhasa, the targets of
heritage vandalism as China seeks to repress Tibetan culture. Holy cities can
be the subject of terrorist attacks as at Kandy in Sri Lanka, and inter-religious
conflict as at Amritsar and Jerusalem. They are equally tempting targets for
tourism commodification of their heritage, in the first instance for the often
captive pilgrimage market.

Paralleling the relationship between heritage and language, religious heritage can also be mislocated. Indeed the two ethnic axes may coincide, one example being the replacement of mainly Protestant anglophone Quebeckers by overwhelmingly Catholic francophone Québecois and the resultant redundancies or misfits in identities. More drastic mislocation is implicit in the fate of European Jews, and has in fact characterized Jewish experience from the time of their original diaspora from Roman Palestine. Although Jerusalem itself is sacred to three rival religions, the adherents of two of those – Islam and Christianity – have experienced mislocation for most of two millennia. Even today, while there is freedom of access to the city, it is under Israeli control, rather than guaranteed through political internationalization. The Israeli reclamation of the Jewish Wailing Wall from Muslim control in their 1967 conquest of East Jerusalem might be seen as a latter-day echo of the Christian Crusades to reconquer Jerusalem and the Holy Land, which were not only among the defining political events of the European Middle Ages but left permanent imprints upon the religious geography of the Middle East. It is not invariably the case, however, that mislocated religious heritage triggers enduring conflict. Perhaps the most expressive act of religious heritage dispossession in European history, symbolized by the conversion of the already ancient St Sophia (Hagia Sophia) into a mosque, was the conquest of Byzantine Christian Constantinople by the Ottoman Muslims in 1453. In its dedication to the creation of a modern secular society, the nationalist government of Mustafa Kemal (Atatürk), who ruled Turkey from 1922–38, secularized the use and thus the meaning of historic religious buildings, most notably Hagia Sophia, which is now a museum rather than the site of overt religious heritage conflict.

Heritage and 'race'

Although they are often difficult to separate, ethnicity and 'race' are distinct social phenomena and should not be conflated. Nor should their derivatives, ethnocentrism and racism (Werbener and Modood 1997). Genetic ideas of 'race' are now largely discredited and 'race', like nation, is essentially interpreted as a social construction, one, moreover, that means different things in different places. Thus:

> By demonstrating the existence of a plurality of place-specific ideologies of 'race' . . . rather than a monolithically, historically singular and geographically invariant racism . . . , the constructedness of 'race' . . . is starkly revealed.
>
> (Jackson and Penrose 1993, p. 13)

It is the very idea of 'race' which has become problematized, rather than the assumption that colour is the primary index of 'race' and that it is the skin colour of minorities which constitutes the problem. Nevertheless, there are still racialized identities and while there may be no 'race' in the genetic sense (hence the inverted commas), there is ample evidence of racism, which 'remains a widespread, and possibly intensifying, fact of many people's lives'. Therefore, the question is not whether 'race' exists but how 'racial logics and racial frames of reference' are constructed and used and with what consequences (Donald and Rattansi 1992, p. 1). Nor is racism simply based on ideas of innate biological superiority because it can also claim the supposed incompatibility of cultural traditions.

Hobsbawm and Ranger (1983) argue that most European national identities are products of the nineteenth century. They are imbued with assumptions of racial superiority and stereotypes derived from the history of colonialism and imperialism and still represent illusions of racial homogeneity. As Gilroy (1987) has famously claimed, there 'ain't no black in the Union Jack' and the absence of particular voices in national heritages is part of the same crisis of representation that attends the gendering of identity and heritage. Lowenthal (1996, p. 196) considers that the focus of western heritage moved through time from a focus on family lineages to 'entire peoples determined by inherent traits'. As a result, 'minority heritage is especially linked with immutable traits' (Lowenthal 1996, p. 197). Indigenous peoples once deemed inferior are now exalted but on precisely the same racial basis. Exactly the same point applies to ethnic groups.

Although the traditional genetic definition of 'race', defined above all by skin colour and physiognomy, remains among the most important contributors to 'visible minority' status, 'race' has received little attention in the heritage debate. One reason is that it is very difficult to define precise boundaries between 'race', ethnicity and nationalism, which are all socially constructed but along a variety of complexly intersecting axes. 'Race', therefore, tends to become subsumed in ethnicity, which clearly constitutes a major gap in our understanding of the social and political connotations of heritage and in deconstructing the dissonance that emanates from them.

Conclusion

It is readily apparent that the fragmented, inchoate nature of identity militates against any straightforward interpretation of the construction of heritage. In addressing the issue of 'whose heritage?' certain motifs of power relationships – national, official, masculine, even white – may appear to dominate. Thus, as we explore in Chapter 3's analysis of the relationships between heritage and nationalism, modernity combated ethnicity in the name of universalism (Friedman 1997). It was those perspectives which were privileged at the expense of other subordinated representations. That subordination, however, has helped create the numerous spaces of resistance identified by contemporary cultural geographers. Although they are concerned with the 'ways in which resistance is mobilized through specific times and places' (Pile and

$\Big| 3 \Big|$
Heritage and national identity

Introduction

In this chapter, the emphasis shifts to address not only the question of 'whose heritage?', but also 'which heritage?' We have already observed that traditional narratives of meaning as they apply to the centralized state are generally recent in origin, bound up with the emergence in the nineteenth century of the quintessentially modernist concept of nationalism as the defining universalizing myth. As Heffernan (1998a) – drawing upon Lefebvre – persuasively argues, space is not an independent given but a mutable and ever-changing product of economic, social, cultural and political processes. Modernity, however, attempted to 'fix' space through the creation of rigidly territorial nation-states, promulgating ideologies which attempted to subsume differences through representations of homogeneity. But all too often, the grail of universal conformity has produced atrocity and genocide as those who do not 'fit' have been driven out or eradicated. Heritage is heavily implicated in these processes as a medium of communication of prevailing myths and counter-claims.

In pursuing the interrelated issues of 'whose?' and 'which?' heritage, this chapter addresses the complicated relationships between heritage and nationalism. Heritage is one means of supporting and defining the ideology as it relates to particular spaces, but also a focus of multiple resistances. In both guises, heritage is further implicated in the meshing of nationalism and ethnicity and the discussion addresses the forces of disinheritance and atrocity that all too often emanate from this inter-dependence.

Heritage and nationalism

As explained in Chapter 1, the origins of what we now term heritage lie in the modernist nexus of European state formation and Romanticism, which is defined in political terms by nationalism. While these nineteenth-century European nationalisms evolved many different trajectories, they shared in the mutual assumption of modernity that all people of 'a similar ethical rationality might agree on a system of norms to guide the operation of society' (Peet 1998, p. 14). Hence nationalist discourses are sited within a sense of limitless change and advance which, in turn, demanded the creation of modernistic, progressive, linear heritage narratives that sought to subsume the diversity and heterogeneity of the everyday world. These were combined with assumptions of long-term continuities of culture, place and allegiance and constructed to lead directly to the contemporary nexus of power, providing the precedents and traditions which underpin the legitimacy of that authority.

Thus we have the emergence of what Gilroy (1993) depicts as the fatal junction of concepts of nationality and culture in the intellectual history of the West since the Enlightenment. As we have explained in Chapter 1, symbolic national landscapes became distinctive home places, in which heritage became configured in certain ways. These represented the dominant beliefs, ethnicities and discourses of progress of the modern era and its invocation of infinite self-directed progress. Hence there was a sense of liberation from tradition, offset, however, by the new disciplinary powers of the emergent state. Modernity was characterized by escalating rates of social and economic change and by deeper and more extended degrees of interconnection between places at a variety of scales as, for example, centralized state economies and global networks of trade and imperialism developed (Ogborn 1998).

In one of the key statements regarding the nature of nationalism, Anderson (1991, pp. 6–7) argues that any nation is imagined

> as both inherently limited and sovereign . . . [i]t is imagined because the members of even the smallest nation will never know most of their fellow-members . . . the nation is imagined as *limited* because even the largest . . . has finite, if elastic, boundaries, beyond which lie other nations . . . it is imagined as *sovereign* because the concept was born in [the] age [of] Enlightenment and Revolution . . . [and] [f]inally, it is imagined as a *community* because, regardless of the actual inequality and exploitation that might prevail . . . the nation is always conceived as a deep horizontal comradeship.

This imagining of an internal national homogeneity – one which draws inevitably upon a particular representation of heritage and a mythology of the past for its coherence and legitimacy – has conditioned western conceptualizations of political space for more than two centuries. Modern national identity became an object bounded in time and space, with clear beginnings and endings and its own territory (Handler 1994) and, through imperialism, evoked an attitude of superiority towards the rest of the world. The power of such narratives depends on their ability to evoke the accustomed, tropes that work by appealing to 'our desire to reduce the unfamiliar to the familiar' (Barnes and Duncan 1992, pp. 11–12), a context in which the inherently conservative force of heritage is central. Although we now recognize the situated nature of nationalism, and no longer visualize it as a fixed primordial identity rooted in the mists of history (Agnew 1997), it has often been glorified in this fashion. Like memory and heritage, nationalisms are contingent, constantly mutating processes, which espouse a language of continuity, permanence and eternal values. They cannot be viewed as monolithic meta-narratives with immutable and predictable outcomes but are, like modernity itself, powerful and durable 'differentiated geographies . . . made in the relationships *between* places and *across* spaces' (Ogborn 1998, p. 19).

The equation of state sovereignty and territorial space produces a geopolitics in which historiography in general – including heritage – acts as a mechanism of dissemination for nationalism and other ideologically loaded discourses. A parallel here is to be found in studies which demonstrate how geography itself can be interpreted as a discourse, its subject matter, textbooks and methodologies underpinning the structures of imperialism and nationalism (Nash 1996; Ploszajska 1999). Whether local or national, official or popular, heritage can function to oversimplify space into idealized constructs of tradition and modernity, although, as we argue throughout this book, such attempts will be subverted by that plurality of meaning which is intrinsic to the meanings of heritage. In terms of the state, a particular time-period becomes imbued with an idealized historical experience, this standing as a metaphor of the state and nation (Agnew 1996). Although that allegory may well lack any congruence with contemporary empirical economic and social conditions (as in the resonances of *Great* Britain), it becomes invested with notions of national heritage. Thus The Netherlands, for example, is still conceptualized culturally through the parameters of a seventeenth-century Golden Age, defined not only by the art of Rembrandt and Vermeer but also through the technology of reclamation from the sea (Schama 1987). Largely a nineteenth-century invention in itself, this narrative served to support the hegemony of a capitalist, Protestant bourgeois class, and provides a cogent demonstration of the way in which the distinctive and historic territory of the nation-state becomes 'the receptacle of the past in the present, a unique region in which the nation has its homeland' (Anderson 1988, p. 24). One function of official heritage is to visualize this homeland.

The rise of the nation-state in the eighteenth and nineteenth centuries was closely connected to Romantic sentiments of the mysticism of place, and of notions of belonging and not belonging. Hobsbawm (1990), who regards nationalism as primarily a principle that holds that the political and national unit should be congruent, sees the essence of 'national' being defined within the cultural realm. Davies (1996, p. 813) agrees, citing the French historian, Ernest Renan, to the effect that the essential qualities of the nation are spiritual in nature. 'One is the common legacy of rich memories from the past. The other is the present consensus, the will to live together'.

Several important qualifications must be made concerning the nature of national heritage. First, 'nationalism favours a distinctly homosocial form of male bonding' (Parker *et al.* 1992, p. 6) as expressed by Anderson's argument that ultimately it is the 'fraternity' of the 'deep horizontal comradeship' of the imagined community 'that makes it possible, over the past two centuries, for so many millions of people, not so much to kill, as willingly to die for such limited imaginings' (Anderson 1991, p. 7). Pratt (1994, p. 30) believes that as a consequence,

> [w]omen inhabitants of nations were neither imagined as nor invited to imagine themselves as part of the horizontal brotherhood . . . rather, their value was specifically attached to . . . their reproductive roles [as] mothers of the nation . . .

Thus it is the common case that the heritage of war, militarism and the armed struggle for national freedom has been to the fore in the invention of the imagined communality of the modern nation-state and its 'one out of many' ideology. A largely masculine iconography of heritage is subborned to the defence of a nation-state, itself almost inevitably visualized and symbolized in the feminine. Second, despite its importance to the modern era, particularly in the West, the hegemony of national heritages and identities has always been compromised by other – sometimes contradictory – allegiances and interpretations already discussed in Chapter 2. Agnew (1998, p. 216) contends that 'the "sacralization" of the nation-state has never been total; even within totalitarian states, sites of religious and local celebration have had their place'. Moreover, as we now consider, the ethnic mosaic, sometimes seen as characteristic of the multicultural postmodern world, has always been so.

Heritage, nationalism and ethnicity

Despite a mutual reliance on a shared history and values, nationalism is not necessarily an intrinsic feature of ethnicity (Anderson 1991). Nevertheless, they share a dependence on heritages constructed as simplifying linear historical narratives, which are imposed on the complexities and ambiguities of the past and used to legitimate armed conflict. As Heffernan (1998a and b) shows, the boundaries of European nation-states still reflect the geopolitics of ethnic exclusion and division of territorialized political identity generally achieved through or as a result of violence and war or in war's aftermath. He observes that:

> [t]he "new" idea [defined in the 1919 Treaty of Versailles] of granting national rights to racial minorities challenged the very idea of the imperialist nation-state and was often inspired by a genuine conviction that small states were more democratic than larger ones.

> (Heffernan 1998a, p. 113)

The 'corrosive' element here, of course, was the belief that 'race' – or ethnicity – determines nationality, the ideology at the heart of Nazism.

Because of their congruence of characteristics, it has become customary to refer to 'ethnic nationalism' and to the ethnification of the nation-state, a process which as we explain in the next two chapters possesses several different dimensions. By definition, this is exclusive, often intolerant and frequently unstable, although it is not the only form which nationalism can take (Graham 1999). Based on representations and heritages, which make membership a matter of blood and equate identity with a national territory that embodies the community of birth and native culture, the primary function of ethnic nationalism lies in its subsumption of diversity and denial of heterogeneity (Shaw 1998). As such narratives rely on their appeal to cultural symbols of identity and collective material goals in pursuit of political goals – primarily control over a state – that denial often takes the physical form of 'ethnic cleansing'.

Hobsbawm (1990, p. 65) argues, however, that very few modern national movements in Europe were actually based on a strong ethnic consciousness, although 'they often invent one once they have got going, in the form of racism'. For example, *L'Action Français*, founded in 1899, expounded a virulent form of racial nationalism, which equated Frenchness with being native-born and Catholic; as was also then true of Irish nationalism, a particular religious allegiance and national identity became inseparable. This more intolerant, dogmatic and ultimately deadly variant of nationalism was characteristic of late nineteenth-century Europe, succeeding earlier more liberal variants, which often originated in the struggle for freedom from reactionary dynastic rule (Davies 1996). When exported through imperialism's networks, the racial hues of such ideas were compounded by notions of European superiority that projected on colonized lands and their inhabitants, 'imperial codes expressing both an affinity with the colonizing country and an estrangement from it' (Daniels 1993, p. 10). Increasingly, for example, '[Britons] defined themselves in contrast to the colonial peoples they conquered, peoples who were manifestly alien in terms of culture, religion and colour' (Colley 1992, p. 5). In Europe, the racial connotations of nationalism were later glossed by fascism and its inherent anti-Semitism, the apogee of racial nationalism in France, for example, occurring during World War II when the collaborationist Vichy government deported French citizens who were Jews to the Nazi death camps in Poland. (It has taken much of the intervening 55 years for France to remember these events, proof of the adage that nationalism is often as much about forgetting the past as commemorating it.)

Historically, the invented, imagined community depended on tropes of cultural exclusivity. Besides language and sometimes religion, its defining characteristics had to be located firmly in readings of the past and place that legitimated the nation's claim to its territory. By its very nature, nationalism embodies a zero-sum conceptualization of power in which possession of territory is absolute and non-negotiable. Only through war can territory be wrested from its rightful owners. That sense of belonging depended on forgetting as much as remembering, the past being reconstructed as a trajectory to the national present in order to guarantee a common future (Gillis 1994). 'History was raked to furnish proof of the nation's age-long struggle for its rights and its lands' (Davies 1996, p. 815), and constructed around the Othering of a common enemy (or enemies).

Great Britain, for example, can plausibly be regarded as an invented nation 'superimposed, if only for a while, onto much older alignments and loyalties' (Colley 1992, pp. 5–6). In one sense *British* national heritage is militaristic, harking back not only to war with the perpetual Other of France and, before that, of Spain, but to a period of imperial hegemony and global power. It is vested above all in the triumphal morphology of London, the imperial capital, in militaristic rituals, and in the close ceremonial relationship between the Royal Family and the Armed Forces. But it is a highly qualified militarism in which gallant defeat is often celebrated as much as glorious victory, while a central motif remains the memoralizations of death and sacrifice, best encapsulated in the cemeteries of the Commonwealth War Graves Commission. As discussed in Chapter 2, these can be read as conveying no real sense of sacrifice to the nation-state, being, instead, essentially apolitical sacred landscapes. They presage, too, in their sombre way, the multicultural nature of the Commonwealth, arguably the most successful transnational institution to emerge from the imperial world.

Englishness, however, seems different. For Lowenthal (1991, p. 213), nowhere else in Europe is landscape 'so freighted as legacy. Nowhere else does the very term suggest not simply scenery and *genres de vie*, but quintessential national virtues'. As Agnew (1998, p. 214) observes, however, even in England, not all is as it seems.

> The visual cliché of sheep grazing in a meadow, with hedgerows separating the fields and neat villages nestling in tidy valleys dates from the time in the nineteenth century when the landscape paintings of Constable and others gained popularity among the taste-making élite . . . Nevertheless, the "invented" ideal of a created and ordered landscape, with deep roots in a past in which everyone also knew their place within the landscape (and the ordered society it represents), has become an important element in English national identity, irrespective of its fabulous roots in the 1800s.

Such allegories of place were constructed through particular readings of religion, art, literature and even music into ideal national or representative landscapes. It is these invocations of heritage which act as a visual encapsulation of a group's occupation of a particular territory and the memory of the shared past that this conveys (Daniels 1993; Graham 1994b; Agnew 1998). The dilemma, however, was that a 'nation of even middling size' had to construct this manifestation of unity 'on the basis of evident disparity'

(Hobsbawm, 1990, p. 91) so that national heritage landscapes essentially subsume diversity, even though they may have little congruence with the realities of everyday life.

Johnson (1993) uses the term, 'hegemonic landscape', to convey this sense of an imagery of ideal place becoming the heartland of a collective cultural consciousness and – despite Rose's warnings against bi-polar models of culture vested in Otherness – this remains a useful concept so long as it does not in itself define a dualistic conceptualization of society. In Ireland, for example, the imaging of the Atlantic West as the cultural heartland of the country was an essential component of the late nineteenth-century construction of an ideology of Irish nationalism (Graham 1997). Strongly reinforced by the intellectual élite of early twentieth-century Ireland, the 'West' became an idealized landscape, populated by an idealized people who invoked the representative, exclusive essence of the nation through their Otherness from Britain. The invented, manipulated geography of the West portrayed the unspoilt beauty of landscapes, where the influences of modernity were at their weakest and which evoked the mystic unity of Ireland prior to the chaos of conquest (Johnson 1993, p. 159). Agnew (1996) believes that such renditions of place are fundamental to a European tradition of over-simplifying space into idealized constructs of tradition and modernity. He warns elsewhere (1998), however, that such imagined places must not be reified, for history does not end with the modernist story of a representative landscape created to secure national identity.

> In England the shock of industrialisation produced a romantic attachment to a rural/pastoral ideal that has outlasted the original historical context. For the United States, the myth of the frontier and the subjugation of 'wilderness' has likewise served to focus national identity around themes of survival, cornucopia and escape from the confines of city life.
>
> (Agnew 1998, p. 232)

Conversely, attempts to delineate an Italian landscape ideal failed, partly because the country lacks the dominant heroic event on which landscape ideals are based. 'Only the recycling of the Risorgimento [the process of unification in the 1860s] serves a similar purpose' (Agnew 1998, p. 232) and it cannot be fixed in place. Instead, there are multiple interpretations of Italianness and its essential landscape, 'rather than a stable, singular interpretation that serves to knit all Italians together'.

The very survival of Italy suggests, therefore, that a national landscape myth is not an essential heritage prerequisite for a state. In part, this is because there is another dimension to national identity, one which can include other attributes of citizenship and territory that are not necessarily congruent with ethnic markers.

Civic nationalism is regarded by many scholars as having derived from the rationalism of the eighteenth-century Enlightenment, whereas ethnic nationalism emerged from organic notions of identity associated with the Romantic movement.

(Shaw 1998, p. 136)

In this civic manifestation, members of the nation self-identify with a common institutional heritage, a single code of rights and a well demarcated and bounded territory. Membership is by residence rather than blood and is legally inclusive (if less so in reality) – at least of those who live within the national territory. Thus the 'American people' is a multi-ethnic cultural mosaic, but one drawn together by the country's institutional framework, the basis of its national identity (Smith 1991). Nevertheless, heritage remains to the fore in the evocation of the state, not least through heroic representations of the West, the frontier and the wilderness. Although subject to extensive revision and contestation of its representations, western history still seeks to be 'a popular history which informs the political discourse of the times, which helps to understand who "we" are' (Mitchell 1998, p. 8).

Heritages of disinheritance and atrocity

The corollary of understanding who 'we are' is that the burdens of heritage are inevitably invoked. In appropriating particular constructions of the past, the representations of certain social groups are privileged at the expense of others. As in nationalism, social inclusion is commonly cemented by processes of Othering that depend on social exclusion, one potent reason for the persistence of nationalist tropes of identity. Although such exclusion may be relatively benign in the sense of being non-violent, it can also extend to deliberate disinheritance and, ultimately, to a heritage of atrocity. We explore these issues largely through the medium of twentieth-century Eastern and Central Europe.

Nationalism in Eastern and Central Europe

Processes of disinheritance do not necessarily have to take extreme forms but the excrescences of ethnic nationalism that have accompanied the collapse of Communism in Eastern and Central Europe provide a grim reminder of the potency of such discourses. In general terms, identity politics in the West are more effectively defined by the precepts of civic nationalism, although as Shaw (1998, p. 136) warns, in reality, however, 'the two forms of nationalism are by no means mutually exclusive'. One reason for this is that ethnic definitions of European states have proved unsatisfactory because the territorial integrity of many states themselves has often been compromised, boundaries having proved to be as contingent as the identities they contain. Germany, for example, finally unified only in 1871, has altered dramatically

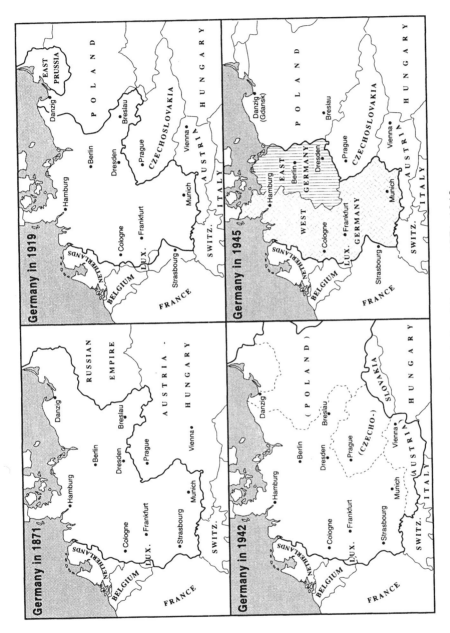

Figure 3.1 The successive alterations in the boundaries of Germany, 1871–1945
Source: After Jess and Massey (1995, p. 166)

in extent several times during the intervening period, each involving a repositioning and reinterpretation of the heritage iconography of the state. After World War I, it lost territory to the newly-established Polish state, only to reclaim this (and more) following Hitler's invasion of Czechoslovakia and Poland in 1938–9. Following World War II, a much shrunken Germany was divided by the victors – the United States, Britain, France and the USSR – between the capitalist Federal Republic (West) and the Communist German Democratic Republic (East). The country's present boundaries were established as recently as October 1990 when West and East were reunited (Figure 3.1). Each ideological – and spatial – repositioning of the German state has demanded an enduring and radical revision of national heritage narratives; as Tunbridge (1998, p. 250) observes:

> A ninety-year-old Leipziger (in 1998) will remember: the authoritarian Second Empire of Kaiser Wilhelm II; the first democratic Weimar Republic; the totalitarian Nazism of Hitler's Third Reich; the state socialism of the GDR; and the contemporary democratic Bundesrepublik.

More widely, the prolonged and shifting processes of European state formation have often imposed states defined by ethnic criteria onto a cultural mosaic, the complexity of which has been further exacerbated by the forced migrations caused by warfare. After the victory of the Red Army in Eastern Europe in 1945, for example, as many as 12 million Germans were forced to migrate west, only to be succeeded by Poles, in turn ejected from their eastern territories lost to the Soviet Union (Tunbridge 1998). Such human costs reflected the reality that because of earlier migrations – either voluntary or forced – and wars, the construction of ethnically defined states in Europe could be no more than an approximate process. Many of the polities created by the Treaty of Versailles proved incapable of defending themselves and were easily swept aside by Nazi Germany (Shaw 1998). In numerous cases, these countries had to be substantially recast following World War II. In the Balkans, the ethnic mosaic was so complex as to prevent the creation of stable national states. The malevolent legacies of ethnic territoriality have been manifest. Boundaries failed in defining homogenous ethnic homelands within the mosaic. Numerous minorities were left on the wrong sides of boundaries and inevitably became – and may still remain – targets for persecution and sources of actual or potential conflict between countries. Most horrifically, the major European peoples not nationally defined, the Jews and Romanies, became the targets of Nazi genocides. By 1945, Hobsbawm claims that the quintessential modernist construct of 'the homogeneous territorial nation' had become 'a programme that could be realised only by barbarians, or at least by barbarian means' (1990, p. 134).

If that is so, the barbarity has persisted to the present day as the geopolitical map of Eastern Europe is transformed in the wake of the collapse of the Soviet Empire. Pilkington (1998) estimates that around 25 million ethnic

Russians have been displaced since 1991, around three million returning 'home' either voluntarily or as a result of force. Vicious conflicts, fuelled by nationalist and ethnic rivalries, as well as religion, have occurred in a succession of former Soviet republics. The wars in the former federal republic of Yugoslavia in 1991–5, and again in Kosovo in 1998–9, reflected the very worst excesses of ethnic nationalism but simultaneously demonstrated that the struggle for national identity is fundamentally related to the historical struggle of subordinated groups for political recognition.

In Eastern Europe generally, the sudden collapse of Communism in 1989 precipitated widespread conflict and an escalation in the politics of difference which had temporarily been contained within the Soviet empire. With that institutional framework gone, national heritages became paramount in a political environment in which there is widespread disparity of wealth and virtually every country contains minority groups inevitably defined by their ethnic origins. The borders drawn on ethnic principles in 1919 produced either multi-national states like Czechoslovakia, which divided peacefully into its two principal ethnic components in 1992, or states with core peoples (Agnew 1996; Figure 3.2). Heritage became a matter of replacing the old monuments of imperialism, for example of the Austro-Hungarian or Prussian empires, with a new heritage of national liberation. This involved the deliberate disinheritance of the minority groups left on the wrong sides of borders (Tunbridge 1994). It was important, for example, to establish primacy of occupation in an area in which medieval society had been dominated by the eastward colonizations of Germanic peoples settling Slav lands. While German archaeology before 1939 sought evidence that justified German expansion, the post-1945 period has been dominated by the search for indigenous origins to social change. This is graphically demonstrated, for example, in the search for urban origins in Poland where explanations based on German colonization were no longer tenable. Consequently, Leciejewicz (1976) argues that the economic and cultural foundations of the Polish state were entirely of native origin, while 'incipient' or 'proto' towns existed between the Elbe and the Oder from the ninth century at the latest, thereby predating the onset of German colonization (Hensel 1969–70). In other words, the academic debate concerning objects, which in themselves may be translated into heritage, can be motivated directly by nationalist prerogatives (and it is only fair to stress that Poland is but an example).

After World War II, nationalism in Eastern Europe was suppressed by the imposition of Communism. Attitudes to heritage were contradictory. On one hand states like the German Democratic Republic (the GDR or East Germany) represented a new world, a break with the past. On the other, the GDR was unable to resist exploiting the past as a source of legitimacy. While West Berlin was consciously developed as a bastion of brash capitalism, East Berlin retained the heart of the old imperial German capital city (Figure 3.3). This was underlined by the GDR's appropriation of the legacy of the city of Weimar, the cultural capital of modern Germany. In reconstructing the

Figure 3.2 Central and Eastern Europe, 1921–1989
Source: Adapted from Shaw (1998, p. 123)

Figure 3.3 The heritage and identity contradictions of the former GDR: Marx and Engels stand in front of its Parliament building in the former East Berlin, while behind is the Dom, commissioned by the Kaiser William II and opened in 1905. Damaged in World War II, the building was restored by the GDR government as part of a policy of appropriation of past German culture to claim legitimacy for itself

ceremonial centre of Berlin and other cities, the GDR proclaimed itself to be the true custodian of German culture, a reading rendered more complex by the simultaneous need to distance itself from the Nazi past. In this reconceptualization, the GDR used preserved concentration camps, notably those at Buchenwald and Sachsenhausen, to demonize both the Third Reich and also West Germany, the latter identified (with some justice) as the refuge of both Nazis and industrialists who had exploited camp labour (Koonz 1994; Tunbridge 1998; Figure 3.4). As Buchenwald was built initially, largely to imprison Communists, the GDR could claim legitimacy by endowing the camp's victims with the mantle of resistance to Nazism.

But once capitalism triumphed and the Berlin Wall tumbled down in 1989, the GDR had no validity as a separate state. In claiming Germanness for itself, it made reunification inevitable, now that its Communist ideology was no longer tenable. Since 1990, democratic united Germany has had to dispute what it felt were misrepresentations in this narrative, without incurring the suspicion of evading the GDR's legitimate charges. In terms of the camps like Buchenwald, it has instituted a much better-funded research effort to create a historically sequential narrative from the 1930s to today. This recognizes those formerly excluded, including the US liberation of Buchenwald and the Soviet excesses of its 1945–50 denazification period. The GDR's heritage interpretation is seen not as wrong but as an interim, incomplete product of the political perspectives and research limitations of its time.

Since 1989, nationalism has re-emerged in Central and Eastern Europe. Rediscovered national heritages reflect back to the pre-Communist era and even, as in the example of Hungary and its capital Budapest, to former imperial greatness in which the country is represented as the bulwark of Christendom against Asia and Islam. The heritage sold to the cultural tourism industry is that of a fifteenth-century golden age exemplified, for example, in the built fabric of Buda and its depiction as a centre of the Renaissance. Budapest also demonstrates neatly that monumental features do not have to be changed physically but may require only reinterpretation. For some fifty years, the dominating statue crowning Gellert Hill represented the city's 'liberation' by the Red Army in 1945 and thus the triumph of Soviet ideology. It was erected originally, however, as a personal memorial to the son of the regent Miklós Horthy, who came to power in 1919 and was indirectly a statement of his regime's nationalist right-wing ideology. Today, in post-Communist Hungary, the monument has yet another incarnation as a symbol of urban pride and renaissance.

Heritage and atrocity

Although Budapest probably functions less as a repository for Hungarian national heritage and rather more as a portrayal of Hungary's new location as

Figure 3.4 Buchenwald, Germany. The monuments are on the site of the former concentration camp huts. The main surviving building, which contains the revised museum, is in the background

a Central European state seeking early entry into the European Union (EU), the wider recent experiences of Central and Eastern Europe serve to perpetuate compelling evidence of the enduring significance of nationalism as the primary mode of identity and of national heritage as a principal means of delineating and representing that identity. While 'ethnic cleansing' may refer to the forcible migration or genocide of minority peoples, it can also refer to heritage disinheritance, destruction and atrocity (Tunbridge and Ashworth 1996). Destruction, concealment and distortion are merely the more obvious ways in which one social group, as an adjunct to its control of territory, can seek to obliterate or marginalize the cultural record of another people, usually as a means of denying the legitimacy of their continued presence or destroying the evidence of their former presence. The historical record is replete with examples – or more accurately would be so – except that the control of that record is central to the disinheritor's objective. Our awareness of heritage disinheritance and its extension into a heritage of atrocity therefore depends on how successfully the disinheritance has been perpetrated or, conversely, challenged.

Atrocity and its heritage may be triggered by political, social or even economic circumstances. Typically, however, it has resulted from particularly hostile constructions of Otherness and, above all, from inter-ethnic hostility: Turks against Armenians; Bosnian Croats versus Serbs versus Muslims; Germans against Jews. The relationship between heritage and atrocity is more complex than might at first appear, involving a bi- or even tripolar web of accusation, counter-charge, excuse and denial. The first party is the victim, a status hardly desirable in life, but one both prized and even contested due to the political rewards stemming from heritage interpretations of horrors now past. The second is the perpetrator, to whom the converse applies; creative changes of identity are merely one defensive tactic used in attempts to avoid the opprobrium of guilt. A possible third party is the bystander, vulnerable to charges of being an accomplice by virtue of doing nothing.

Pre-eminent in any discussion of the heritage of atrocity are the events which occurred during the Jewish Holocaust and the related events on the Eastern Front in World War II. In the role of victim are the Jews, but also the Romanies, Soviet and other prisoners of war, and many among the civilian populations of the countries occupied by the Third Reich. As these groups may aggressively compete for primacy of victimization, the actual remains or sites of the death and labour camps themselves have become part of Europe's contested heritage. Auschwitz – perhaps the pre-eminent symbol of the Jewish Holocaust – has been the subject of a 'steady Catholicizing process' in which it stands increasingly as a 'symbol for Poland's role in Catholicizing Europe, in the past, now, and in the future' (Charlesworth 1994, p. 591). This was first manifested in the erection of a 'papal' wooden crucifix outside Auschwitz I as a sign of defiance to Jewish organizations. In 1998, the dispute escalated as right-wing Polish Catholic nationalists planted several hundred further crosses, demanding their right of ownership to a place of death as a symbol of their fatherland. As some 90 per cent of Auschwitz-Birkenau's estimated 1.5 million victims were Jews, this claim is bitterly resented by Jewish organizations and the Israeli government. The additional crosses were removed in 1999, although the eight-metre-high papal cross remains as a symbol of Polish martyrdom. The perpetrators in this case included German Nazis, but also their locally recruited co-combatants and collaborators. Among the bystanders were an assortment of Eastern Europeans and even Allied governments, who knew of the slaughter of the Jews.

The relationship between heritage and atrocity extends to the behaviour of entire states. Israel has successfully appropriated Holocaust victimization into its national heritage identity, most vividly symbolized by the Holocaust museum and memorial at Yad Vashem. Even then, however, Jews are in conflict over whose version of the Holocaust should be preserved in the images contained there. For example, in discussing an image of naked Jewish women about to die, Dear (1997, pp. 230–1) writes:

> Orthodox Jews in Jerusalem . . . objected to the display of dead or near-dead people, on the basis that the victims are being degraded yet again by their nakedness. Defenders of the photographs . . . objected to the sanitization of Nazi cruelty that would be implied by the removal of the images.

Internationally, Israel's behaviour in the Middle East is sanctioned by its global capital of victim-goodwill, while the attitudes of other states towards it varies in accord with their own roles in the Holocaust: Germany as perpetrator; France or Poland as part-collaborators; parts of the western world as bystander; and much of the Middle East as innocent derivative victim. In accepting the perpetrator's role, the then-Federal Republic of Germany committed itself constitutionally as a haven for the oppressed (until recent extremist backlashes against immigrants) and a model of external non-intervention.

The heritage of atrocity, wherever it occurs, has a predictable geography. As with Yad Vashem, the appropriation of victimhood is likely to involve shrines in the most sacred, usually the most visible, places from the standpoint of the group in question. From a perspective of contrite bystander or concerned 'world citizen', a claim to co-responsibility in perpetuating atrocity memory may likewise produce high-profile shrines. Thus the Holocaust Memorial Museum in Washington, D.C., reflects the United States's perception of itself as the 'arsenal of democracy', as well as the reality that it is home to much of the world's Jewish population. Again, we can cite the commemorializations of Jews and the Holocaust, which are part of the new Berlin. In stark spatial contrast, places of perpetration of atrocity tend to be peripheral and remote. In 1940, the secret Soviet execution of some 26 000 Polish officers took place in the isolated forest of Katyn near Smolensk, while the slaughter of Kiev's Jews at Babi Yar in 1941 occurred in a gorge outside the city. The Nazi concentration and death camps were generally sited in rail-accessible locations, largely in Poland, but generally remote from the major cities (Gilbert 1997; Figure 3.5). Except for the speed of the Allied advance in 1945, all traces of the camps might have been obliterated, as some largely were. The site of the death camp at Treblinka, for example, is now marked only by a memorial. Notwithstanding such efforts at concealment, sufficient material evidence has survived – or even been rebuilt in what Gilbert (1997, p. 277) refers to as 'zealous restoration, to say the least' – to constitute a material heritage of atrocity.

The widespread realization that the physical destruction of a people can be promoted by the deliberate destruction of the symbolic past on which their identity depends has continued to promote heritage atrocity. Among

Figure 3.5 The geography of the Holocaust
Source: adapted from Heffernan (1998a, p. 169)

numerous examples are the on-going attempts by the Turkish government to destroy the surviving physical heritage in eastern Anatolia of the Armenian Christians, a people decimated by massacre early in the twentieth century and subsequent migration. This example pales, however, in the context of the wars that have accompanied the disintegration of the former Yugoslavia during the 1990s (Figure 3.6). Ó Tuathail (1996, p. 219) describes the Bosnian war in particular, which killed as many as 200 000 people between 1991 and 1995, as 'an irreducibly modern war over space, territory and identity', characterized by 'brutal and criminal campaigns of "ethnic cleansing"'. But it is not sufficient simply to kill or drive out a people from their territory. The symbolic keys to their heritage, a fundamental basis of identity, become military targets. The Serbian devastation of the Bosnian National Library in Sarajevo and the shelling of the Croatian city of Dubrovnik – a UNESCO World Heritage Site – in 1991 were among 'hundreds of attempts to extirpate the cultural memory which that archival and built heritage represents' (Tunbridge 1998, p. 256). Nor was human and heritage atrocity the prerogative of the Serbs alone. The Croat destruction of the Stari Most Bridge in Mostar is perhaps the most famous example from the Yugoslavian wars, which illustrates the wider point that the physical destruction of heritage is a fundamental aim of war, repression and eradicating a people's claim to territory.

Meanwhile, in Israel, Christian and Muslim heritage artefacts have been destroyed in what some regard as a conscious process to create a monolithically Jewish state (Dalrymple 1997). This example has a certain bitter irony, given that, in Europe, similar events took place during the Holocaust when synagogues and other structures of Jewish religious association were vandalized and destroyed, or appropriated and adaptively reused for unsympathetic purposes (Gruber 1992). More recently, however, there have been attempts to redress former heritage atrocities and try to re-create a place for Jews in Europe. Despite the present contestation of Auschwitz, it is now officially recognized in Poland that the death camps are in the first instance a heritage of Jewish victimhood. The infamous *Kristallnacht* in Germany in 1938, the best-known instance of systematic destruction of Jewish-built heritage, has been memorialized by the restored New Synagogue in Oranienburgerstrasse, Berlin, while the Jewish Museum, opened in 1999, is – together with the restored Reichstag – among the city's most emotive set-pieces in its reconstruction as the capital of a unified Germany – the 'Berlin Republic'. Nazi Germany also systematically looted cultural artefacts from the victims of the Holocaust. Many of these objects were hoarded in Prague, where they were to be exhibited as the relics of an extinct culture; today, they are contained in the city's Jewish Museum and are the object of a more sympathetic heritage tourism, by Jews and others. In other European cities as diverse as Budapest and Groningen, the preservation of synagogues by non-Jewish communities can be seen as some attempt to atone for the past, while the restoration (indeed commodification) of Kraków's former Jewish ghetto, Kazimierz, has been greatly stimulated by the 'Schindler tourism', which has followed the

Figure 3.6   The new geography of the former Federal Republic of Yugoslavia

making of Steven Spielberg's film, *Schindler's List*, in itself an adaptation of Thomas Keneally's book, *Schindler's Ark* (1982).

Conclusion

Thus the zero-sum geopolitics and heritages of modernity and the nation-state still persist, as does the potential for such constructions of identity to spill over into an orgy of heritage destruction and ethnic cleansing. None the less, it is apparent that nationalism can maintain universalizing myths only at the cost of privileging a particular representation at the expense of subordinating or actively suppressing many others. The ensuing processes of resistance have been a principal cause of contestation and war. In Chapter 2, however, we briefly examined the heritage analogies of landscape and museology and explained the ways in which the academic study of these fields has evolved into notions such as polyvocality, hybridity and the subversion of previously hegemonic representations and messages. Cultural geography in general has embraced similar notions, so that it is not a material force but an intellectual arena of numerous and contested ideas and beliefs. It is already apparent from the analysis of heritage and nationalism that 'out of many one' ideologies can only temporarily and ineffectively subsume diversity and contestation. But, it is vital to remember that the national domain does not disappear in this flux. Rather it remains as one inherently powerful form of identity, a key element in the contemporary renegotiation of space and place.

|4|
Heritage, identity and postmodernity

Introduction

Although we contend that the national scale remains pre-eminent in the definition and management of heritage (*see* Chapter 8), the contemporary debate on a geography of heritage has to be located within the burgeoning literature on postmodern societies. Postmodern knowledges are framed by their multiple resistances to homogenizing meta-narratives such as nationalism, and to the appropriation and suborning of diversity through the mechanisms of imperialism and colonialism. In its celebration of fluidity, plurality, heterogeneity and multiple socially constructed identities and meanings, postmodernism has brought a politics of ambiguities and complexities to the discipline of geography, one which embraces a greater awareness of the contradictions of the world and aspires to a markedly more nuanced treatment of those contradictions.

None the less, all too often, geographies of resistance or landscape become little more than repositories of academic complexities, ignoring the need for judgement and values in a world in which people continue to suffer oppression, to hurt others and to die in the name of free trade, class, gender, religion, ethnicity, nationalism and much more. Undoubtedly, postmodern perspectives have made us more aware of the complexity, subjectivity and contingency of history and heritage, and the repercussions of complicated pasts for diverse presents. But it is important that, in considering the role of heritage in this context, we go beyond the elegant but empty metaphors of too much contemporary geography and ground our analyses, as Lefebvre (1991) urges, in the contestation and reclaiming of the actual spaces of everyday life. For Lefebvre, 'space is produced and reproduced, and thus represents the site and the outcome of social, political and economic struggle' (Keith and Pile 1993, p. 24). Heritage is a key element in those processes of the production and reproduction of power relationships.

In this chapter, we discuss the complex and nuanced nature of identity politics in the postmodern world and examine the relevance of place and heritage to that debate. We argue against placeless identities and in favour of multiple layerings of hybrid senses of belonging. A dynamic sense of place is mirrored in heritage landscapes which carry a multiplicity of meanings and significations, and cannot be interpreted simply as hegemonic representations foisted on a supine population by an ideology in which meaning has been appropriated by dominant social groups. Critics then represent this hegemonic ideology as the centre of their objections, opposing it with a counter-hegemonic opposition that focuses on struggle and resistance and is often narrowly framed in racial terms. An emphasis on contestation does not render such an analysis irrelevant, for power relationships in societies still reflect attempts by élites to render certain values as common-sense and therefore hegemonic (Rose 1994). But the dynamism of postmodern interpretations passes beyond the binary or bi-polar nature of dominant ideology into a plethora of possibilities. We seek, therefore, to explore the ways in which a postmodern geography of heritage – a hybridity of heritages – deconstructs modernism into a chiaroscuro of multiple layerings of identity, and the heritage meanings that both express and support this complexity. The key to this discussion is the concept of heritage dissonance, which provides a basis for the analysis of multicultural societies that comprises Chapter 5.

Heritage, place and postmodernity

Despite our argument that the national scale still remains the dominant focus for heritage, many cultural theorists see nationalist place-oriented constructs of identity as ever more irrelevant to a postcolonial world in which mass migration has created complex, multicultural societies, thereby disrupting the justification for allegories of belonging constructed around place. Thus Bhabha (1994) proposes a postnationalist process of 'DissemiNation', in which new communities of interest are evolving, testimony to the construction of changing identities and transnational communities of interest that undermine and eventually negate the 'out of many one' ideology of nationalism and the nation-state. He denies the uniformity of the 'imagined community', arguing instead for an alternative 'modernity' in which 'organic' ideologies are neither consistent nor homogeneous and subjects of ideology are not unitarily assigned to a singular social position.

Place has little role in such analyses but geographers, too, have moved towards conceptualizations that deny the continuing relevance of place identities. Harvey (1989), for example, argues that time-space compression and the advent of globalization are dissolving space and fragmenting identities. The response, he argues, is an increase in xenophobia and the resurgence of reactionary place-bound politics (such as those of post-Cold War Europe discussed in the previous chapter) as people search for old certainties and struggle to construct or retain a more stable or 'bounded' place identity. In particular, Harvey points to the emergence of 'local heritage' as one such attempt to fix the meanings of places, while enclosing and defending them. To some extent, this reiterates Wright's argument (1985) that the securing of the past as a cultural presence was one of the major themes of Conservative governance in Britain during the 1980s, the aim being to defuse political tensions by erecting a unifying dominant culture of the nation. Both Harvey and Wright, however, underestimate the chameleon nature of a constantly evolving and mutating heritage.

It is Harvey's argument that the complete domination of multinational global capitalism, and the mobility of information, investment and capital has destroyed modernity's expression of itself through space. While the victims of modernity's conceptualization of space were given a sense of where they were, and thus a context for 'grounding their resistance',

> In the era of multinational capitalism, with its relentless relocations and forced redistributions of labour and resources, it is no longer clear where the centres of power or the sites of struggle are . . . the means to orientate oneself spatially may be precisely what are missing from the postmodern world, in which, to take one instance power seems not to reside in nation states but is relayed and distributed across a global network of multinational corporations and communicational structures.
>
> (Connor 1997, p. 255)

It is less than apparent, however, that people ground their lives and resistances in such notions of global power. Moreover, this is a highly privileged conceptualization, which depends on access to the means of communication. Deprived of the latter, and confined by poverty and oppression to locality, it is difficult to imagine the world's poor and oppressed conceptualizing themselves in terms of time-space compression. Even then, among the more privileged, the stuff of everyday life remains structured in more intimate and localized conceptions of place. This is probably less reactionary than a reflection of the human inability to grasp or relate to global processes that seem remote to everyday life. Harvey's ideas also assume implicitly the enduring hegemony of the hydrocarbon economy, unsustainable though that is, both in relative terms of environmental carrying capacity and absolute terms of resource exhaustion. Globalization is as much a contingent and ultimately ephemeral process as modernity, one reason why we can dispute Harvey's claim (1989, p. 337) that 'one of the prime conditions of postmodernity is that no one can or should discuss it as an historico-geographical condition'.

In his enthusiasm for dissolving rather than decentring space, Harvey overstates the case. More persuasively, Gregory (1994) contends that different people in different places are implicated in time-space colonization and compression in different ways.

The production of space is not an accidental by-product of social life but a moment intrinsic to its conduct and constitution, and for geography to *make* a difference – politically and intellectually – it must be attentive *to* difference.

(Gregory 1994, p. 414)

Similarly, Massey (1994, 1995) argues that there is nothing inherently reactionary about identification with place, even though – as we have seen in Chapter 3 – this can take unpleasantly reactionary forms. She sees space identities as fluid and dynamic, place being more than a bounded, enclosed space defined by its opposition to an Other beyond. Rose (1994) concurs, seeing the representation of places as both constituted by, and legitimating, social power relationships, while arguing for a hybridity of culture and therefore for a multiplicity of interpretations of place. More recently, Harvey (1996) himself has moved to accepting that:

> Place, like space and time, is a social construct . . . entities achieve relative stability creating space, permanencies come to exclusively occupy a piece of space for a time, and the process of place formation involves carving out permanencies which turn out to be contingent. Place then has a double meaning, as position, and as entity or permanence constituted within a social process. Place can also be understood as the locus of imaginaries, as institutionalizations, configurations of social relations, material practices, forms of power and elements in discourse . . . Social beings individually and collectively invest places with the permanence necessary for them to become loci of institutionalized social power. Harvey now sees the politics of place construction ranging across material, representational, and symbolic activities.

(Peet 1998, p. 222)

Heritage is at the core of those activities. In essence, Harvey has moved to the same ground as that defined in the concept of heritage dissonance, one occupied by uncertainty, complexity and contestation of meaning at any one time and through time. This stands as the antithesis of what Lefebvre (1991) terms 'police space', enforced 'over the irregularity and complexity of space in everyday life' through the collusion of Marxist theory and industrial capital. For Lefebvre, a necessary antidote lay in the study of the local and everyday 'production and transformation of meanings, and especially the meanings of, and expressed through, place' (Connor 1997, p. 257). Thus the multiplicity of meanings that attend a single manifestation of heritage are encoded in an array of landscapes of power and resistance (Pile and Keith 1997; Osborne 1998), often at the local scale. Place remains and as Driver and Samuel (1995, p. vi) contend, the histories of communities and local places must be understood and represented in the present 'without falling prey to introverted (and ultimately exclusionary) visions of the essence or spirit of places':

If conventional notions of place have been destabilised, what are the alternatives? Can we understand the identity of places in less bounded, more open-ended ways? Can we write local histories which acknowledge that places are not so much singular points as constellations, the product of all sorts of social relations which cut across particular locations in a multiplicity of ways? What are the ways of telling the story of places that might be appropriate to such a perspective? How are we to reconcile radically different senses of place? Such questions arise not simply within the projects of local history, but within all those varieties of writing concerned with places and their pasts.

Not least do they arise with the writing of the text of heritage, most pressingly – as we discuss in Chapter 5 – within the context of multicultural societies.

Thus we have a duality of perspectives on postmodernity which interact with a geography of heritage. First, some theorists are too ready to pronounce the despatialization of the world; second, we can reiterate again that any subject of heritage carries with it the potential for multiple expressions of meaning and identity. None the less, we believe that there are limits to Foucault's conceptualization of heritage 'as an unstable assemblage of faults, fissures and heterogeneous layers that threaten the fragile inheritor from within or underneath' (cited in Matless 1992, p. 51; *see* Chapter 2). One of the most effective critiques of postmodernity is to be found in the work of the German philosopher, Jürgen Habermas. He claims 'that there is a universal core of moral intuition operating at all times with an inherent human interest in emancipation and especially in communication without domination'. Taking the analogy of speech, Habermas argues that '[a]greement between people is achieved through the recognition of the validity of . . . truth claims and in turn their claim to reason' (Peet 1998, p. 243). It follows that the 'ideal' speech situation can be recovered. In heritage terms, this could reflect constructions of meaning that are not formulated around modernist conceptions of domination, legitimation and place-boundedness, but rather reflect the mutuality of esteem and recognition of the validity of other people's claims which underpins the complex notion of multiculturalism (*see* Chapter 5). Livingstone (1992, p. 342) believes that critiques of postmodernity, such as that offered by Habermas, suggest that 'it is surely possible to follow Foucault in seeing the wisdom of sticking close to the particular, to the local, to lived experience without adopting his Nietzschean model of truth', in which standards of judgement can be assumed but not explained. For Peet (1998), Foucault dissolves history into islands of discourse, filling the spaces of history with absolutely contingent occurrences. Thus there is no place for over-arching meaning or, as Best (1995) argues, for the universality and continuity in which Habermas grounds social theory and the conditions for advancing human freedom.

Importantly, too, we can set aside the progressive chronological implications of a modernity being subsumed by postmodernity, such a construct being, of course, a quintessentially modernist idea. Postmodernity is matched by postnationalism and postcolonialism, possibly unfortunate terms that suggest societies have moved beyond these constructs and their repercussions. Thus postnationalism, for example, is often used to refer to revisions or renegotiations rather than to the ending of nationalism, which – as we have seen – remains a powerful force, albeit leavened by a multiplicity of other dimensions to identity. In the context of heritage, post-Fordism and postindustrialism 'might be considered as a part of the attempt to disassociate ourselves from these pasts – a clinical operation to remove these unsightly calluses, sanitize them, and place them in a theme park. The society of the "post" is a society without a past' (Walsh 1992, p. 177). Moreover, neither modernity nor postmodernity have been – or are – shared by the world in a global chronology. The very interconnections between places that are at the roots of Harvey's arguments about time-space compression also serve – paradoxically to the terms of his thesis – to underscore the multiple differential experiences of places and peoples in both historical and contemporary circumstances. Those knowledges include war, oppression, atrocity and famine, as well as the hegemony of global free-market capitalism.

Therefore, how does postmodernism illuminate the debate on heritage? In terms of the issues raised above, our arguments reject the postmodernist denial of pursuing a moral or political agenda designed to make the world a better place for us to live in (Cloke *et al.* 1991). It is in this sense that we disagree with Foucault's claim that 'nothing is fundamental: this is what is interesting in the study of society' (cited in Matless 1992, p. 48). The key elements of the foregoing discussion centre, not on the denial of values or morals, but on the complex and nuanced ways in which heritage is implicated with identity and the meaning of lived experience through the interconnections and differential experiences of the world in which we live. Four points in particular can be isolated from the general discussion:

- the production of place is intrinsic to the conduct and constitution of social life (Gregory 1994);
- place identities are fluid and dynamic (for example, Massey 1994) although this does not imply some form of transition to the argument that the rapid speeding up of time and space is dissolving any sense of place identity at all;
- there exists a hybridity of identities in which the representation of places is both constituted by, and legitimates, social power relationships (Rose 1994);
- places are invested with the permanence necessary for them to become loci of institutionalized power (Harvey 1996).

A hybridity of heritages

In summary, production and consumption at the interfaces of heritage, identity and place is highly fragmented but not incoherently so. Notions of hybridity and multiplicity provide the key to the relationships between these three entities. We can identify four such multiplicities: the multiple construction of identities; the multiplicity of social groups comprising any one conceptualization of society; the multiple consumption of heritage and place; and the multiple layerings of place that challenges the former hegemony of the nation-state.

A multiplicity of identities

Turning first, then, to identity, Hall (1996, p. 4) sees the construction of diverse multicultural societies, and the concomitant fragmentation of belonging, as pointing to a world in which identities are 'never singular but [are] multiply constructed across different, often intersecting and antagonistic discourses, practices and positions'. Such a conceptualization is, in part, a reaction to the perceived hegemony of nationalist discourses in the recent past. But identity has never been framed entirely within those bounds. Modernist identity was concerned with more than nationalism but, equally, postmodern identity remains interconnected with territorial allegories of belonging that inevitably draw upon the allegories vested in the past as formulated through heritage. Hall's claim that identities are 'multiply constructed' has perhaps always been so, not least because migration and population movement – the forces which he claims characterize the postcolonial world – have undermined notions of ethnic space for centuries. While the degree of integration and speed of change has increased enormously in the later part of the twentieth century, the asymmetries of power and the reciprocal exchanges that are now termed globalization have been shaped by the global interconnections which developed and deepened in tandem with modern European industrial and urban development (Nash 1999; Ogborn 1999). The origins of globalization are thus part of the same processes as the development of modernity and nationalism. Consequently, the power of Hall's analysis rests in the contention that a multiplicity of places and their meanings are located among the 'intersecting and antagonistic discourses, practices and positions' which he identifies as the key to postmodern society, rather than in the validity of any assumptions that this polyvocality postdates the modern era.

A multiplicity of social groups

Second, cultural representations of heritage, identity and place are produced and consumed by a multiplicity of groups, even within the same bounded space. As we have seen, the focus of contestation may rest on attempts to create hegemonic representations and counter-efforts to undermine or subvert these. For example, at the very local scale, a study of the inner London neighbourhood of Stoke Newington showed that place imageries were informed by a complex mixture of class and racial attitudes. White working-class residents of the area both welcomed gentrification as a means of 'bolstering a local politics of race(ism)', while recognizing that this process and its related local heritage movement, 'built around the iconography of a mythical village England', was undermining their own local heritage (May 1996, p. 210). In turn, there was little evidence among the incoming new class of either a regressive, bounded sense of place as suggested by Harvey (1989), or the more progressive sense of place advocated by Massey (1994). In moving towards a conceptualization of multiple place identities, this particular study produced no real evidence of the less exclusionary understandings associated with postmodern attitudes.

More widely, segregated identities survive in an apparently homogenizing world, not least because postmodern re-evaluations of non-national levels and constructs of identity are constantly undermined by the survival of old cultural and ethnic hatreds and often racist exploitation of minorities (Tunbridge 1998). But no matter how many groups and nuances of identity between them, and indeed within them, there still exists a coherence of internal belonging. This is complicated, however, because groups are not necessarily defined by hegemonic principles and thus an individual may belong to several, each representing a different facet of her or his identity. Thus the internal coherence may be restricted in scope. None the less, a particular manifestation of belonging – nation, religion, gender – is likely to be dominant in an individual's self-identity, although this is subject to change through the passage of a life-time.

It is now customary to use the term, multicultural, to refer to more complex and fluid postmodern societies. The strength of modernism derived from the universalist ideas that transcended cultural differences. These could have negative manifestations, as in the excesses of nationalism, but they also embraced social justice, equality and individual rights (Friedman 1997). Multiculturalism attempts the same but in the name of hybridity and cosmopolitanism, thereby denying the hegemony of previously privileged perspectives and the recognition of previously marginalized identities. Migration is crucial to this process and to the creation of diasporic identities which help undermine the imagined coherence of the nation-state.

Hybridization is often seen as the solution to nationalist agendas but, equally, it can be argued that the evolution of postmodern multicultural states has promoted the processes of ethnification, ethnocentrism and racism (Werbener 1997). Friedman (1997) sees processes of indigenization and regionalization combining to create senses of ethnic primordality and ethnification, leaving the nation-state besieged from within and without. Thus hybridity may fail to move beyond the ephemeral and contingent, while merely masking long-term social and political continuities. In the real world, political agency is 'constituted, not in flux and displacement but in given historical locations', by having a coherent 'sense of place, of belonging, of some stable commitment to one's class or gender or nation' (Ahmad 1995, pp. 16 and 14). Consequently multiculturalism is not necessarily progressive and is, moreover, commonly articulated within the national context. Cultural hybridity has limits and anti-hybridity discourses continue to stress cultural boundedness: rather 'than being open and subject to fusion, identities seem to resist hybridisation' (Werbener 1997, p. 3). Furthermore, if the 'forsaking of modernism, which generates a return to roots, leads to a strengthening of countervailing subnational and ethnic identities' (Friedman 1997, p. 72), multiculturalism can be held to represent an abandonment of modernist ideas of assimilation. The outcome of hybridization may actually be greater conflict and dissonance.

Multiple production and consumption

Third, heritage and place – if not identity in the same way – are simultaneously multi-sold and multi-consumed. While the dichotomy between cultural and economic consumption may appear to be the most apparent manifestation of this process, in marketing terms both dimensions are heavily segmented into an array of not necessarily easily reconciled sub-markets. Each has its own pattern of demand and heritage constituency (as defined by meaning), each has its own form of consumption. These will reflect the whole gamut of identity indicators – class, education, gender, ethnicity – and a wide variety of socio-economic indicators, such as disposable wealth, propensity to travel, and household composition. The meanings and interpretations to be abstracted from any heritage assemblage are therefore highly fragmented. The very limited evidence on this, however, does point to a coherence of response within particular social groups, the classifications and interpretations placed upon artefacts imposing a rationality upon the objects that will reflect the wider epistemologies of heritage producers and consumers.

Multiple layerings of place

Finally, there remains the multiple layerings of place, a highly complex set of processes occurring at all sorts of scales, and one which we treat here in some depth because of its fundamental importance to the discussions on heritage that appear in subsequent chapters. It is widely held that the nation-state is under attack from below and above. We have already observed, for example, the importance of locality in the example of Stoke Newington above. At the much wider scale of Europe, although the strategies of European integration were not created originally in opposition to the nation-state, but as part of the post-war rehabilitation of a number of those polities (Bideleux 1996), the EU has been characterized as the world's first truly postmodern international political entity, distinct from the national and federal state forms of the modern era, but in some respects reminiscent of pre-modern territorialities (Anderson 1996; *see* Chapter 10). This hypothesis, sometimes referred to as 'new medievalism', speculates that the growth of transnational corporations and networks, combined with sub-state nationalist and regional pressures, might produce overlapping forms of sovereignty analogous to the complex political arrangements of medieval Europe (Bull 1977; Graham 1998b). Sovereignty would again cease to be a state monopoly. Meanwhile, as we have also seen, it is held that global 'time-space compression' is radically reconstructing our views of space, and leading to an accelerated unbundling of territorial sovereignty with the growth of common markets and various transnational functional regimes and political communities, which are not delimited primarily in territorial terms.

Anderson, however, considers this argument an overstatement, referring elsewhere (1995) to 'exaggerated reports' of the death of the nation-state. First, even in the EU, the unbundling of territoriality and sovereignty is limited and partial, affecting different state activities very unevenly. The politics of economic development is the sphere where state power has been most affected by globalization. Moreover, while territoriality is becoming less important in some fields (for example, financial markets), the state remains the principal spatial framework for many aspects of social, cultural and political life, including heritage, not least because of the enduring power of language differences. Second, Anderson argues, the EU, although a new political form, is itself territorial, and in many respects traditional conceptions of sovereignty remain dominant, whether exercised by Member States or by the EU as a whole. Thus it may be that although the political control of space is being renegotiated in contemporary Europe – as indeed it has always been – we are seeing *re*territorialization rather than the *de*territorialization implied by Hall and Bhabha. Perhaps the most challenging geographical manifestation of these concerns is to be found in Soja's powerful argument (1989) that space is filled with politics and ideology, a perspective later extended (Soja 1996) in his adaptation of Bhabha's concept of Thirdspace. To Peet (1998, pp. 224–5), Soja 'wants to set aside either/or choices and contemplate the possibility of a "both/and also" logic which effectively combines postmodernist with modernist perspectives', the aim being to build on 'a Firstspace perspective focused on the "real" material world, and a Secondspace perspective that interprets this reality through imagining representations, to reach a Thirdspace of multiple real-and-imagined places'.

From accounts such as those of Anderson and Soja, we can abstract the idea of multiple layerings of identity and place with potentially conflicting supranational, national, regional and local expressions, in turn fractured by other manifestations of belonging – religion, language, high culture – that are not necessarily defined in terms of those same spatial divisions. Inevitably, therefore, identity is socially and geographically diverse rather than neatly bundled, and nationalism can be seen to exist largely to structure such heterogeneity into simplifying representations – synecdoches – of sameness. To explore this point further, we use the example of France.

The impression that France is somehow a 'natural' state, defined by 'natural' boundaries on the Rhine, Alps and Pyrénées, is primarily a perspective of seventeenth-century politics, the country having grown only slowly, spasmodically, and largely through war, to attain those frontiers. The defining feature of that territory is its heterogeneity, a relationship encapsulated in the idea of the *pays* (literally an area with its own identity derived, not only from divisions of physical geography, but also from ethnic and linguistic divisions imposed on a region by its history) as the geographical mediation of synthesis and continuity, the product of human interaction with the environment over many centuries. For Braudel (1988, p. 41), France is a 'patchwork' country, a jigsaw of regions and *pays* in which 'the vital thing for every community is to avoid being confused with the next tiny "*patrie*", to remain *other*'.

How, then, was the national unity of France invented to reconcile this geographical mosaic? This can be understood only if it is recalled that territorial identities are not absolute and never have been. Rather, they are layered one upon the other, frequently so in antagonistic discourses, each stratum defined by different sets of criteria. Hence the fierce localization of the French *pays* and its administrative equivalent, the *commune*, is overlain by, if not always fully reconciled with, the *départements*, superimposed onto the older alignments after the French Revolution but redolent of localized identities because they were generally allocated the names of rivers and mountains. Subsequently, the *départements* were amalgamated into regions such as Languedoc-Roussillon or Midi-Pyrénées, the original scheme being devised in 1910 by the geographer, Paul Vidal de la Blache (Heffernan 1998a; Figure 4.1). That such scales of identity are defined largely by administrative and financial functions serves only to emphasize the enduring importance of place-oriented politics in everyday life. Beyond that again is the national scale of identity, which in France essentially takes a civic form. 'French nationality was French citizenship: ethnicity, history, the language or patois spoken at home, were irrelevant to the definition of the "nation"' (Hobsbawm 1990, p. 88). Democratization, the 'turning of subjects into citizens', was crucial to this process and the engendering of a patriotism that shades into nationalism.

Thus it is readily apparent that sub-national dimensions to belonging constitute a very ambiguous and fractured form of identity, a conclusion germane to constructions of identity-laden heritage. The south of the country – the Midi – is partly defined by the linguistic divide between Teutonic northern France (*lange d'oil*) and the Latin, Mediterranean south (*langue d'oc*) (Figure 4.2). But the Midi itself is divided into a number of cultural regions with their own distinct dialects and cultural heritages. To the west of the Rhône, Occitan, for example, is one of the factors that still distinguishes Languedoc-Roussillon from Provence to the east, two discrete regions with very different histories and contrasting trajectories of belonging. Languedoc-Roussillon, however, is an administrative region, which bears only a passing

Figure 4.1 Paul Vidal de la Blache's scheme for a regionalization of France, 1910
Source: adapted from Heffernan (1998a, p. 105)

resemblance to historical circumstance. It is very much smaller in extent than the area of the *langue d'oc*, while Roussillon only became incorporated into France as late as the seventeenth century, having been part of the ceaselessly mutating medieval kingdoms based on Catalonia and Aragon. Nor can contemporary Languedoc-Roussillon claim to be a coherent cultural entity, its southernmost portion asserting a much closer trans-Pyrénéan affinity – based on a common historical narrative – with Catalonia than with any part of France at all. The unofficial heritage of political graffiti sprayed on walls, reads (in Catalan), 'Neither France nor Spain'.

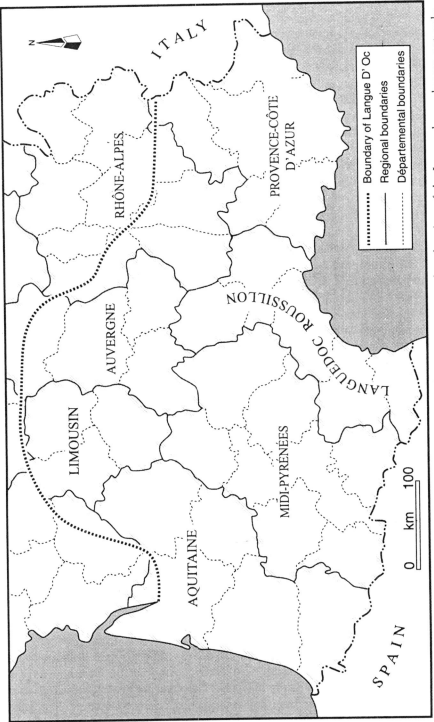

Figure 4.2 Administrative boundaries in the French Midi. The contemporary cultural region of the Languedoc embraces not only Languedoc-Roussillon but also much of the Midi-Pyrénées

Despite these inconsistencies, the identity and heritage imagery of contemporary Languedoc is heavily informed by depictions of the savage oppression suffered by the region in the early thirteenth century, when Capetian France, centred on the Île-de-France around Paris, allied with the Papacy to launch the brutal Albigensian Crusade against the Cathar church. Ostensibly justified by the need to extirpate heresy, the underlying – and ultimately successful – political agenda sought to secure the submission of the Count of Toulouse to the French crown and more fully integrate his territories within its domain. Today, the Cathars, and their fortress eyries in the Pyrénées, allied somewhat incongruously to rugby and the contemporary monumental architectural splendours of Montpellier, the regional capital, have become quintessential heritage symbols of a reborn regional cultural consciousness that seeks both to promote continued Languedocian resistance to Parisian ascendancy over the terms of Frenchness but also to assert the region's growing self-confidence and self-reliance (Ardagh 1999; Figures 4.3 and 4.4).

At the same time, however, despite these complex manifestations of a fragmentation of place-centred identity, it would be foolish to underestimate the enduring importance of that Frenchness as a central motif of the country's heritage identity and one which has had a global impact through the imprint of colonialism. France remains divided by the vitriolic debate on precisely who qualifies for membership of the nation. The *Front Nationale* and its blatant recourse to anti-immigrant rhetoric is the principal contemporary expression of a long legacy of right-wing intolerance in the country. In particular, it exploits the presence in metropolitan France of peoples of North African descent (largely Muslim). On one hand, they can be seen as symbolic of a new multicultural France that negates the 'out of many one' conceptualization of nationalism, but does not deny their allegiance to the French state for which they died in large numbers during World War I, as the Islamic grave stones in French military cemeteries attest (Figure 4.5). Their presence also requires France to acknowledge the savage Algerian War of 1954–62, which killed an estimated one million Muslim Algerians in the name of the *présence française* (Horne 1977). It does well to remember again that multiculturalism is commonly articulated within the national context, which was precisely what occurred when France won the 1998 Soccer World Cup with a team containing many first- or second-generation immigrants. Conversely, for the *Front Nationale*, immigrants from Francophone North (and West) Africa stand as the Other within, an affront to a true Frenchness still essentially racist in its definition. In sum, the complexities of territorial identity in France are not amenable to explanation through the medium of nationalism alone. Place is still fundamental to belonging, but this relationship is expressed today – as indeed it always has been – in a heterogeneous and nuanced fashion. While the terms of the interconnections between spatiality and identity have changed, that does not render allegories of place irrelevant, nor modernist nationalist representations of heritage redundant.

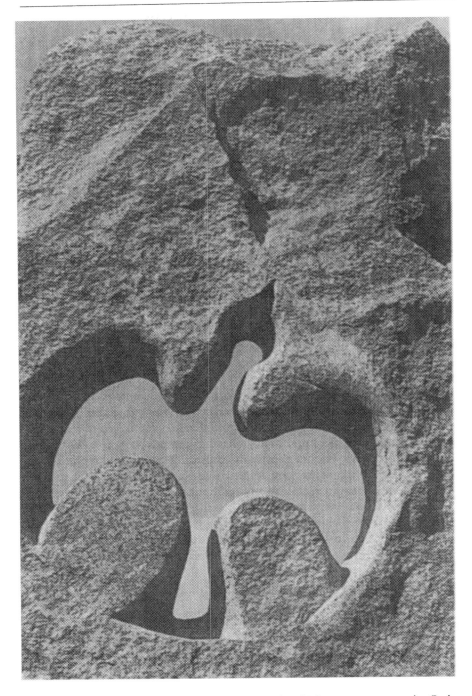

Figure 4.3 The monument at Minerve, Hérault, which commemorates the Cathar martyrs burnt to death after its fortress fell to the forces of the Albigensian Crusade in 1210

Figure 4.4 The hill-top Cathar fortress of Montségur, Ariège, which surrendered to the forces of France and the church in 1244, has become the pivotal focus of the resurgence of interest in the Cathars as a symbol of regional identity

France, like any other country, therefore displays a complex array of relationships between heritage, place and identity. The consequences are equally complex processes of inclusion and exclusion which complicate the processes of constructing a multicultural state, in itself a contested concept. Within this matrix of intersecting but not necessarily compatible allegiances to place, combined with equally complex geographies of resistance, it is not difficult to see how the same heritage objects take on a multiplicity of cultural and identity significations and interpretations, as well as being the focus of the 'tourist gaze' (Urry 1990). While being careful not to exaggerate the death of the national, the example of France demonstrates the fractured nature of modernity and the ultimately ineffective nature of nationalism in subsuming differences.

Towards a synthesis

The relationship between heritage, identity and place can now be seen as intensely heterogeneous and full of nuances and ambiguities. Hybridity is all, not least because of the increasingly complicated interconnections of a globalizing world, itself a product of the modern era. But hybridity and complexity are not synonyms for incoherence. Place remains a fundamental icon of identity but one individual self identifies with multiple layers of place and with other manifestations of identity, not necessarily spatially defined. The point is, however, that this was always so. Nationalism imposed

Figure 4.5 The gravestone of a Great War French Muslim soldier, Rancourt Cemetery, Somme

representations of homogeneity only for a while, and while dominant in some societies, it never completely subsumed regional and other more localized place identities. Thus Braudel (1990, p. 669) argues that France's diversity is not unparalleled: 'Germany, Italy, Britain, Spain, Poland can all lay claim to diversity'. So too can smaller countries. Pursuing the same symbiosis of physical environment and human society, Ireland's most influential geographer, Estyn Evans (1981), believed that even fractious Ulster could be reconciled as a single theme with many variations, its personality deriving from the fusion of many small *pays*. Through a unity defined by diversity, Evans sought a communality in Ireland's past to which all its present inhabitants might subscribe (Graham 1994c, 1996).

It is also the case that – as observed in Chapter 2 with the example of Italy – some societies entirely failed in constructing national iconographies of place. People may well identify with constructions of identity, like ethnicity or gender, that ostensibly have no necessary setting in place. But while never singular, these communities of interest overlap and it is in place that they so do, not least because the abilities of the global economy to operate through electronic communications and languages is not matched in the cultural realm. Even music, for example, apparently global, is produced and consumed – like heritage – within complex economic, cultural and political frameworks in different places at different historical times. As Leyshon *et al.* (1998) demonstrate, the globalization of music production and marketing is accompanied by the use of music in localized resistances and constructs of national identity.

Therefore, we argue that place remains intrinsic to the nature of identity and heritage. At an entirely more prosaic level, this is also the case in a cultural tourism market in which heritages are consumed through the collection of sterotypical images and debased cultural iconographies. Place is a fluid, dynamic and hybrid entity occurring at many scales from the global to the very local, and in their heterogeneity and complexity, identities and heritages reflect that same diversity of constructions of place. But as we have suggested, to assume that this is a repercussion of an imagined post-nationalist era is both to underestimate the enduring importance of nationalist tropes of identity but also to exaggerate the extent of their past hegemony. Nevertheless, representations of place are often created for reasons of empowerment and investing the contingent with a material, representational, and symbolic iconography of permanency (Harvey 1996). As we explore below, such processes are no longer directed primarily at the national scale.

Dissonance of heritage revisited

If the production of heritage, identity and place is polyvocal, so too is the interpretation of this complicated set of interrelationships. The multiple readings and interpretations of hybridity are congruent with heterogeneous, multicultural and pluralistic societies orchestrated by complex forces of migration and time–space compression. But these carry with them the potential for privilege or suppression, for inclusion and exclusion. Whose heritage is represented; whose is elided? Thus no matter how polyvocal, hybrid and complex the rendition of identity might be, heritage's implication in processes of empowerment ensures that it also becomes the focus of resistances at many scales and in many places.

These issues can be addressed more precisely by revisiting the concept of heritage dissonance discussed in Chapter 1. Simply, all heritage is someone's heritage and inevitably not someone else's. The central theme of this book is that heritage cannot exist as a universal absolute. Ultimately, because it is what and where we say it is (the pivotal variable being 'we') then one person's heritage is the disinheritance of another. That such disinheritance may be asserted by either party, or by neither, and be experienced on a spectrum of emotional intensity anywhere from disregard to passionate commitment, does not alter the inherently partisan quality of whatever is designated as heritage. Moreover, this designation, and the identity of those who recognize or appropriate it, and those who do not or cannot, is in itself subject to the shifting crosscurrents of time. Heritage dissonance can be defined as the mismatch between heritage and people, in space and time. It is caused by movements or other changes in heritage and by migration or other changes in people, transformations which characteristically involve how heritage is perceived and what value systems are filtering those perceptions. The most pervasive source of heritage dissonance lies in the fundamental diversity of societies. At one extreme (as explored in Chapter 2), these divisions become hatreds and hatreds beget atrocities, victimizing both people and their heritage values. Atrocities create the most emotively macabre heritage in themselves, raising the quintessential dissonances discussed in the previous chapter; in this respect the post-Cold War reconceptualization of the former Nazi concentration camps is arguably the most difficult resolution of heritage dissonance yet attempted.

The complexities of dissonance are further exacerbated by the contemporary expansion in the meanings and scope of heritage, and the concomitant multiplication of conflicts between its uses. From the occasional designation a century ago of isolated buildings as 'national monuments' or 'historic landmarks', the scope of heritage has progressed through area conservation initiatives to comprehensive management efforts for the built environment, and to the recognition of valued continuities in the entire natural and human world. This continuing expansion of the heritage portfolio has correspondingly enhanced the potential and actuality of dissonance, not least because it is inseparable from economic commodification. Those seeking profit from heritage have triggered a further set of dissonances as they target a range of markets with a variety of different heritage-based place-products at varying scales. This has generated a profusion of messages reflecting different values and purposes, which conflict both with each other and with the diverse and unpredictable ways in which such messages may actually be received by consumers, whether or not they are the intended targets.

Thus the same heritage artefacts may preserve a record of cultural creativity, provide an instrument of political manipulation and present a source of economic enrichment. Societies may literally stand or fall by the effectiveness of their political use of heritage, while that material is simultaneously the subject of tourism and economic commodification. The agents of these different uses pursue quite distinct and potentially conflicting agendas aimed at particular markets. The recorders of cultural creativity, taking an altruistic stance on their task as guardians of artistic or historical treasures, may look askance at ideological or commercial exploitation, while the shapers of national identity may be indifferent to international tourism markets and lack the commodifying entrepreneur's business acumen to exploit them. Nor are the heritage producers necessarily in harmony with each other within any one use category, for all markets are segmented. Underlying the often multiple dissonances of use is the simple reality that those who preserve, manage and interpret heritage are rarely those who put it to use. Nor need the objectives of these producers and of the users be shared. There is in any case no clearcut user objective, since all users have their own motives, goals and institutional positions.

Although the grounds for heritage dissonance are manifold, certain scenarios form recurrent geographical patterns. One is the phenomenon of the national cultural minority. In Europe, for example, the complex array of regional cultural outliers and 'misplaced' political boundaries, accented by distinct dispersed (but mainly urban) minorities subjected to past atrocity or present intolerance, creates a rich medium for dissonance based upon cultural grievances and opposing nationalisms. Again, in postcolonial states, the principal dissonance is between new national identities based upon revised and unifying heritage values, and tourism economies, which perpetuate colonial heritages in order to sell them to visitors from former metropolitan countries who recognize their own identities therein.

Conclusion

The polyvocal world of multiple places, multiculturalism, hybridity, cosmopolitanism and internationalism is seen as a positive counter-position to the negativities of modernist nationalism and its commonplace insistence on bi-polar or binary representations of the world. But multipicity is not in itself inherently less conflictual, creating instead a markedly enhanced potential for dissonance. Nor can the fluidities of postmodern society be seen as substitutes or replacements for nationalism, which remains a vital element of place identity and heritage. It is crucial to remember that the resolution of other dimensions of diversity is often contested, and on occasion achieved, within the national or state context. The fragmentation of the relationship between place and identity has been overstated because of equally exaggerated claims of the modern hegemony of nationalism. As we have sought to explain, this has imposed a dominant and sometimes hegemonic interpretation of identity and heritage upon a state, but nationalism has rarely suppressed, and then only momentarily, all other dimensions of identity and heritage, whether vested in place or not. In Chapter 5, we explore the repercussions of these arguments through a complex set of examples. Heritage is contested along many political and social axes, and also, of course, between them. In essence, the remainder of Part II addresses the question: how can heritage be framed and managed in multicultural societies with unappealing, even unspeakable, pasts and contested presents?

|5|
Multicultural heritage: from dissonance to harmony?

Introduction

In this chapter, we pursue the issue of heritage dissonance in multicultural societies, moving from the broader debate of the previous chapters to specific examples of the complex cultural dimensions to heritage. We have argued that heritage is a crucial factor in the creation of space identities, which while remaining intrinsic to social life, are increasingly hybrid, fluid and dynamic, if also simultaneously regressive. None the less, some space identities at least must maintain an illusion of permanency as they fulfil an enduring role in power relationships. Because of that inherent dynamism, heritage is polyvocal although the selection and transmission of messages raises the question of privileged viewpoints. The very quality of hybridity means, however, that heritage always maintains a subversive quality. In its analysis of dissonance and multiculturalism through an array of examples, this chapter engages with Soja's ideas concerning the reconciliation of the real material world and imagined representations of space. In a cultural politics of difference, there is a thirdspace of 'multiple real-and-imagined places', a site of counter-hegemonic resistance. It is 'a common ground of multidisciplinarity, where we can be historical and spatial and critically social simultaneously and without a priori privileging of one or another viewpoint' (Soja and Hooper 1993, p. 200). The evidence presented here, however, concerning the contestation of heritage, suggests that while there may well be a multiplicity of real and imagined places, it is less easy to set aside the issue of the privileging of particular interpretations. The chapter begins with a brief discussion of the practical difficulties of managing dissonance and continues with a series of case studies which examine these problems in greater depth.

The management of dissonance

The practical resolution of heritage dissonance can scarcely be a simple matter, given the myriad economic, social and political functions of heritage. It is one further complicated by the multiplicity of spatial scales at which the institutions of heritage management operate and their motivations. At the local scale of the tourist-historic city, for example (Ashworth and Tunbridge 1990), management has to reconcile tourist and resident needs for heritage while, at the national scale, the cohesion of the state is usually the chief frame of reference, taking precedence over both regional identities and tourism needs. Internationally, UNESCO, particularly through the medium of World Heritage Sites, pits the ideas of universal heritage values (themselves at times the subject of intractable dissonances) against the self-interest of the various host states, chiefly concerned with national-scale priorities.

As we return to the dissonance issues raised by the different scales of heritage management in Chapters 8–11, it is sufficient here to note two points. First, it is questionable if a world heritage can be successfully maintained, given the absence of an effective governing body to assert the management of dissonance. Second, the maintenance of national heritages in diverse societies depends on a fine balance of management. National identity can be showcased in capital cities, while local perspectives from national norms may be represented in regional centres, possibly incorporating regional differences rather than promoting centrifugal tendencies.

In a more general context, it may be possible to manage dissonance by locational separation of the heritage messages. For example, the dissonances which permeate the postcolonial world can be partially addressed by deflecting the tourist interest in colonial heritage to peripheral locations in or beyond the urban centres and their nation-building agendas. However, so much colonial heritage inevitably resides in city centres that this policy is not always realistic. Alternatively, the management of dissonance can be attempted *in situ* by varying the heritage messages projected to different segments of the market (Ashworth 1998). One set of messages might be communicated through the built environment and particularly in its iconography, while others are conveyed by the printed and electronic media. It is likely that the former will emphasize the political realm, while the latter focuses upon the tourism economy, although no simplistic dichotomy can be assumed, given the multiple complexities of heritage use. Different messages, or at least emphases, can be relayed to residents as against culturally diverse visitors, some of whom who may indeed have past associations with these places which are dissonant to their present inhabitants.

The wider the cultural and economic differences between visitors and residents, the more extreme is the potential dissonance but also – paradoxically – the more obvious are the possibilities of market separation to mitigate this. For example, foreign visitors to Turkey associate most strongly with Greek, Hellenistic and Byzantine Christian heritage which may mean little to Islamic Turkish residents. The Turkish state (represented significantly by a single Ministry of Culture and Tourism) has thus to promote one heritage (and set of heritage sites such as Troy, Pergamon or Ephesus) to tourists for economic reasons, and a different Ottoman or 'Kemalist' heritage (for example, at

Bursa, Konya or Ankara) to residents for reasons of political legitimacy and social cohesion.

With respect to the critical contestations emanating from human diversity, the management of heritage dissonance takes two contrasting forms. In the first instance, a minimalist approach can be followed in the face of apparently irreconcilable group differences, as in Cyprus or Northern Ireland. This recognizes as heritage only those features which all groups can accept, or be persuaded to accept. Such a 'lowest common denominator' approach may be positively pragmatic, since it avoids both conflicting definitions of – and choices between – specific group heritages and also the costs and space which an attempt to memorialize all possible claimants might require. The minimalist approach, however, invokes several difficulties. First, it implies strict control in the interests of conflict avoidance, but the question arises as to who in a democratic society can apply such control. Clearly there must be agreement among the many generators of heritage messages that their voices should be muted, if not harmonized, in the common good. Second, the approach is particularly compromised by the flow of time which we have identified as a prime source of dissonance. Past messages cannot readily be eradicated nor present heritage expansions easily accommodated. Finally, there is an obvious loss of cultural variety and potential economic resources, not least for tourism.

Alternatively an inclusivist approach can be adopted, whereby all heritages are at least accepted and perhaps even actively cultivated across a spectrum. This might range from indifferent tolerance to interactive sharing, either intermittently (as on St Patrick's Day in New York, where anyone can become 'Irish for a day') or continuously. The active cultivation of inclusivist options provides a logical redress of dissonance in the absence of overt antagonism, since all can be flexibly accommodated. Even those who identify with formerly exclusive or dominant heritages can be compensated for their loss of hegemony with the prospect of cultural enrichment and economic gain from a tourist-marketable diversity. Contemporary marketing messages in heritage tourism indicate a widespread tendency to season formerly exclusive heritages with whatever systematic extensions might competitively broaden the market (technically 'product line differentiation'), and promote greater economic participation as well as the social and political goodwill of formerly marginalized minorities. One notable illustration is provided by the inclusion of black, French and other minorities into formerly 'Scottish' Nova Scotia (McKay 1994). An inclusive strategy, however, does not provide the panacea for dissonance. Sooner or later a judgement has to be made as to the balance and emphasis that should exist between the plural components of heritage, and this is likely to be contentious. Ultimately, the issue returns to such key questions as who decides the balance and emphasis of inclusion, and how can the decision rise above the ephemera of fashionable values or charismatic figures?

The possibility of reconciling dissonance through an inclusivist management strategy is fundamental to the relationship between heritage and multiculturalism and its democratic sustainability. As we have seen, multiculturalism is not the simple, uniform ideology that is sometimes supposed. Dissonance inevitably results when the answer to the now-familiar question 'whose heritage?' is expressed in terms of a particular cultural group. Many societies have identified and interpreted their heritage, consciously or otherwise, in terms of the dominant social values of a majority cultural and political identity. In the colonial world, conversely, the dominant heritage was that of the minority élite.

Such dominance in heritage values is very tenacious in many societies. That the dominant group may change may be of little comfort to those excluded. Often this exacerbates rather than resolves the accompanying tensions as such transfers of power are often accompanied by aggressive assertions or re-assertions of dominance. As explained in Chapter 2, virulently aggressive reassertions of dominant heritage have followed the end of the Cold War. Suppressed but competitive nationalisms have resurfaced in Eastern Europe and, as in the former Yugoslavia, led to atrocity and war, in which the annihilation of opponents' cultural heritage has constituted deliberate military strategy. Furthermore, the break-up of the Soviet Union in the early 1990s has left the previously dominant Russian identity marginalized on an unprecedented scale in most of the former constituent republics other than Russia (and even within it, as in Chechnya) but, conversely, has encouraged a reassertion of a specifically Russian identity in the heartland of Russia itself (Pilkington 1998).

Similar events accompanied the decolonization of the Third World, formerly dominant European heritage values having been generally marginalized and suppressed, while local inter-cultural tensions have been released. European marginalization is most evident in Asia and Africa, often through changed priorities in the face of demographic or economic pressure, as much as from the desire for new indigenous symbolisms. Even in the long-independent states of Latin America, however, a postcolonial reordering of heritage priorities is occurring. Indigenization of identity is widely resurgent, most clearly where the indigenous population is in a majority, as in Mexico and Peru.

The conspicuous tensions and conflicts in many postcolonial Third World societies reflect both ancient ethnic animosities and also the propensity of European colonizers to play upon these by more or less conscious policies of 'divide and rule'. The most flagrant example was the internal colonialism practised by the apartheid regime in South Africa, which found its principal geographical expression in the ethnically assigned 'homelands'. Ethnic resurgence by conservative tribal groups in Africa does not greatly affect the heritage of the built environment. Aside from notable exceptions such as the ruins of Zimbabwe, its more durable elements are in the cities, which reflect African labour without much African identity. This resurgence, however, does certainly affect the sacralization of artefacts. Both in Africa and Asia, inter-cultural tensions have often been exacerbated by the perception that one or more indigenous, usually minority, groups had previously been favoured. One example is the reassertion of Hindu nationalism in India, accompanied by partisan name-changes and the destruction of the mosque at Ayodhya in 1992. Politically, this movement is not only anti-Muslim (and recently anti-Christian) but appears to be partly a response to separatist nationalism among the Sikhs, which had earlier resulted in the desecration of their Golden Temple in Amritsar. Another case influenced by the colonial legacy is the Sinhalese-Tamil conflict in Sri Lanka, in which the 1998 bombing of the Buddhist Temple of the Tooth in Kandy was an assault on heritage sacred to the postcolonially dominant Sinhalese.

Such partisan rivalry has sometimes been intensified when one group is an exotic colonial importation. Indian minorities in Africa, the West Indies and Fiji have commonly experienced marginalization of identity and exceptionally expulsion, frequently associated with resentment of their economic status. In Malaysia, the now dominant Malays have consistently denied equal standing to their formerly immigrant ethnic Chinese (and Indian) compatriots, a process matched by the systematic cultivation of a Malay, and Muslim, national heritage at the expense of both colonial and Chinese identities (Shaw *et al.* 1997). The much smaller Chinese minority in Indonesia continues to be directly victimized in periods of unrest. Singapore is a rare exception in its suppression of Chinese (here the majority), Malay, Indian and European partisan values in favour of a fabricated national identity, a strategy which – as is discussed below – has generated a different set of heritage dissonances. A further if seldom examined repercussion of postcolonialism is the continued perpetration of (technically internal) colonial dominance by states themselves liberated from European control or encroachment. Two examples are Indonesian cultural repression in West Irian and East Timor, and the Chinese subjugation of Sinkiang and Tibet, which – in the case of Tibetan Buddhist monasteries – has marginalized local heritage to the point of destruction. Many of these unacknowledged perpetuations of colonialism are associated with religious or other ideological hegemonies.

Thus it is evident that the price of cultural hegemony 'or monoculturalism' in plural societies is too often (though not invariably) oppressive intolerance or even atrocity. Nevertheless, the widespread and sometimes violent assertion of partisan cultural values, as in the larger human issues of which heritage is the footprint in time, has been countered – with varying degrees of effectiveness – in some influential societies. As in the case of France discussed in Chapter 4, the western democracies are experiencing a new-found cultural diversity as a result of global immigration flows, while belatedly acknowledging the rights, notably to land and heritage, of marginalized indigenous peoples. In the official celebration of multiculturalism, heritage becomes the critical medium for the preservation and intergenerational transmission of the appropriate values, rather than of unilaterally dominant or conflicting ideologies. Throughout North America, Australasia and Western Europe, multiculturalism has become an increasingly prominent ideology, promoting recognition of different cultural groups in many dimensions of life, and in their heritage records.

As discussed in Chapter 4, however, multiculturalism as either a set of social attitudes or a collection of government policies is variously understood and thus frequently contested in its detail, or even as an overall objective. It can mean little more than an awareness of the existence of intercultural complexities, leading perhaps to the adoption by a dominant culture of a few selected exotic elements from minority cultures – dismissed by Buckner (1994) as the 'pizzas and polkas approach'. Such multiculturalism offers no significant threat to the dominant culture, which may even see itself as enriched by these additions. A more active and expensive approach is for governments to offer support for the expression and maintenance of minority cultures. While this strategy may be supported by the majority, it can also promote processes of ethnification which may separate rather than unite. Multiculturalism can also be conceived as an attempt to replace the existing dominant culture with something new. This in turn could be an enhanced version of a previously dominant culture ('the core and variants model'), a composite of all existing cultures ('the mosaic model'), or the merging of existing cultures into a new identity ('the melting-pot model'). The case studies which form the remainder of this chapter explore this complex spectrum of multicultural societies and their heritage representations

Multiculturalism and heritage

United States

No other nation can compare with the United States in terms of the size and cultural diversity of a population derived overwhelmingly from immigration over the past four centuries. It is conventionally visualized as the ultimate human 'melting pot', even if in practice assimilation has been uneven, particularly so for visible minorities. This status has not, however, traditionally been identified with a concern for multicultural sensitivity beyond the Constitution's guarantees of individual freedoms, most notably of religion. The Statue of Liberty's famous exhortation to the nations of Europe:

> Give me your tired, your poor, your huddled masses yearning to breathe free, the wretched refuse of your teeming shore, send these, the homeless, tempest-tossed, to me . . .

carried a promise of personal liberty and equality before the law, and perhaps of economic exploitability, but no particular respect for group cultural identity or rights. Americans old and new were, and are, expected to honour a supreme national foundation mythology, involving the pioneering of democratic values forged in the independent frontier experience and successfully wrested in the Revolutionary War of 1775–82 from the grasp of a tyrannical, imperial British parent. All cultural origins have been subordinated to this unifying ideology, instilled throughout the education system and civil and political institutions.

The heritage reflections of US national ideology are pervasive and omnipresent. The most revered are those of the American 'Revolution' – the origin of national democratic virtues – and the Civil War, deemed to have defended them. Accordingly Boston, with its Freedom Trail connecting sites associated with the Revolutionary War, and Williamsburg, the seat of the Virginia colonial assembly, where political opposition to the British imperial power was largely focused, are particularly treasured to the great advantage of the former's tourist-historic economy and the latter's unparalleled restoration (Ashworth and Tunbridge 1990; Figure 5.1).

Signatories of the Declaration of Independence are an especially place-marketable human heritage, even if (as in Virginia and the Carolinas) they were slave-owners whose descendants confronted the national ideology in the Civil War. Paradoxically, the heritage of the imperial oppressor, Great Britain, has a disproportionate presence, both as the focus of opposition and as the main original source of the population and value systems which founded the nation. Those of early British descent largely remain a patrician group readily identifying – despite its ambiguities – with this originating European heritage. The people who followed them, however, were expected to identify with a national heritage which, inevitably, had less – if any –

Figure 5.1 Williamsburg, Virginia: the main street with inn and horse-drawn tourist wagon in a 'frozen' streetscape

personal meaning beyond the constitutional fundamentals, or the possibility that one of their own was numbered in the nation's founders. Among the many agents of heritage creation, the National Parks Service is the foremost guardian of a centripetal national heritage identity, to which all have been proclaimed as contributors.

Given this clear and strongly projected national identity, it is ironic that the United States has more recently become the focus of dissent over entrenched social values, a discord which in itself has achieved the status of a new hegemony subsequently diffused to other countries. Established values in US society have been challenged as unrepresentative, especially of the disadvantaged. Beginning with the Civil Rights movement in the 1960s, which combated the racial prejudice against black Americans rooted in the legacy of slavery, other visible minorities, including native Americans and Hispanics, together with minority groups defined, for example, by sexual and ability characteristics, have challenged the national foundation mythology and/or its derivative values. The feminist movement has perhaps been the most pervasive force intersecting with the wider culture of dissent in its depiction of social, and derivatively heritage, values as the creation of an entrenched white male hegemony.

The calls for affirmative action to redress disadvantage have introduced tensions into the national heritage edifice, as it is renegotiated into representations that identify and reinterpret heritage to include those who might hitherto have been implicitly or explicitly disinherited. In historic sites such as Williamsburg and Charleston, the heritage of slavery has moved from a state of sanitization, or even complete exclusion, to one of reinterpretive inclusion, if albeit still criticized as inadequate or inaccurate (see, for example, Ferguson 1991). This process is not driven by socio-political reasons alone, as the economic advance of the descendants of slaves provides the market incentive to produce heritage which they will consume. Again, the restitution of the heritage of native Americans, after decades of denigration in Western movies, is inseparable from their claims to land and resources. These have profound implications for the conservation of 'natural' landscapes, especially in the national parks and other protected areas of the western United States, where multilateral tensions and shifting alliances have developed between conservationists, native Americans and resource development interests. Meanwhile, a significant if not yet resolved demand for a greater memorialization of women dates back to the 1930s when Rose Arnold Powell campaigned unsuccessfully to have Susan B. Anthony, the heroine of the United States' 'long crusade for women's suffrage, up there on the granite [of Mount Rushmore, South Dakota] with the four presidents' (Schama 1995, p. 385), Washington, Jefferson, Lincoln and Teddy Roosevelt. More recently, the challenge to national heritage values has extended to conflicts over heritage representation of homosexuality, and – as observed in Chapter 2 – tensions over whether the monumentalization of President Franklin Roosevelt in Washington, DC should depict him in a wheelchair.

The national heritage edifice has not, however, been fractured. Despite insurgent voices, themselves reflecting the mainstream heritage of free expression, the renegotiation of US heritage values along a more inclusive trajectory has largely co-opted minority perspectives into the central structure. In a polyglot society, it is not difficult to highlight the black Americans who died for the national cause in the 'Boston Massacre' of 1770, the Civil War battles or later conflicts. Conversely, neither is it more difficult to disinherit black than white dissenters from the Revolution, the denigrated Tories who, as United Empire Loyalists, were to constitute the core population of English-speaking Canada, where they have left an equally manipulable heritage resource.

The enduring power of this national heritage and its centrality to the United States' superpower world view does not, paradoxically, stifle discordant regional heritages. Radford (1992) argues that the memorialization of the Confederacy and Civil War in the southern states is regionally as well as nationally divisive, as is the romanticization, even lionization, of the Old South – or 'Dixie' – in globalized popular culture from *Gone with the Wind* to country music. But of course the enduring recourse to the symbols of the Confederacy, especially by right-wing groups, no longer threatens national survival. It certainly provides local heritage colour and could be regarded more benignly as just one of several regionally volatile manifestations of multiculturalism, acknowledged but firmly contained – while being profitably commodified – within the national edifice.

Canada

Notwithstanding its superficial similarity to the United States in the eyes of overseas visitors, Canada is a very different political entity. Its European settler heritage is bipolar and linguistically divided. This challenge to a centripetal national identity is accentuated by the historic definition of the French pole through its language and the English largely by the negative criterion of its rejection of the American Revolution. The combination of this human centrifugality and the hostility of the natural environmental made the founding and subsequent survival of the nation an enduring improbability. Initially it was intelligible only in reaction against the Other of the United States and its simultaneous protection by Britain, the imperial power. Throughout the first century of its political unity (1867–1967), Canada existed reactively to Britain and the United States, and lacked any clear national identity cemented by an unequivocal national heritage. Its expansion to the Pacific and Arctic, and the more recent absorption of idiosyncratic Newfoundland and Labrador (1949), accentuated this condition. While this condition of inadequate identity largely continues, Canada has been actively grappling since its Centennial with the national challenge and has arguably made progress towards a distinctive self-definition, even if some view this goal as unattainable. This representation is cast primarily in terms of a multiculturalism distinct from both the United States and Britain, so much so, indeed, that the sustainability of Canada as a nation has now become closely identified with the sustainability of multiculturalism itself.

The background to Canadian multiculturalism originated in the increasing resistance of the Francophone majority in Québec to a predominantly British national iconography, which, while not comfortably defining Canada, had remained a convenient distancing factor from the United States and a means of uniting diverse cultural groups long after the zenith of the British Empire had passed. It was a comfortable imagery for the socio-economically dominant white Anglo-Saxon, Protestant élite and more or less so for many of the cultural and racial minorities. However, Québec's secularization from its conservative Catholic background and growing national aspirations came to a head in the 'Quiet Revolution' of the 1960s. Even before the 1967 Centennial, it was clear that Canada's survival depended upon its renegotiation away from the British imagery in favour of a higher profile for French Canadians and for their language. The Royal Commission on Bilingualism and Biculturalism (1963) initiated a radical policy of bilingualism throughout the federal government and much of the education system. Simultaneously, changes in global migration trends meant that the traditional flows from Britain, and Europe generally, were drying up. Although Buckner (1994) has argued that the supposed ethnic composition of the population has had little meaning in understanding ethnic identity in Canada, the growth in migration from the Third World clearly introduced a new diversity, leading, by 1972, to a politically pragmatic federal government's espousement of multiculturalism. Apparently a logical extension of biculturalism, this policy was destined to conflict with that earlier representation. Multiculturalism entailed a commitment of federal resources to the enhancement of distinctive cultural identities through the support of festivals, 'heritage language' instruction, and all that was required to incorporate recent immigrants into the national project, as defined by the federal government. This schema edged closer to realization in 1982, with a newly negotiated constitution, complete with a Charter of Rights and Freedoms. The latter guaranteed equality, not only to recent minorities but also, as in the United States, to the native peoples and to otherwise defined disadvantaged groups.

The multicultural initiative reflected an immigration rate generally far higher relative to the national population base than in other western countries, albeit disproportionately visible only in the three largest cities, Toronto, Montréal and Vancouver. Multiculturalism has undoubtedly helped recast Canada from a nation traditionally prejudiced against discernible minorities (Morton and Granatstein 1995) into one of the world's most open and tolerant societies – if most particularly so in its own estimation. Ethnic tensions have been clearly moderated, although not eliminated. The major 'English' Canadian cities have evolved in a generation from bland redoubts of puritanical tradition to what are widely (if contestably) perceived as oases of colourful cultural diversity, suitably lubricated by reformation of drinking laws and culinary tastes. Minorities have found an increasingly secure place, while the cities have developed a previously unimagined tourism economy, in which cultural diversity can be marketed as heritage, over and above the identification of historic resources in the built environment.

These gains have been won, however, at a price. Most seriously, multiculturalism has exacerbated rather than soothed the separatist sentiments of francophone Québecois, who feel that they have become trivialized from co-founding nation to simply one among many ethnicities. In 1998, the resistance of Chinese-speakers to the 'racist' enforcement of English or French as immigration requirements threatened the ultimate survival of bilingualism. This demonstrates the potential conflict between concepts of multiculturalism, and prevailing attitudes in Québec and also the more conservative parts of 'English' Canada. More generally, discontent exists over the contradiction between equal and different treatment of minorities, compounded by perceptions that official preoccupation with those minorities is at the perceived expense of majorities, however these might be defined. This hypersensitization of minorities has bred a competitive, even victim, group mentality which has obstructed the creation of a credible collective Canadian identity (Mallet 1997). Ironically, minority representatives themselves sometimes protest the trivializing of their values by multicultural generalization or commodification (Dyer 1998).

Canadian multiculturalism must be considered in its national cultural context as a settler society (Pearson 1994), which is that of a 'mosaic' in the terms of the spectrum discussed earlier. The heritage implications of multiculturalism have inevitably been profound, equally inevitably fraught with dissonance, and have affected all but the most locally introverted public and private agencies involved with the conservation and marketing of heritage (Tunbridge and Ashworth 1996). The urban tourism marketing of cultural heritage diversity, visible in the streetscape, festivals and profusion of ethnic restaurants, bars and shops, has reached its apogee in Toronto. Here 'village' identities are now recognized largely in ethnic terms, often exaggerating the human reality, while conveniently substituting for the past squandering of the city's built 'English' heritage. Provincial governments, museums and heritage organizations have mostly recast their perspectives, although regional dissonances reflecting divergent cultural realities remain significant. Unsurprisingly, the most fundamental manifestations of heritage multiculturalism are to be found in the products of the federal agencies, above all those of the national parks agency, Parks Canada and the National Capital Commission (NCC) and other Ottawa-area bodies.

Parks Canada, for example, has devised a 'systems plan' which seeks a balanced representation of the country's natural and cultural diversity in the ongoing acquisition of national parks and historic sites. While this has been criticized as unworkable (Ashworth 1993) because of the difficulties in uncontentiously selecting or apportioning relative importance, much agility is being shown towards greater inclusivity in the reinterpretation of existing heritage sites. Thus in the most recent expression of an elastic sequence of imperial and national reinterpretations of the same core heritage resource, the United Empire Loyalists, who broadly initiated the British heritage in Canada, are now reimaged as culturally diverse Americans who rejected the founding ideology of the United States (Tunbridge and Ashworth 1996).

The showcasing of the national heritage reaches its peak in the National Capital Region centred on Ottawa. Here the NCC has the critical mandate of persuading all Canadians that they possess a sufficiently shared heritage to stay together. This entails the management of iconography and the built environment so as to accentuate commonalties and patriotic pride, a quintessentially political use of heritage and thus inevitably ridden with dissonances. The NCC's national role is supported by other agencies such as the Canadian Museum of Civilization, to which falls the task of reconciling all cultural claims to the construction of the national edifice. It attempts, as do other museums world-wide, to side-step dissonance through a mode of presentation in which multicultural inclusivity is realized through a series of ethnic tableaux. These lack any all-embracing structure that pretends to depict an evolutionary progression of cause and effect; people and cultures simply appear and disappear (Tunbridge and Ashworth 1996).

Unlike the United States, Canada has no uncontested defining core heritage to which newly recognized components could be co-opted. On the contrary, it has sought to define itself in part by its differences from its neighbour, the American 'melting pot' having been officially eschewed in favour of a 'mosaic' with no centripetal coercion, indeed no centre. Unofficially, of course, minority cultures thrive and are tourist-marketed in both countries. But the expectation of common language and loyalty is less insistent, indeed less capable of insistence, in Canada, where sectional freedoms might be regarded as a virtue made of necessity. Legislators in the United States are well aware of the 'Canadian problem' of linguistic centrifugality and potential disintegration of identity. Whereas speeches in Chinese are now made in the British Columbia legislature, California and other US states with substantial, largely Spanish-speaking minorities have either implemented, or are considering, laws recognizing only English as the official language, meanwhile restricting funding for education in minority languages. Interestingly, some of the strongest support for such measures comes from second- or third-generation descendants of non-English-speaking immigrants, who equate economic and social success with anglophone education. Conversely, much of the opposition to such measures comes from the traditional English-speaking élites upholding the constitution's liberal freedoms. This US wariness over the extremes of multiculturalism certainly poses the question as to how far the apparently generous Canadian model is in itself sustainable, let alone constituting a model for other societies (*see also* Chapter 11).

Australia and New Zealand

The cases of Australia and New Zealand are markedly different from Canada's human centrifugality. In certain respects, the two countries contrast mutually in that Australia's Aboriginal population is of North American proportions (under 2 per cent), while New Zealand's Maori population approximates 10 per cent of the whole. In other ways, however, they share distinctive qualities.

First the populations of both countries retain clear majorities of British ancestry and the United Kingdom remains the largest single source of immigrants (as of 1996). In contrast, in 1991, although approximately 20 per cent of Canadians were of wholly British and a similar proportion of French origins, the proportion of British immigrants was insignificant in the country's immigration flows. Second, both Australia and New Zealand derive a far more distinctive identity and social cohesion from their insular, isolated and exotic natural environments than is possible for Canada, where natural regions are continuous into the United States and the general environmental regime is shared with much of the northern hemisphere. Third, the global location of Australia and New Zealand is also fundamentally distinctive. The two countries are as remote as is possible from their main population sources but comparatively close to East Asia. With the breakdown of imperial trade ties as the United Kingdom has reoriented itself towards the EU, both have been obliged to develop economic ties with Asia. This has been closely associated with the abandonment of racial exclusivity in immigration, the 'White Australia' policy having been ended in the 1960s, so that, collectively, Asian immigrants now dominate.

Finally, as in Canada and elsewhere, both countries are experiencing a socio-economic reordering in favour of indigenous peoples, one that is particularly intense because of national circumstances. In New Zealand, the demographic and political prominence of the Maori people places them among the leaders in the global trend towards restitution of native land and associated heritage values (particularly place names). In Australia, the 1988 Bicentennial of British settlement was accompanied by Aboriginal activism and national conscience-searching over their treatment, followed by the legal disqualification of the doctrine of *terra nullius* whereby their land had been appropriated as effectively unoccupied (Mercer 1993). This legal renegotiation of Aboriginal rights has been reinforced by the recognition of their cultural precedence in the landscape (Head 1993; Jones 1997). In the case, for example, of the Old Swan Brewery outside Perth, the legend-based Aboriginal heritage claim to its site, although legally contested, served to eliminate this prime restored riverfront industrial heritage resource from leisure reuse during the 1990s, and even precludes any references in tourism promotional literature (Jones 1997; Figure 5.2).

These distinctive characteristics go far to explaining the relatively late, but nevertheless intense, multicultural re-evaluations of society and heritage identity in Australia and New Zealand. Other factors have also contributed. As elsewhere, political opportunism has played a role, particularly in Australia where multiculturalism has provided a convenient tool for the republican movement, which has deeper roots in anti-establishment and

Figure 5.2 Perth, Western Australia: the Old Swan Brewery site is surrounded by a security fence and marked by warning signs barring access

anglophobic attitudes. These date from the convict origins of the early settler population and republican Irish values and are demonstrated in the manipulation of the history of Australian involvement in the world wars. In sum, the Australian case clearly illustrates the uniqueness of ingredients and the particularity of the agenda that underlie multiculturalism in any specific geographical manifestation. Although its philosophical underpinnings and influences can be construed as a global phenomenon, multiculturalism cannot be carbon-copied from place to place. This is apparent in the new Australian willingness to respect Aboriginal heritage artefacts, which may be landscape features or interpretations invisible to European perceptions, or place names reflective of a tiny minority of the present population. While the multicultural recognition of both Aboriginal and Asian values has engendered a predictable right-wing political backlash, the speed and intensity of its application during the 1990s (paralleled by other dimensions of social inclusion, notably of women) would be difficult to imagine in other societies such as Canada. Indeed the re-negotiation of Australian multiculturalism is sufficiently dramatic that it arguably constitutes a globally exceptional act of deliberate heritage self-disinheritance.

The significance of this process in heritage terms is similar to, but often more sharply dissonant than, multicultural manifestations elsewhere. The dramatic (and contested) return of land ownership and resource rights to the Aborigines entrenches their heritage values in the unique Outback landscapes, that are at the heart of Australian identity. Conversely, the urban landscapes, which are the daily reality of most Australians, are overwhelmingly the product of a British settler society, indelibly reflective of Europe and closely parallel to those of other British settler societies around the world. Morphological features including, for example, corrugated iron roofs and cast-iron lattice balconies, are particularly akin to those found in New Zealand and southern Africa. These townscapes are also heavily imbued with a shared imperial iconography. The Aboriginal imprint is usually transient at best, and Asian immigrants are only beginning to make an impact, although continental Europeans have produced a significant adaptive heritage in the larger cities. Thus the townscape is usually markedly at variance with the new multiculturalism, especially so in the mass of smaller urban centres. Even if it is more diverse in the larger cities and also in ports such as Fremantle, Western Australia (Jones and Shaw 1992), local conservation interests remain focused on colonial Victoriana. Highly capitalized heritage commodification in the major cities also accentuates established values, classically exemplified by The Rocks on Sydney Cove and nearby Millers Point, which remain the 'Birthplace of Australia' to the dismay of current academic fashion (Waitt and McGuirk 1996) but to the delight of many tourists. Relatively placeless waterfront redevelopments, such as Sydney's Darling Harbour, make multicultural references, but framed in generic contexts that are intent only on retail profit. Place marketing, to which heritage promotion is central, perpetuates an alleged white, élite (and male) bias, as in Newcastle, New South Wales (Winchester *et al.* 1996). However, striking – if controversial – new heritage representations are now being promoted by leading public agencies in major cities, one prime example being the Museum of Sydney, built on the site of the first Government House, but relating its heritage significance largely from the Aboriginal point of view.

Nevertheless, the discordance between most Australian urban heritage environments, that largely sustain past social values, and the multicultural message emanating from governments and opinion leaders, presently remains. As occurs elsewhere, however, this dissonance may be partially bridged by reinterpretations of existing heritage. The monuments to the sacrifice of the First World War, ubiquitous in Australia as in New Zealand and elsewhere in the former British Empire, are especially susceptible to such reinterpretation as, almost from their inception, they have carried overtones of a national identity forged in a 'trial by ordeal', as well as their more usually overt message of sacrifice to the common imperial cause. The Australian memorials are now increasingly seen as symbolic signposts of nationalism, particularly where they concern the ill-fated landings on the Turkish mainland at Gallipoli in 1915, which has become widely interpreted as a callous British sacrifice of ANZAC (Australia and New Zealand Army Corps) lives. Two examples of sites which are susceptible to such anti-imperial resacralization while not requiring any overt alteration are provided by the ANZAC memorial overlooking Perth from Mt Eliza, a Gallipoli-like bluff adjoining

Figure 5.3   Perth, Western Australia: the war memorial overlooking the city from King's Park

Kings Park (Figure 5.3), and the Mt Clarence memorials overlooking Albany and King George Sound, the Western Australian rendezvous for troopships bound for Gallipoli.

Western Europe

While we have already considered French multiculturalism in Chapter 4, it is useful here to widen out the discussion to consider Western Europe more generally. As the birthplace of nation-states defined on ethnic principles, Western Europe is an excessively rigid cultural framework upon which to attempt to superimpose multicultural reconstructions of heritage identity. However, it has a pressing need both to achieve national minority heritage reconciliations and to evolve towards a continental heritage identity which will embrace majorities and minorities alike (Tunbridge 1998), an objective which demands a multicultural reweaving of the European heritage tapestry. The task of minority reconciliation has three prominent facets. First is the existence of spatially concentrated minorities, defining themselves primarily in linguistic or religious terms, who are the legacy of centuries of cross-cultural currents and displacements upon which national boundaries were arbitrarily superimposed. Second, and most daunting in terms of atonement for past atrocity, is the former existence of Europe-wide minorities, Jews and also the Roma or Gypsies, who were nearly exterminated during the German Nazi regime. Finally, perhaps the most pressing minority reconciliation issue concerns the later twentieth-century postcolonial immigration into Western European cities of peoples doubly alien to mainstream heritage in their absence of European and Christian roots and their frequently visible Otherness. This migration has occasioned right-wing nationalist backlashes in a number of Western European countries including Germany and – as we have seen – France. More generally it has fuelled centrifugal national preoccupations with culturally distinct immigrant flows from different source areas (King 1995).

It is very much the case that the poorer areas of most larger Western European cities have been partly appropriated by immigrant groups, who have much in common with one another in their socio-economic and spatial relationships with host populations, from whom, in turn, they are gradually securing greater or lesser degrees of acceptance. Kesteloot and Mistiaen (1997) have examined a Turkish district of Brussels in terms of an evolutionary model, which develops through successive stages from an internalized ethnic minority niche, through an externally interesting exoticism, to an internationalized economic assimilation. While the model is concerned purely with the socio-economic impact of ethnic restaurants, it triggers more intangible questions concerning the material expression of an evolutionary model of heritage adaptation which might exist in parallel. In Kreuzberg, the main Turkish district of Berlin, for example, the restaurant streetscape is characterized by a superficial modification of the German tenement environment in which signs and graffiti betray a tone of insurrection against German citizenship laws and right-wing hostility. While local conditions vary, recent European minority heritage can be more widely expressed in such dissonant terms, at least as an evolutionary phase from which assimilation might ultimately ensue.

The initiative for public multicultural policy lies substantially at the local government level and to this extent is geographically uneven. While the United Kingdom, for example, has lately fostered a cultural revival among its ancient regional minorities (notably the Welsh), some of its urban authorities, such as those in Tower Hamlets and Newham in East London, have more generally sought to recognize their diverse recent minorities. Despite often explicitly racial violence, the streetscapes in such areas can be among the best global examples in their projection of a peaceful multicultural environment, expressing both very diverse minority heritage values and official respect for those values visible in the form of adequate public maintenance and even ornamentation. In many British cities, including London, Leicester and Bradford, the adaptive reuse of religious buildings (notably a Huguenot meeting house to synagogue to mosque) provides another example of adaptive and new multicultural heritage imprints upon the townscape, imprints which conservation efforts are unequivocally seeking to retain (Taylor 1997).

It is worth noting that some heritage adjustments in favour of recent immigrants have involved an enrichment of the collective heritage without necessarily raising any substantial issues of dissonance and reconciliation. One example is the statue of Raja Rammohun Roy, the nineteenth-century Indian humanist, which was completed in Calcutta and erected – by civic instigation – in Bristol to mark the fiftieth year of Indian independence. It is aligned with another statue of Queen Victoria in front of the city's Council House and has a bridging cultural relevance to both immigrant and host societies, in that the Raja was an English and European-influenced leader of Indian social and religious reform, who died and is buried in Bristol. While such cases are still unusual, the creative potential of heritage certainly allows for a more extensive sifting (and selective projection) of hitherto under-utilized resources to build multicultural bridges, particularly since – as with Gandhi's legacy, for example – the values involved can implicitly or expressly include more than the cultures directly implicated. Moreover, such bridging heritage, invoking a minimum problem of dissonance management, is likely to be more successfully created from subjects associated with contemporary progressive values, rather than political or military power.

Whatever heritage adjustments might occur in cities, a deep-rooted national and regional identification with landscape heritage is particularly characteristic of Europe (see, for example, Lowenthal 1994). It is a moot point how far minorities might be permitted to share this identification, unless they are anciently associated with it. Kinsman (1995), for instance, relates the difficulties encountered by a black English photographer in 'her' countryside because those she meets there react negatively to her as an alien from the inner city who visibly has no business there. The wider problem encapsulated in this particular case of encompassing Western European minority heritages into multicultural reconstructions sometimes appears intractable, given the durability of regional conflicts, the legacy of atrocity surrounding ancient dispersed minorities, and sensitivities over recent immigration. However, pragmatic local accommodations already exist, albeit limited and urban-focused, although Taylor (1997) contends that economics and demography will reduce the synonymity of multiculturalism and the inner city. Underlying contemporary processes, precedents have long existed in Europe for multicultural tolerance as well as its converse; Williams (1998), for example, notes the religious plurality of the historical Polish-Lithuanian state. The successful recasting of national heritages in terms more inclusive than narrowly perceived traditional nationalisms could thus recognize the dynamic evolution of European cultures and their architectural expressions (Taylor 1997), and would also mark a decisive breakthrough in the quest for a multilateral continental European heritage. The attainment of such a multilateral European heritage objective will centrally depend, of course, upon the success of direct and cognate initiatives by the EU as it evolves from a Western European into a pan-continental entity. The European Commission supports minority language rights and advocates a common educational policy, leading Williams (1998) to ask whether the EU will become the first postmodern, postnational-sovereignty, multicultural political system of the twenty-first century. He suggests that for the optimist this represents the accommodation, openness and diversity of a highly developed pluralist society. For the pessimist, however, it is a recipe for conflict, inefficiency and the artificial reproduction of often misleading cultural identities (and one might add the possible suppression of socio-economic dissent). We return to these specific issues in Chapter 10 and to the continuous implication of Europe's heritage as both mirror and catalyst of the larger issues involved.

Singapore

Singapore represents a radically different scale and context from the above cases, and a very distinct variant of multicultural trajectories. After independence from British colonial rule as part of Malaysia in 1963, Singapore's ethnic Chinese majority rejected the selectively Malay national identity of that new state, and it became separately independent in 1965. Since then Singapore has been expressly created as a non-majoritarian city-state in which all its cultural components have been subordinated to a new identity, one effectively shaped by authoritarian state-directed mechanisms. The new state identity was bonded with an unprecedentedly comprehensive urban renewal programme in which most of the existing urban fabric was replaced

Figure 5.4 Singapore's multicultural heritage I: the colonial Singapore Cricket Club on the Padang with the modern financial district behind

Figure 5.5   Singapore's multicultural heritage II: renovated shophouses mark one attempt to reconstruct the past

by standardized high-rise accommodation, which simultaneously upgraded living conditions from the previous 'slums' (sanitary considerations being critical in the equatorial climate) and largely suppressed visible inequities and differences among the population. The social stability and economic success of the city-state owe much to this questionably democratic policy of a virtually one-party political system, which has sought to impose its national ideology in many spheres of life (see, for example, Kong 1995).

However, the heritage cost of the urban redevelopment so motivated has been severe. Limited and carefully managed cultural heritage expressions (in restorations and redevelopment) have maintained the minimum continuities required for social stability. Nevertheless, these proved insufficient in preventing cultural resentment (Kong and Yeoh 1994), while tourists largely perceived Singapore as the 'supermarket of Asia' and a place increasingly devoid of heritage identity. Efforts to tourist-commodify the diverse surviving religious buildings were resented as alien re-evaluations (Kong 1993), while nation-building attempts to strike a balance in street-name changes, between Chinese, Malay, Indian and English language and heritage associations, proved unintelligible and insensitive to local realities. The townscape became littered with remnants of a series of different meaning systems, a process which illustrates the complexity of the postcolonial landscape as cultural text (Yeoh 1996, 1999; Figures 5.4 and 5.5). By the 1980s the extent of previous demolition was forcing selective 'pastiche' reconstruction, in order to reconstitute a sanitized 'Chinatown' and the like for tourist consumption.

In this respect Shaw *et al.* (1997) regard Singapore as the end-stage in a broader evolutionary model of ex-colonial Indian Ocean ports.

Singapore's ideologically and economically motivated erasure of memory and the subsequent pastiche efforts towards invention of tradition are eloquently discussed by Powell (1997). He observes that pockets of resistance to the officially planned redevelopment continue to exist, less in surviving unaltered structures than in the persistence of traditional spontaneous activities such as informal street markets. Further, Kong and Tay (1998) discuss the emergence of a Singapore children's literature, among other forms of cultural expression, in which adults selectively recollect and idealize the lost world, particularly the traditional *kampung* community, in contrast to the perceived sterile and hostile modern high-rise housing estates. In Singapore's case, it is evident that the extent of state reimaging of identity in pursuit of a particular multicultural vision has been so drastic as to engender disorientation and disaffection among the population, not to speak of economic costs. For this reason, and notwithstanding its economic success, Singapore does not appear to offer a model for wider application.

South Africa

In this discussion of multicultural societies, we turn finally to South Africa, which is treated at some length, not least because it constitutes perhaps the most dynamic contemporary example of multiculturalism in progress. The country remained under minority political, socio-economic and consequently heritage control until the 1990s. The goal of affirming a multicultural agenda in the postapartheid era is not merely one of addressing inequalities of social justice, but of ensuring the survival of democracy and perhaps of the state itself. While there are limited parallels elsewhere in Africa (notably Zimbabwe, see Tunbridge and Ashworth 1996), South Africa's distinctive qualities, especially of scale, population mix and historical depth, require it to chart its own heritage path.

During some 340 years of white minority rule beginning with the early Cape Colony, South Africa was generally perceived by Europeans as a settler society comparable to other regions of extensive European overseas settlement (Lester 1999a and b). This created a mindset which was reinforced daily by a visible heritage closely comparable to that of other settler societies. Further, the Great Trek, whereby, after 1836, many Boers of mainly early Dutch descent temporarily escaped British rule and created frontier societies, also invoked the parallel of the American West. The result was a heritage mythology construed as divinely ordained, but also one of overt racial domination (Christopher 1994). In the landscape outside the cities, the most pervasive aspect of this heritage is the imprint of European settler agriculture in field patterns, farmsteads and the innumerable trappings of a rural economy in which the veldt and, for example, the Canadian prairies differ primarily in their provisions for workers' accommodation.

Small communities complement the Europeanness of this economy: in Kwazulu-Natal, for example, Weenen perpetuates Dutch water control systems, while Richmond more characteristically echoes its British namesakes in Tasmania or Ontario. Some are classics of imperial Victoriana, now recycled as hotel complexes, as at Pilgrims Rest (a former mining village in the then Transvaal) and Matjesfontein (a health resort in Western Cape) (Bell 1993). More specifically, the landscape memorializes European heritage in two key respects: the monuments to white supremacy and those to inter-European conflict. The former include the memorials to battle victory (or even heroic defeat as at Isandlwana) of the Anglo-Zulu War in Kwazulu-Natal. Their apogee, however, is the powerful symbolism of Boer hegemony represented at the decisive battle site of Blood River (1838) (Figure 5.6), and in the Voortrekker Monument commemorating the Great Trek, which in radiating overtones of cultural supremacy (if not fascism) from a hilltop overlooking Pretoria, provides the ultimate rallying point for contemporary white Afrikaner extremism. Inter-European conflict is reflected in both memorial and relic, well preserved in the often dry environment, of the Anglo-Boer War (1899–1900), which ultimately permitted South African union. In contrast, the visible heritage of the indigenous peoples has been confined to the usual settler formula of limited peripheralized reserves, here the 'homelands' disbanded only in 1994. Its primary commodification has been in the form of craft products and tribal dancing.

European heritage, however, has been concentrated in the cities, which were deliberately denied (as far as possible) to Africans by a white minority conscious of its particular vulnerability in holding onto power. White dominance of city centres, with their icons of control identity, was entrenched under apartheid after 1948. In cities otherwise clearly moulded by and for a European settler population, Coloured and Indian minorities were granted marginalized slivers of space and localized identity, while Africans were confined to peripheral townships. Apartheid was the climax, however, of a much longer effort to attain more or less racial exclusivity in which the status of the city centre as white 'sacred space' was intrinsic, particularly so in Cape Town, the 'Mother City' (Western 1985, 1996). As South Africa's colonial urban evolution occurred primarily during the nineteenth century, it is scarcely surprising, as throughout the British Empire, that the country's cities should exude a Victorian imagery. This has been overlain in the twentieth century with the same World War monuments to imperial sacrifice and national awakening that abound in the other former British Dominions. While the largest cities have inevitably experienced structural metamorphosis, medium-sized and smaller centres often remain redolent of European diaspora heritage. Pietermaritzburg (Kwazulu-Natal), for example, is a globally exceptional manifestation of Victoriana (Figure 5.7). Although a Boer foundation, it acquired and preserved a heritage 'cocoon' as a British colonial, then provincial, capital, which was markedly dissonant to the surrounding impoverished and violent Kwazulu homeland until the end of the apartheid era (Haswell 1990; Tunbridge and Ashworth 1996).

Figure 5.6   Blood River, Kwazulu-Natal, South Africa: life-size, cast-iron simulation of the Boer laager at the decisive battle in 1838

The advent of majority rule in 1994 brought a new constitution with human rights protections which replaced privileged group status with guarantees of individual rights, and government commitment to the rapid improvement – in all respects – of the conditions of the non-white population, and of other marginalized groups, most particularly women. Although it remains imperative to deliver material evidence of change, multiculturalism is critical to South Africa's survival as a social democracy, and in avoiding civil war and national disintegration. Consequently, all sectors of the population have a stake in its success. Indeed the multicultural adjustment of South African heritage was an important concern of the African National Congress (ANC), even before it succeeded to government in 1994. The National Monuments Council, which had designated essentially white heritage, has since been reconstituted and largely replaced by agencies at the recast provincial level, providing a mechanism for releasing tensions created by regional heritage dissonances. In contrast to the archetypical postcolonial scenario, white heritage is being generally respected, although associations with the worst excesses of apartheid, such as statues of the former Prime Minister, Hendrick Verwoerd, have been removed if not destroyed. White heritage, however, may be subjected to reinterpretation to accommodate majority viewpoints, which in some cases value it inversely for its oppressive associations. Similarly, the sites of European-African conflict and even of the Anglo-Boer War are now acquiring additional memorials to non-white participants

Figure 5.7 Pietermaritzburg, Kwazulu-Natal, South Africa: an enduring white South African heritage – a statue of Queen Victoria stands in front of the colonial legislature

and perspectives (Tunbridge 1999). These renditions of multiculturalism seek a more broadly based inclusiveness, in which the birthplaces and other associations of African leaders and anti-racism heroes will now join the Indian temples and Coloured heritage (such as the Malay Quarter in Cape Town) which the old order had ultimately recognized. Museums, albeit inevitably underfunded, are also gradually developing a key role in the dissemination of interactive multicultural values.

The first monument in the new paradigm was a statue of Gandhi, unveiled in Pietermaritzburg in 1993, in the presence of the ANC leadership. Commemorating the centennial of his racist ejection from a train carriage there, the event which began his lifelong campaign against colonial rule, this monument is an overt statement of non-violent opposition to racism which is peculiarly apposite to contemporary South Africa (Figure 5.8; Tunbridge and Ashworth 1996). The greatest heritage challenge, however, lies in the interpretation of Robben Island off Cape Town, the most important new National Monument because of the imprisonment there of Nelson Mandela (*see* Chapter 11).

Apart from the obvious issue of maximizing consensus, the development of a multicultural heritage in South Africa is fraught with serious difficulties. First is the dissonance that may well exist between national political and tourism uses of heritage, both critical to the country because of the urgency of

Figure 5.8 Pietermaritzburg, Kwazulu-Natal, South Africa: Gandhi's statue in Maritzburg Mall, Church Street; he walks away from the railway station, invisible in the background

political nation-building and of the economic exploitation of a hitherto underdeveloped resource. The commitment to broader inclusion, rather than replacement of existing heritage, should lessen this dissonance by comparison with other postcolonial societies, but new interpretations will inevitably create some further discord. One prominent example concerns Cape Town's Victoria and Alfred Waterfront, a 1990s commercial success based upon the reclamation and sanitization of a pre-apartheid British imperial heritage, combined with subsequent universal pastiche elements (Figure 5.9) (Worden 1996). Initially, this ignored the heritage of the Africans, convicts and under-classes, who had built and populated the district, and shunned Robben Island which had been accessed from it. Moreover, the development has refocused Cape Town's tourism away from the city centre, and has substantially marginalized new and alternative local grassroots heritage initiatives elsewhere such as the District Six Museum (Worden 1997). Older corporate initiatives, including Johannesburg's Gold Reef City and the Kimberley Mining Museum, similarly commodify Victoriana very effectively with broadly comparable significance for the larger heritage connotations (Berning and Dominy 1992; Tunbridge and Ashworth 1996). While corporate heritage and waterfront ventures can be criticized globally for similar reasons, this does not alleviate the consequent problem, in South Africa's fragile condition, of an inherent misfit between the socio-political requirements of a revised heritage and its economic exploitation. One significant antidote is found in the African-run township tourism, which has appeared in metropolitan peripheries when social conditions permit.

Second, the general development and consumption of urban heritage in South Africa is being seriously impaired by the growth of crime in the cities. The path already trodden in Nairobi and Harare is being followed in Cape Town and Pietermaritzburg, where the momentum from the Gandhi initiative and its multicultural relevance has faltered in an atmosphere of growing avoidance of the city centre, even by day. Thus recent heritage recognition has tended to be of individual African leaders in inevitably peripheral locations (Tunbridge 1999). In this threatening urban environment, the corporate heritage initiatives have, however, acquired a paradoxical significance. On the one hand, they offer relatively defensible space in the urban geography of security. The Victoria and Alfred Waterfront has, for all its heritage sins, provided the leading multicultural gathering place in the 'new' South Africa, and it attracts a wide spectrum of international and domestic patronage (including ANC leaders) behind the former dock gates where entry is at least broadly scrutinized. On the other hand, this contributes to the draining of life and heritage significance from Cape Town's city centre, thereby jeopardizing the national multicultural heritage project, for which the public stage of the city centre is as indispensable as it is for democratic well-being in general.

Figure 5.9 Victoria and Alfred Waterfront, Cape Town, South Africa: Table Mountain is in the distance

Conclusion: multicultural reality, theory and democratic sustainability

Prior to investigating the possibility of some form of synthesis of the sheer diversity of these case studies, one further complication has to be addressed. While the case studies have been dealt with largely at the holistic level, it is necessary to briefly reconsider the implications of the multiple layerings of place and identity considered in Chapter 4. Excepting odd examples like tiny Singapore, national realms of heritage dissonance are further complicated by the existence in most multiculturally aspirant states of.regional or local areas in which the application of even tailored multicultural heritage policies had best be honoured in the breach rather than the observance, if possibly violent backlash is to be avoided. In Québec's case, this is so obvious as to be central to the entire argument with respect to Canadian multiculturalism.

Even where national disintegration is not an immediate challenge, however, national multicultural policies may have to bend a long way to accommodate regional heritage perspectives. In Canada, Québec apart, Newfoundland, the most recent province (1949), maintains a uniquely insular identity with strong Anglo-Irish and monarchist ties, no immigrant minorities and lingering suspicion of mainland values. Conversely, in British Columbia, the Pacific Coast identity, shared with the United States and Asian minority values, favours multiculturalism but introduces dimensions remote to most eastern Canadians. South African regionalism is at least as prominent and also prone to bloodshed. The newly decentralized level of provincial power over heritage and much else is an attempt to balance regionally concentrated ethnic tensions (Lemon 1995). To this end multicultural aspirations must take second place to local monocultural primacy if violent separatism is to be averted, for example, by Zulu nationalists at the provincial level of Kwazulu-Natal, or by extremist Afrikaners in local areas they can control (such as the decaying town of Orania, Western Cape, which was bought by a right-wing foundation in the early 1990s and declared an Afrikaner *volkstaat*). In Europe, as we have seen in Chapter 4, monocultural regional heritage primacy and autonomy is again a common feature.

Moreover, the regional dimension apart, the sheer complexity of essentially operationalizing multicultural societies through heritage is exacerbated by the distinct differences apparent in the case studies, which undermine any attempt to erect a general model. The United States is relatively centripetal whereas Canada is centrifugal; Australia and New Zealand are displaying multicultural flexibility in the face of presently limited diversity, while Western European states are typically yielding less despite the manifest multiplicity of needs to do so. Singapore has been centrally assertive, while South Africa strives to address its urgent needs for reconciliation within the constraints of democratic mechanisms. All these examples are suspect as general role models of multiculturalism; all are challenged or compromised in their own jurisdictions. Accordingly it is clear that there is no multicultural panacea to the human and heritage problems of reconciling cultural diversity. But equally there is also no alternative to the continuing quest for broadly multicultural solutions to the world's social diversity.

In pursuit of this dilemma, Kallen (1995) has developed a fourfold model of cultural integration (Figure 5.10). In order of what might be considered maximum to minimum hegemony of any one group, he envisages:

- paternalism, in which one dominant culture subordinates minorities (or even majorities, in the most classic colonial relationship);
- dominant conformity, in which one dominant culture absorbs all (typical of the European nation-state model);
- 'melting pot', an integration of all into one new composite culture;
- mosaic, a pluralism of multiple but distinct cultures in one political entity.

Clearly, this particular conceptualization envisages a sequence broadly similar to the multicultural spectrum discussed earlier. What it does not fully

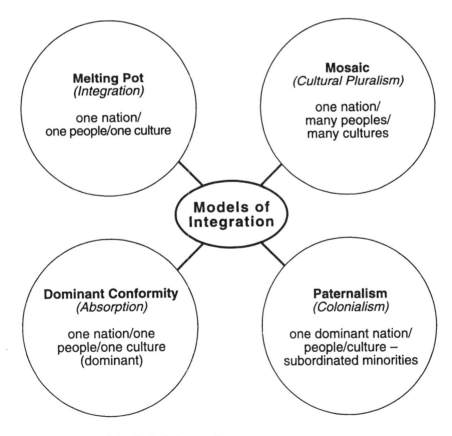

Figure 5.10   Models of ethnic integration
Source: adapted from Kallen (1995)

recognize is that the examples discussed here point to a continuous spectrum of possibilities, liberally compromised with nuances of local agenda and circumstance.

In relating this model to issues of language and religion in Europe, Williams (1998) discusses the difficulties of multiculturalism and considers the conventional promotion of individual rights versus an increasingly favoured group rights approach. The latter would protect the status of specified minorities, while providing the most explicit and durable foundation for the mosaic option of multiculturalism by inhibiting the 'dread hand of homogenization' (Williams 1998, p. 197) and perpetuating the worth of diverse identities. There are, however, serious problems with the concept of group rights not readily apparent from Williams's discussion. Given the postmodern insistence on the fluidity and hybridity of societies, who within or outside any alleged group is mandated to speak for its existence, let alone its views?

One example suffices to illustrate the heritage dilemma. Should minorities, if offended at incumbent heritage, be empowered to eliminate or reinterpret it? In 1996, leaders of native Canadian organizations demanded the removal of the kneeling Indian scout at the foot of the monument in Ottawa to the first European explorer, Champlain, on the grounds that it demeaned indigenous people. Although the issue has since been circumvented, the wider point concerns the implications of any such minority group veto over aggregate multicultural heritage. While acknowledging the antecedence of the native people, and their particular group cohesion resulting largely from historical injustice, their veto may not fairly reflect the view of all who might identify with the minority, but of activists among them and even – as in this example – the outcome of activist political rivalries. More fundamentally, the rest of society is marginalized by the decision and may be affronted, even disinherited, by its own arbitrary exclusion. Beyond this, the precedent is created for removal or reinterpretation of any part of the collective heritage resource at the behest of any minority or special interest, however defined.

In the quest for peaceful and creative coexistence, the ultimate constraint to multiculturalism in any liberal political order, and even in more authoritarian scenarios, is democratic sustainability. Multiculturally interactive social and heritage values originating among intellectual élites, cultural geographers among them, are liable to be remote from popular aspiration and correspondingly perceived not as liberating but as coercive. Thus Habermas (1996), for example, argues that majority culture must be decoupled from political culture. Similarly, if majority values are affronted by a 'tyranny of the minority', it is likely that multicultural initiatives will be rejected electorally. The task for those advocating multiculturalism is therefore to craft nationally, regionally or locally sensitive approaches to social and heritage equity, which can command or persuade majority support at the appropriate spatial scale. 'Majority' can be defined in terms of mainstream or coalition values. While popularly acceptable pragmatic multiculturalisms might vary around the world, they would share the common denominator of a minimum mutual respect across the diversity of population and values, and specifically between minorities and majorities, however defined at any point in time.

Heritage policies to achieve these goals would ideally work towards a balanced, proportionate inclusion of minority elements and interpretations, the objective being to obtain social profit from celebrating – and economic gains from selling – heritage diversity. However, in the apparently intractable Belfasts, Sarajevos or Jerusalems of the world, any recognition of a common heritage might require a minimalist approach, accenting only that which is held in common and nurturing social harmony at the expense of profitable commodification of divisive heritage resources. Ultimately, each and every resolution of heritage dissonance, particularly the nuances of multicultural inclusion, must be separately thought out for its appropriateness and acceptability in time and place. As we have discussed for heritage in general, however, such resolutions are qualified by their dependence upon how the messages they project are variously received by those who reflect upon them. Precisely how this ideal of heritage management and its complex variety of spatial scales might be realized is addressed in Part IV. Before dealing with that raft of issues, it is necessary to consider the economic commodification of heritage, another potent source of dissonance given its conflicts with the cultural realm which we have been examining here.

PART III

The economic uses of heritage

6

Heritage and economics: an ambiguous relationship

Introduction

While heritage is part of the way in which cultural politics are operationalized, it exists simultaneously as an economic commodity. Historically, the
economic functions of heritage have generally been presented as subsequent
or secondary and often barely tolerated uses of monuments, sites and places,
which have been initially identified, preserved and interpreted for quite other
reasons. Most extant heritage artefacts, collections, buildings, sites and places
would continue to exist, fulfil most of their current functions, and be
endowed with much the same values by contemporary society, even if it
could be demonstrated that they possessed no intrinsic economic worth and
made no contribution to economic well-being. Indeed there is a strongly felt,
and frequently articulated, view that any attempt to attach economic values
to heritage, and to other cultural products and performances, is at best a
pointless irrelevance and at worst an unacceptable soiling of the aesthetically
sublime with the commercially mundane. In such a view the activities, objects
and values of heritage should not appear in the market place and even the
terms used in this chapter, such as resource, product, price or consumption,
betray a commercialization that attracts distinctly derogatory connotations in
debates about the contemporary functions of heritage. There are two reasons
why this reaction cannot be dismissed out of hand. First, it is a sustainable
argument. Few historic buildings have actually been saved from demolition
by dominantly economic arguments, while policy discussions frequently
revolve around conservation and development as alternative, opposing and
exclusive options. Second, it must not be forgotten that many of those active
in the field of the conservation of the built environment are inspired principally by moral-aesthetic or socio-cultural motives rather than the search for
economic gains. Nevertheless, however uncomfortable it may be for many
observers, two simple propositions form the basis of a counter argument
which justifies the approach adopted in Part III.

First, heritage costs money. Although the crusade in western countries to save relict artefacts from the past, mostly because of their unquestioned intrinsic worth, has been crowned with quite spectacular success, it has also produced numerous unpredicted consequences, many of which are economic. At the level of the individual monument or historic district, the ever-lengthening lists of protected monuments and ever-widening extent of preserved districts impose large, growing and open-ended financial commitments, whether these are borne by owners, occupiers, users or by society at large. Continuous maintenance costs money, as does, indirectly, the inconvenience of employing sub-optimal structures for modern functions. Conservation can also mean forgoing profitable opportunities to develop alternative uses of buildings, sites and areas. Large sums of capital – often concealed, inequitably distributed and difficult to calculate – are trapped in investment in the products of the past rather than in the developments of the future. Arguably, this is especially so in Europe where the processes of preservation and conservation first began.

Second, heritage is worth money and also earns it, even if this economic value was not the reason for its creation nor the prime justification for its maintenance. This value can be utilized to provide a return in profits, incomes and jobs. In Canada, for example, it has been estimated that building restoration delivers 27.8 jobs for each million dollars invested compared with only 12.8 for the less labour intensive new building (Weiler 1998). Such benefits may extend far beyond the individual building or site, providing an economic support, not just for the heritage structures concerned, but for whole regional and even national economies. Releasing these values is neither automatic nor easy and how it has been – or could be – done forms the substance of much of Part III. Heritage's capacity to earn compensates for its capacity to cost. To claim that Robin Hood is worth many hundreds of millions of pounds to Nottingham, whether he actually existed there, somewhere else, or not at all, may be condemned as crass commercialization and a bowdlerization of the past. It does, however, help shape a local identity, project a place image and directly support an industry that in turn makes the conservation of Nottingham Castle, as well as many other smaller structures whose connection with the fabled outlaw is historically tenuous, economically worthwhile. If the perceived past has such real contemporary economic values, then it can be priced. In turn, places compete for possession of such a resource and the resulting products compete for consumers within markets.

These two simple propositions alone make it essential that heritage is approached as an economic phenomenon and part of a wider economic system. It may be very difficult to accept that cultural heritage resources are often ultimately dependent upon the sale of fun products in a branch of the commercial public entertainment industry. Yet if we try to ignore this apparently unpalatable conclusion, the effectiveness, or often even the chances of survival, of that heritage cannot be maximized. In attempting to outline an economics of heritage, this chapter subjects the topic to various types of economic analysis, most of which were not originally designed for this purpose. Subsequently, Chapter 7 broadens the discussion to consider the various roles of heritage within economic development strategies at various spatial scales.

Economics of heritage

Any analysis of the economics of heritage immediately confronts the consequences of the fundamental paradox outlined above, namely that economic motives were of secondary importance in the creation of heritage and of primary importance in its maintenance. This has a number of important implications. First, the value of heritage artefacts, experiences and places is clearly more complex than that of most goods and services in an economic system. Not only is the definition of such a value more difficult, so also is its calculation. What cannot be valued cannot be priced and cannot be traded and yet it is precisely these values that are exploited within economic development strategies. Second, values and prices are the essential mechanism that allows markets to exist and operate. Yet there are many difficulties in identifying, understanding and intervening within the market, or more properly many different markets, for heritage. Once again, however, it is precisely this intervention that is required if heritage values are to be released and utilized.

Third, there are also ambiguities in the production system. The resources used in the production of heritage products may, as a result of their origin, be currently maintained and even owned by individuals and institutions quite different in type, intent and working practices to those managing their marketing and use. An inherent weakness of regarding heritage as a product, in comparison with many other goods and services, is that it lacks a production system, at least in the usual sense of an integrated control with an agreed purpose from resource use through production to sale and consumption.

Finally, the consumption of the heritage product is essentially an experience which relates so distinctly to the individual consumer that it provides another dimension to the question, 'whose heritage?' which largely determines what is heritage. Consider a visit to a Gothic cathedral such as Chartres or Rouen, where the same arrangement of stone and glass may result in consumers experiencing the aesthetic beauty of an artwork, a sense of identification with a place or people, a spiritual or educational enrichment, or just a novel and entertaining use of time. If the products consumed are these – and many other experiences – and not merely architectural detail or historical narrative, then it is quite literally the interpretation or, more accurately, the significance of the interpretation to the individual consumer, which forms the product. If this is so, then the convenient distinction between producer and consumer as two independent actors in the economic process begins to disintegrate.

All these factors lead to difficulties, or rather peculiarities, in treating heritage as a product. To complicate the matter still further, many heritage products are places. The place itself is the product, whether at the scale of the historic region or town, or simply a site, a point in space whose value is ascribed by some historical event that occurred there. Heritage place products thus have all the characteristics of places, which are social, political and economic, as well as the characteristics of products (Ashworth and Voogd 1990, 1994a and b). Thus although heritage fits very ambiguously and incompletely into economic modes of analysis, the past, its monuments, artefacts and exhibits, its visitors and experiences can be freely replaced by near synonyms such as resources, supply, products, demand, markets and consumers as a means of analysis, even by those who may be reluctant to accept the implications of pursuing such an approach further.

The value of heritage: the price of heritage

The value that we place on heritage, and therefore the nature of the demand for its products and experiences, is more complex than that for most goods and services in that demand cannot be equated only with direct consumption. Heritage acquires value in a number of different ways, a factor which in turn determines how this value can be measured through price. Much heritage is produced to satisfy deferred, option, existence or bequest demands, especially for the uses discussed in earlier chapters. Such demands are no less real or effective than direct participatory demand. Large sums of money are contributed towards the maintenance of national collections, or the rescue from imminent disasters of international heritage, by those who never have directly experienced them or never will. These people obtain benefit from the maintenance of an option to do so, from the mere continued existence of the heritage, or from a desire that it be saved for future generations.

Therefore, a need exists for a 'compound evaluation of the value of heritage ' (Bizzaro and Nijkamp 1996a), calculated by Stabler (1996) with the equation:

$$\text{Use value (direct + indirect) + existence value + option value} \\ \text{+ bequest value = Total value}$$

The pricing of heritage would follow logically from this equation and thus the price of a building or a heritage town could be calculated by determining the aggregate of the prices of each of these values. To these values, which can be expressed in monetary terms, however incompletely, Bizzaro and Nijkamp (1996a) have added the intrinsic but inexpressible values, to arrive at a 'social complex value'; this, however, by its nature can play no part in the calculation.

If the problem of determining value is primarily a conceptual one, then the difficulty of actually assigning prices to heritage is largely practical. It stems from the absence of a market driven by an open market pricing mechanism, as for most other goods and services. Direct use values can of course be directly priced: a visit to a museum or heritage theme park can be priced and sold in competition with a visit to a cinema or amusement park and thus give some indication of the comparative value placed upon such a visit. However, with heritage facilities, the indirect use and other values are often so much larger than the direct that a strong argument exists – as in the long-standing discussion on entry fees to museums – for not charging prices that lead to a loss of visitors. Even if such fees increase direct revenues, the total values of visiting the heritage object would decline.

Methods of calculating values that are not directly traded in a market place, including those developed for measuring aspects of the environment, such as clean air or attractive landscapes, could also be applied to heritage. These are compared at length in Stabler (1996) and can be summarized here under four headings.

- *Hedonic pricing*, which assumes that heritage values are capitalized in real estate prices and thus the heritage component in a price can be isolated by comparing otherwise similar properties. However, the impacts of monument listing or heritage area designation upon property values are rarely straightforward (as discussed below).
- *Travel-cost pricing* implies that the costs of visiting a site or facility reflect the value put upon it. It has a common-sense justification, especially in tourism, where visitors may have travelled over extensive distances. The total value generated by a particular site could be calculated by adding together the costs incurred by the visitors, however these are measured. This technique assumes, nevertheless, that each journey has a single determinable motive and that the heritage experience is not just an incidental part of a wider holiday package.
- *Contingent pricing* requires individuals to place a value upon heritage in a hypothetical contingency, often a demolition auction where real buildings can be saved from catastrophe by imaginary cash donations. This technique is popular with, for example, the assessment of the negative environmental impacts of developments upon a large number of potentially affected individuals, because it allows small but widespread impacts to be considered. It is thus compatible with trends towards a more democratically accountable and participatory planning system and is popular in environmental impact assessments but, of course, the technique assumes that reactions in real situations can be predicted by reactions in hypothetical ones.
- *'Delphi' methods*, whereby a selected panel of experts or 'stakeholders' are questioned, could be viewed as a restricted if more easily obtained form of contingency pricing, although their outcome depends on the initial choice of 'oracles' consulted.

While some may resist the pricing of the self-evidently priceless, the inability to assign a realistic – or any – monetary value to the heritage option seriously disadvantages it in situations in which choices have to be made, for example between new building or renovation, between a heritage and a non-heritage use of a building or site, or more generally between categories of public expenditure. At the prosaic level of company board or council meetings, placing a price on heritage may be the only way to assure its survival in competition with other priced alternatives, even if its value to many people goes far beyond any price that could be allocated. It should be noted that cost-benefit analysis is not in itself a means of establishing prices but requires that prices have already been fixed, by these or other methods, so that total costs and benefits can be calculated.

Who invests? Who profits?

The relationship between the costs of investment in heritage and its return may seem similar to any other form of investment. A building or area is preserved, restored and renovated by an investor, who then reaps the potential benefits from this activity, realizing a profit or loss on the transaction indicated by the rate of return to capital. There are a number of reasons, however, why this simple relationship is not only more complex with heritage than other investments but frequently cannot work at all. The three most important of these are encapsulated in the terms: externalities; public goods; and front-loading.

We have already seen that the costs and benefits of heritage accrue much more widely than merely to those who own or occupy it. As with many other aspects of the environment, these externalities are not just extra marginally complicating factors to be considered in the calculation but are frequently more important than the internalities in such 'merit' goods.

Second, in common with some other services, much heritage is produced as a public good. It has the characteristics that its consumption cannot be restricted only to those directly paying for it and, equally, much consumption is compulsory in the sense that occupiers or users of spaces such as historic townscapes must experience them, whether they desire to or not. The argument that many of the benefits are necessarily collective rather than individual is the justification for public intervention, but is also central to the problem of dividing costs and benefits between public and private sectors.

Third, there is the substantial front-loading of investment costs over time. A preserved, restored and renovated building – or area – will release its benefits over many years, or even generations, while the investment needed to obtain these primarily occurs at the beginning. Although – as argued below – the commitment to maintenance costs is continuous, while restoration is an unrelentingly recurring process rather than a once-forever expenditure, it is, nevertheless, rarely possible to restore buildings, and almost never to restore neighbourhoods, through small incremental investments. Technical and architectural factors normally preclude partial restoration of buildings, while neighbourhoods need a critical mass of investment to stimulate interest and involvement, thereby creating the impression that something is being done and that current investment will yield future returns on a rising market.

Lichfield (1988, 1997) has noted another peculiarity of monument and conservation area designation, namely that it is a sudden and externally imposed condition that immediately alters, for better or worse, the existing investment environment. Benefits, if any, will accrue through the lifetime of the property or even longer on the site, but the arbitrary imposition of restrictions and foregone development opportunities fall only on the existing, and not subsequent, presumably aware, owners. This helps explain the paradox that listing of historic buildings can often lead to an initial fall in property and land values, despite the longer-term rise in the value of the conserved area as a whole.

Some of these characteristics are illustrated by the 'neighbour's dilemma', a variant on a widely known problem in decision-making (Table 6.1). Scenario 1 is the base, describing unrestored properties in which owners A and B and the community as a whole have made no investment in and reap no return. In order to improve the situation, individual owners may invest in and receive some return from their restored property through a rise in its value but, equally, a return is conferred on the non-investing neighbour whose property is rendered marginally more valuable as a result of the increased value of the neighbourhood. One neighbour thus free-rides while depressing the expected value of the other's restoration, which thus fails to realise its full

Table 6.1   The neighbour's dilemma

Scenarios	Actor	Investment	Return	Balance
1 No Investment	A	0	0	0
	B	0	0	0
	Community	0	0	0
2 Individual Investment	A	M [0]	L [L]	– [+]
	B	0 [M]	L [L]	+ [–]
	Community	0	L	+
3 Joint Individual Investment	A	M	M	0
	B	M	M	0
	Community	0	M	+
4 Community Investment	A	0	L	+
	B	0	L	+
	Community	M	L	–
5 Individual + Community Investment	A	M	H	+
	B	M	H	+
	Community	M	H	+

Actors: Neighbour A/Neighbour B/The Community.
Levels of Investment/Return: Low/Medium/High.
Balance: Negative (–)/Zero (0)/Positive (+).

Source: based on Hardin (1968).

return and be profitable (Scenario 2). Overall the investor loses and the non-investor gains and thus neither neighbour has the incentive to invest unilaterally. Joint investment (Scenario 3) would lead to each neighbour receiving moderate returns and thus at least breaking even, while the community as a whole benefits through the improvement in the area in which it has not invested and is therefore 'free-riding'. The difficulty is to reach this mutually beneficial position when individual self-interest discourages it. Direct investment by the community can lead to two outcomes: one (Scenario 4) when no matching investment is made by owners who therefore gain on balance at the expense of the community; and another (Scenario 5), where community investment stimulates individuals to invest with all actors receiving high returns and profits.

The lessons from Table 6.1 are clear. Some form of public intervention is needed to redress the failure of the property market, which, if left to itself, is unlikely to arrive at the most desirable condition for either individual owners and users or the wider community. Equally, such intervention will be most effective when it stimulates rather than acts as a substitute for individual investment. There are various ways in which this intervention in the economic system is exercised in practice, reflecting the spectrum of balance between public and private sectors struck in different societies.

Direct purchase, restoration and use by the community defines one pole of the spectrum of public-private involvement. It is ironic that this most interventionist of approaches is actually pursued most strongly in societies dominated by free-market political and economic systems. In the United States and Canada, the strength of the idea of individual property rights renders it difficult to legally enforce collective value on individual owners but, paradoxically, confers on governments the same rights to do what they will with their own properties. For example, the National Capital Commission (NCC), the Canadian federal government agency charged with turning Ottawa into a national show-case capital, has – in the absence of a federal district authority, as in the United States or Australia, and in the presence of provincial governments which jealously guard their territorial jurisdictions – achieved its objectives primarily by the acquisition of key properties and strategic land corridors.

A variant on this strategy of direct public investment is the establishment of agencies, initially publicly funded, which operate a rolling programme of purchase, restoration and resale on the free market. In this way a small initial state investment is constantly recycled through the market and its effectiveness multiplied, with the additional possibility that selective public initiatives will signal an opportunity and thus trigger further private initiatives. In The Netherlands, for example, the 'national restoration fund' finances individual restoration projects, which are then resold. Many cities have also established *stadsherstel* agencies, financed initially by local government grants and thereafter by their turnover of improved properties. In other countries, particularly the United Kingdom and Ireland, there is a tradition of private 'civic trust' involvement of individuals and local sponsors in the property market. As with the Dutch *stadsherstel* agencies, these institutions attempt to lead through example and thereby become a focus of stimulation but also technical experience and risk assessment.

The effectiveness of this strategy is limited by the state of the property market and the freedom of such agencies to operate within it. One quite extreme case, which illustrates a more general problem elsewhere, is the disappointing outcome of the work of the Heritage Foundation for Newfoundland and Labrador in the provincial capital of St. John's (Sharp 1986, 1993). An extensive downtown area was declared a conservation area in 1977, the intention being to encourage the restoration and maintenance of largely late nineteenth-century, wooden, owner-occupied residential property. The trust was empowered and financed by the provincial government to operate a rolling programme and ultimately purchased and restored some 28 properties, mostly occupying key sites within the conservation area. Subsequently, the programme was abruptly terminated, existing properties sold at a loss and further funding denied, leaving St. John's with the dubious distinction of possessing both the largest and most unsuccessful conservation area in Canada (Sharp 1986, 1993). This case demonstrates that heritage conservation does not necessarily result in profitable returns, nor will it necessarily be widely supported by both local economic and political interests once the initial political reluctance and financial obstacles have been overcome. In the case of St. John's, the short-term property market was insufficiently stable to guarantee financial solvency, while there was also political reluctance to pursue conservation policies that might have discouraged alternative economic strategies that offered more immediate returns in local employment. In particular, the provincial government failed to enforce conservation by-laws relating, for example, to building materials, which might have encouraged a general rise of property values in the conservation area.

A no-win situation can also be reached whereby profitable returns on a rising property market are a signal to parsimonious local governments that no public funding is necessary, while, conversely, poor returns on a falling property market are taken as evidence that government investment will be wasted. In any event active involvement in the property market requires the support of other public planning and confidence building measures (see, for example, Cuming and Weiler 1997) if conservation areas are to be seen as sufficiently attractive to encourage private investments.

Moving towards the private end of the spectrum, most mixed economies reflect society's collective interest in heritage preservation and restoration through state encouragement and support to private agencies and individuals, who attempt to maximize their financial returns. Such public investment 'leverage' can take the form of direct grants or fiscal concessions, but may be no more than investment in street furniture and new signage. A minimalist approach can be very successful, as occurred, for example, in many British cities in the 1970s (Larkham 1996). Local authorities had only to declare the existence of conservation areas, thereby signalling their intent to improve public spaces. In so doing, they demarcated locations of future areas of rising property values, encouraging private investment to move in to accomplish the self-fulfilling prophecy. Urban restoration seemed to require no more public expenditure than a line on a planning map and an announcement in the press. The key to further success is clearly dependent on the rate of take-up of individual improvement grants and this, in turn, will depend on the state of property markets at a specific time and place. The process of gentrification, for instance, which has been important in restoring and revitalizing many inner-city neighbourhoods in European and North American cities since the 1970s, was driven both by economic conditions which made investment in the renovation of older properties profitable, accompanied by a whole series of demographic and sociological circumstances, that allowed fashionable lifestyles to be related to inner-city communities and their older properties (see Ley 1996).

Finally the state can reduce its role to one of being no more than a protector of the public interest through measures to limit or mitigate the negative external effects of private restoration investment. For example, it became clear in the 1970s, especially from the experience of major French restoration programmes such as in the Paris Marais (Kain 1975, 1981) that, almost inevitably, the designation, preservation and renovation of the physical fabric led to changes in the local economic landscape and, consequently, in the social structure of urban neighbourhoods. Many local authorities in Western Europe were tempted to intervene to prevent these processes occurring, either through ideological conviction, as in the cities of the Italian Romagna (Cervellati and Scannarini 1973), or simply because public authorities do not like to experience unforeseen and unpredictable side-effects to their actions. The result was numerous regulations such as rent controls, resale restrictions, security of tenure and even the legal right of inhabitants to return to restored properties, all designed to protect existing residents from the economic effects of restoration. The paradox here is that there may be a political or social argument in favour of limiting what is seen as economic speculation, while it is that very speculation – individual profit-seeking investment – which is required if restoration programmes are to be largely privately funded. Thus the economics of the preservation of communities may be quite different from, and even conflict with, the economics of the preservation of their houses.

Heritage in economics

Some attempts have been made to model the place of heritage within wider economic systems. While all these are incomplete, they do provide a way of looking at heritage that is useful, not least as a precondition for management intervention.

The windfall gain model

The windfall gain model is the schema most widely applied, whether consciously or not, to the economic uses of heritage. It is assumed that the heritage facility or place already exists to satisfy some other purpose but can also accommodate economic uses as a supplementary demand generating additional incomes. There are three conditions here, none of which are necessarily automatically tenable. First, it is presupposed that the extra economic function can be added harmoniously to the existing aesthetic, political or social ones at no extra cost, without competing with, displacing or reducing the value obtained from the other uses. Second, it is assumed that the addition of the marginal use has no impact upon the resource, which it does not exclusively consume or indeed alter, damage or distort to the detriment of other current or potential users. Finally, and resulting from the management of the consequences of the first two conditions, it is inferred that the extra demand is conditional in the sense that it is welcomed, or at least tolerated, unless or until it is detrimental to other uses or to the resource itself. This implies that the extra demand can be monitored, segregated and subsequently regulated.

In essence, therefore, the windfall gain model assumes the existence of 'free-ridership', although who is obtaining the free ride varies according to how the model is interpreted. If an economic activity is making use of a heritage facility, which it has not created and for which it does not pay a user fee, as is generally the case, for example, with much tourism use of historic townscapes, then a commercial activity is free-riding. This is the argument that underpins much of the opposition to tourism uses of heritage and the proposition that local tourism taxes should be applied in recompense. If, however, a heritage facility or the local authority in whose area it is located is earning returns from users who maintain that heritage complex in existence so that quite different purposes can be pursued (for example, by contributing to local identities or place images), then the position is reversed and it is these other heritage functions of museums, monuments or historic districts that are 'free-loading' on their paying customers.

These tensions are often expressed as a conflict between locals and outsiders. For a local performance, museum or gallery, which already exists and will continue to so do for a local market, the outsider is at best a clear gain and, at worst, no extra cost, at least until physical capacity is exhausted and locals are displaced or priced-out. Conversely heritage facilities created for, or currently economically sustained by, external demand – for example London theatres or many Arts festivals – can additionally be used by residents who, in that sense, become the 'free-riders'.

The turnstile model

This variant on the windfall gain model is particularly attractive from the viewpoint of the individual heritage facility. Here it is accepted that different groups of consumers have quite different reasons for the consumption – and indeed expectations – of the experience: in marketing terms, different 'buyer benefits' are being conferred by the same product. This is assumed to be irrelevant to the facility selling its product to whoever passes through the turnstile, although the danger of the approach lies in this very assumption that the same product is being consumed by each group of consumers. This is not the case, however, as, for example, the interpretation of heritage collections or sites may vary according to the predispositions and expectations of the different visitor groups. They are consuming their heritage, not that of the heritage producers, and thus the products will be as varied as the markets.

To exemplify this point, we consider briefly the heritage tourism uses of Venice (Figure 6.1). The city's heritages of architecture, urban design and historical associations have an enormous and influential world-wide option demand, demonstrated by the popular response to international appeals since the 1970s to 'Save Venice' (O'Riordan 1975; Fay and Knightly 1976). However, the potential activation of this option demand, which further increases the number of actual visitors, is paradoxically part of the conservation problem rather than its solution. For whom, and from whom, is Venice being saved? Tourism is certainly a welcome extra income, helping to cover the costs of maintenance of what are, by virtue of their physical location in a lagoonal environment, extraordinarily costly resources. The growing numbers of tourists, however, cause increasing physical damage (although in this case the marginal increase is probably not significant) and, more important, displace other users, either physically or by bidding away scarce resources (particularly housing) from them (Burtenshaw *et al.* 1991; Ashworth and Ennen 1998). The cumulative result is a decline in the resident population, the facilities to support them, and the crowding out of what are regarded as more worthy scholarly and artistic users of the heritage.

Two principal economic strategies are possible in such a situation of increasing demand for a product in seemingly or short-term fixed supply. The first is to reduce demand by allowing the price to rise; the second is to increase supply. The nature of the heritage place-product renders both difficult but neither impossible. Raising the price of Venice to visitors depends upon segmenting the market, favouring higher yield hotel-based visitors, while taxing or restricting access for less profitable day excursionists and those staying in lower priced accommodation. A combination of selective de-marketing, planning controls on the development of tourism facilities and, above all, physical controls on motor vehicle access and parking facilitated by the causeway link with the mainland, are all options that have been attempted with varying degrees of success (van der Borg 1990; van der Borg *et al.* 1996). Differentiating among consumers on non-economic criteria is more difficult but the idea of issuing a 'Venice Card' for access to heritage sites, favouring those with more 'serious' motives as well as those with higher expenditure, has been suggested. Both depend, however, upon sufficient knowledge of the nature of the different markets and their patterns of consumption, and

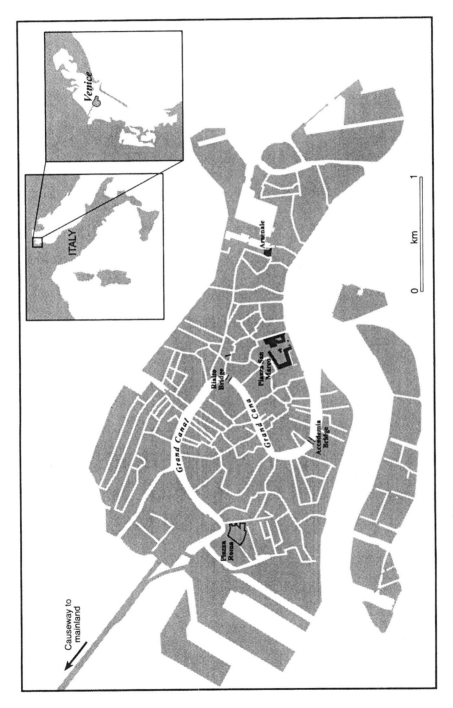

Figure 6.1   The lagoonal city of Venice

management skills in monitoring and regulating the use of the place-product through either economic or physical instruments. As in Venice, the latter most usually take the form of attempts to regulate carrying capacities, but differential pricing, which depends on the ability to segment and separate markets, is also a possibility. Foreign tourism to Egypt, for example, is highly dependent upon Pharaonic heritage, best symbolized by the Giza pyramids and Sphinx outside Cairo. Until recently, this resource was accessible without charge but the logic of the user contributing to the maintenance of the facilities used is now manifest in entry fees. These in turn potentially exclude the poorer local residents for whom the area had been a popular excursion site. The result is differential pricing of the same resource, theoretically based upon nationality or, in practice, on language and appearance (Evans 1998). The point in many such cases is that resource managers are recognizing different users of heritage, prioritizing among them in various ways, and engaging in differential pricing often based upon the different values held by customers.

The second option, that of increasing supply to satisfy increasing demands, seemingly raises the objection that place-products are intrinsically unique: there is one Venice which is not replicable. Heritage place-products, however, are not necessarily in fixed supply. A peculiarity of heritage consumption is that the same product can be consumed simultaneously or sequentially by many different consumers without necessarily reducing the quality of the experience. Good place management can increase capacities, while the extreme selectivity of heritage users in space and time generally allows much room for expansion. In Venice, a very high percentage of total heritage consumers comprises tourists on summer weekends in a small area around the Piazza San Marco and the circuit from Piazza Roma over the Accademia and Rialto bridges. Expanding the product-range in time or space is thus an option; for example, the huge former naval Arsenale could be appropriated as a major heritage tourism resource (Mancuso 1993). A further possibility, dependent upon the degree of interchangeability of heritage place-products, lies in the creation of more 'Venices', a process already occurring in the Veneto itself – as at Chioggia – or in the string of former Venetian colonies from Capodistria, through Ragusa to the eastern Mediterranean and Aegean.

The case of Venice offers lessons both of hope and despair to the countless other such heritage cities searching for similar solutions to similar, if less well publicized, problems. The pessimistic view is that the accumulated aesthetic capital created by art and history can be activated as resources for heritage industries but such industries are essentially parasitical in so far as they do not, and maybe cannot, add to that capital (Mosetto 1993). Similarly, the uniqueness of the individual heritage place-product makes it inevitable that the finest examples will be 'cherished to death'. Alternatively, the very peculiarities of heritage place-products, their capability of being multi-used, and their consumption through so many different interpretations both on- and off-site, offers considerable scope for intensification, substitution and management intervention using a wide range of economic, marketing and physical planning instruments.

A commodification model

Commodification is simply the creation of tradeable commodities from resources, in this case selected elements from the past, which previously were not traded (Ashworth 1991b). The simple analogy with manufacturing industry can be used to demonstrate the nature of the relationships between the component parts and thus the role of heritage as an economic resource (Figure 6.2). Such a model has three main components – resources, products and markets; three processes – resource activation and maintenance, product assembly and marketing; and three main groups of actors – resource caretakers, product assemblers and consumers of the experience.

The heritage resource is a selection from and a reflection of the events, personalities, historical, literary and mythological associations of the past. Selection is central and has been performed in part by the vagaries of time and human memory, but principally by the deliberate choices of those who have preserved, enhanced, rebuilt and re-created. Resources are not a fortuitous endowment determining their use but are activated by potential uses for them.

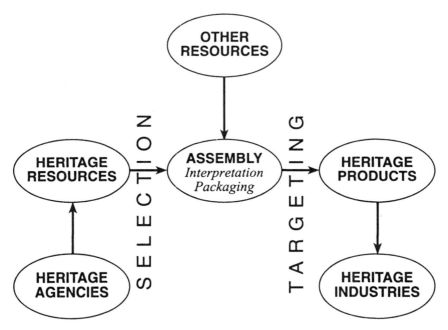

Figure 6.2   Components of the heritage industry

The assembly process by which resources are converted into products is one of interpretation and packaging. This is not merely the bringing together of a given set of resources but a means of selecting resources and transforming them into products. Selection, interpretation and packaging involve a series of choices about which product is being produced, and thus which resources are to be used in which ways.

The end product, in this case various heritage packages, has a specific meaning which is not synonymous with the existing built environment, or even an aggregated set of buildings, spaces and cityscapes. It is a product defined by, and intended to be consumed by, specified markets. Thus quite different products intended for quite distinct markets can be created from the same sets of environmental resources by varying the assembly process and, more especially, the interpretation. In addition, it is worth reiterating that although the resources may in part be derived from the landscapes of the historic past, the industry being described here is a modern one, satisfying contemporary demands for contemporary products. Its effectiveness can therefore be assessed only in those terms.

Several implications arise from the argument that the heritage product is defined by the consumer. Most important, however, is the conclusion that different markets can thus create different products from the same resources, which are then sold to different consumers at the same physical locations. This is an aspect of the 'multi-selling problem' that is intrinsic to all place-products, and one which raises numerous planning and management issues (Ashworth and Voogd 1990; *see* Part IV).

The producer performs this critical transformation process and it is clear from each of the stages outlined above that deliberate choices about resources, products and markets are being made. This raises the possibilities of using the commodification process in the pursuit of particular urban planning and management goals. The critical point is that in the case of heritage, no producer exists in the same sense as in the production of most other commercially marketable goods. The manufacturing analogy breaks down as generally quite different producers are responsible for each of the separate stages described above. Management choices essential in resource creation and maintenance, interpretative selection and packaging, and market identification and targeting are all being made by varying organizations for quite different objectives.

An economic systems model

Much concern in heritage is focused upon the maintenance of the resource itself so that it can continue in existence and potentially contribute towards currently unknown future products for prospective markets yet to be defined. An appreciation of the impacts upon, and what many would see as the threat to, the resource base itself requires that the closed production system of the commodification model be placed within a wider context. This accepts that resources are affected by their use and can even be exhausted in various ways. In addition, it must be understood that the production and consumption of heritage products have substantial impacts outside the closed system. In other words, some sort of development model must be sought which links the production process with the resources that it uses, in this case historical resources which, it must be reiterated, have many different uses. Certainly, a central tenet of such models is that development occurs, as distinct from mere resource preservation, but that such development is capable of serving a variety of goals, many of which are only vaguely, or cannot yet be, defined over the long rather than the short term. At its most straightforward, this is primarily a type of development that secures the long-term survival of the system by encouraging its regenerative capacity for renewal (Nijkamp 1990).

Such models and the concepts underlying them have been developed principally for natural rather than man-made resources. Many of the characteristics of heritage resources are similar, however, to those of the natural environment to the extent that much of the discussion in this chapter so far could have been applied equally to natural phenomena: indeed, it is now generally accepted that the natural cannot be separated from the cultural realm. A natural landscape and a cityscape are valued in similar ways, and provide similar experiences to socially similar consumers: indeed, they are frequently in both joint supply and joint demand. Therefore simple diagrams borrowed from models of natural resource exploitation can be applied to heritage resources. Figure 6.3 demonstrates the basic Dutch model (Ministry of Housing and Physical Planning 1989) for guiding national policies for the

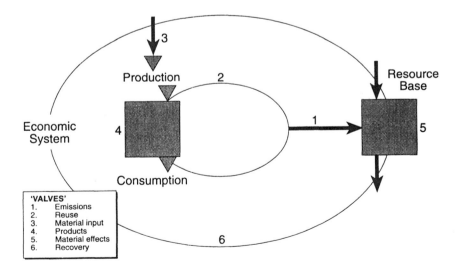

Figure 6.3   Dutch model for guiding national policies for the sustainable use of natural environmental resources

sustainable use of natural environmental resources. A notable aspect of this simple model is the identification of specific so-called 'valves', essentially points in the system at which deliberate intervention is possible with the objective of maintaining an overall balance. This system can be quite easily transposed to heritage by placing the heritage 'industrial' system within a broader context of a 'total' heritage system, which traces the flows of costs and incomes between production and resources. Such a model focuses attention on the relationship of the resources with the production system. Its purpose is not only to promote understanding, but also to provide the basis for the development of instruments of intervention. Sustainability has become a popular guiding principle in devising policies for the management of human impacts upon aspects of the natural environment and here it is pursued as a means of focusing upon the management of the heritage use system as described so far. The six points of potential intervention in the system outlined in Figure 6.3 can be simplified and regrouped into the four most relevant to this form of management. They are: resource valuation; output equity; carrying capacities; and self-balancing systems.

Resource valuation

The way resources are valued is common to all definitions of sustainable development. Historical resources commodified into heritage products are required to satisfy both a demand for direct consumption and a demand for possession or only continued existence. At the very least, this valuation of resources is likely to complicate their current utilization for tourism and may often result in a conflict between use now, or use later. Clearly, sustainable heritage development has to reconcile a range of quite different types of valuation of the resources it wishes to employ, complicated by the question of the legal and moral ownership of such resources.

In the exploitation of natural resources, a distinction is made between renewable and non-renewable resources; this may have some relevance here to heritage management although much depends upon the resolution of the following contradiction. In one sense, as we have seen, every heritage resource is in absolute fixed supply (there is only one York Minster, Heidelburg or George Washington). Indeed, one of the most important uses of heritage has ostensibly been the forming and propagation of the singular character of places through the uniqueness of their heritage. It has already been argued, however, that the conservation movement can create the resources it conserves, in so far as its stimulation of an awareness of historicity endows value to objects or buildings which previously had no such ascribed value. There are in this sense many more heritage resources now than a century ago, while the accelerating tempo of heritage resource creation is a well-remarked contemporary phenomenon (see particularly Hewison 1987). For example, England alone has 29 874 buildings listed as Grade 1 and 2*, and even they account for only 8 per cent of the country's total listed buildings (English Heritage 1999). Clearly an advantage of many heritage resources is that they are not in such relatively fixed supply as are such natural resources as oil fields, water-falls, or the Grand Canyon.

Although heritage resources are hypothetically inexhaustible in that there is no fixed past which is being commodified to serve contemporary demands, in practice, nevertheless, specific resources at particular times and places can be consumed to the point of exhaustion. Urban space, for example, is obviously finite, and the usable space encompassed by buildings or even cities is most evidently so. Actual physical land-use conflict between different users of the space upon which historical sites and monuments are located is the most obvious problem. Many such conflicts are amenable to solution through the exercise of existing planning controls and management policies (Ashworth and Tunbridge 1990), which, as argued above in the case of Venice, often involve more balanced exploitation of heritage resources within the space available.

Most strategies for sustainable natural resource exploitation stress a number of management principles, the most fundamental of which is the principle of parsimony in resource use. Currently, heritage resources are 'wasted' on a very large scale in a number of ways. Most obviously, the majority of museum artefacts, art gallery possessions, and even monumental buildings are not accessible to any sort of public use but merely preserved in store as a sort of reserve. Even those resources that are actively used are generally only consumed at a level well under their potential capacity, and for short time-periods. In natural environmental resource management policies, stress is laid on the possibilities offered by renewal, recycling and recuperation. The relevance of renewal and recycling to heritage resources is obvious. Much of the content of heritage industries is in essence a recycling of the past. Renewal, in the sense of repair, renovation and even reconstruction has always been an intrinsic, if controversial, part of heritage resource preservation. Recuperation, however, implies the operation of natural regenerative processes, which will have significance only to historical landscapes and sites where the 'green' environment plays a major role. Finally, heritage resources are more mobile than is often thought and relocation can often be an effective strategy for protecting resources, which would otherwise be damaged or destroyed, while also achieving a more profitable use. Artefacts, art works, and even bodies have been distinctly peripatetic over time, in response either to threats to the resource or to the demand for them. Even substantial buildings can be moved to less threatened or more productive locations, quite routinely so in North America and increasingly also in Europe. The use-values of a Venetian *palazzo* in Australia, or London Bridge in Lake Havasu, Arizona, were enhanced by their relocation to these resource-poor but high demand locations. Arguably (if unfashionably so), the Parthenon frieze (the Elgin Marbles) is a better protected and more accessible (and free) heritage experience in the British Museum in London than it would be on the Athenian Acropolis. Thus many threats to the over-use of heritage resources can and could be resolved by moving, rearranging and, within limits, extending or even duplicating them.

Output equity

Sustainable development also requires a revaluation on the output side of the model. Production is assessed against a series of output goals aimed at attaining certain equities or balances. The importance of intergenerational equities in devising policies for the management of natural resources is equally inherent in the idea of heritage. Past, present and future uses are theoretically harmonized, although in practice this is less easy to achieve, mainly because of the difficulty of assessing the nature of future demands. In addition, a necessity exists for 'intersectoral equity', reconciling the variety of contemporary uses through policies that prevent the depletion of the resource by one use to the detriment of other uses. The intrinsic multi-use of heritage makes this idea particularly relevant.

Consider, for example, the frequent conflict in objectives between heritage as a tourism resource for an export market and its role as a major component in local place identity and civic consciousness. The interpretations and packagings of heritage resources for export tourism and for local consumption are likely to be different, if only because tourists differ from residents in their knowledge, expectations and requirement of the same local resources. The difficulty is not that employing heritage resources for tourism inevitably distorts some notion of truth or authenticity by producing a 'pseudo-event' (Boorstin 1964): it is more simply that different markets require alternative products. Different 'pasts' are being constructed from the same historical resources and it is not always practical to separate the various market segments. Maintaining such output equities is, of course, a matter for political compromise for which there are no universal rules of guidance.

Carrying capacities

The link between resource valuation at one end of the model and equity outputs at the other can be made through the two ideas: 'carrying capacity' and 'automatic systems adjustment'. The former concept, long used as a management tool in pastoral agriculture, has a superficial attraction for the management of the users of limited space or fragile resources, as is frequently the case with the individual heritage site or building (see among others Wall 1983; Graefe *et al.* 1984; Westover and Collins 1987). It assumes that users have many of the behavioural characteristics of pastoral animals and that the resources have the attributes of pastures, the objective being to maximize numbers while maintaining the long-term sustainability of the resource base. Heritage sites and cities can then be managed by controlling the size of the 'herd' grazing upon them and also, although less usually, increasing the carrying attributes of the 'pasture'. Situations of underutilization, capacity and saturation can then be recognized, often in association with such ideas as 'product life-cycles'.

There are, however, problems with the basic analogy. Capacity is not determined solely by the characteristics of the resource, because heritage users vary greatly in their valuation of heritage resources and their uses of them. For some preservational users, a single additional visitor is too many, while, conversely, for some tourists many thousands of fellow visitors would not detract from the quality of the individual site or experience but rather enhance and legitimate it. Again, some of the places where heritage tourism occurs are large multifunctional cities, which physically are extremely robust, while being characterized by a varied and diverse economy and society capable of absorbing large numbers of heritage users without difficulty.

Furthermore, historical resources, once they have been transformed into heritage by interpretation, can, as argued above, be moved, extended and even replicated to a degree inapplicable to many natural resources. Carrying capacity, therefore, is not only capable of being influenced by its management but is in practice largely determined by that management. In short, carrying capacity is an optimizing model which depends for its outcome on a prior determination of what is to be optimized (Mathieson and Wall 1982). In the case of heritage use, a wide variety of possible outcomes exists depending upon the compromises reached between the aims of the heritage industries, the individual consumer, the custodians of the historical resources, and the public interests of the place itself. In practice, carrying capacity is not so much seeking an answer to the question: 'how many users can the resources bear?' as to 'what do the actors involved want to achieve?' Thus carrying capacity can be a specific rather than general management tool, once objectives have been determined. There may be no valid general statements of the capacity of a heritage city, but hotels, car parks, and even museums, cathedrals, *piazzas* and boulevards do have physical capacities at specific times, which in practice may determine, or can be used to determine, the physical capacity of a heritage site or city. The danger with this approach, of course, is that such manageable physical capacities may not coincide with other optima, including the limits of existing societies' capacity to absorb the demands of tourism without provoking negative reactions. In particular, it is frequently the secondary supporting tourism services (most usually accommodation or vehicle circulation and parking space) that are most easily used to provide controllable capacity figures, rather than the primary heritage facilities for which it is often more difficult to monitor and control visitor access. Thus there may be surplus capacity in the city as a whole while, simultaneously, specific heritage sites are suffering irreparable damage.

Thus this deceptively attractive management idea of carrying capacities provides general statements which have little logical foundation and, worse, are of limited value in most heritage environments. Even when used to determine the incidence of specific problems of congestion, considerable care is required in their application. To return to the case of Venice, attempts have been made to establish the physical capacities of the Lagoon City (van der Borg *et al.* 1996) and monitor the occasions when this has been exceeded. In this case, the unique physical location and causeway access enables both this measurement and the possibilities for remedial action by controlling access. Florence, by contrast, demonstrates the worst-case scenario of multilateral environmental overload of both primary heritage facilities and secondary supporting services, which a comprehensive management attack on all fronts (including coach access, museum opening, geographical redirection to under-used resources) has not yet sustainably resolved.

Self-balancing systems

A question that could be, but rarely is, posed by a discussion of carrying capacities is whether they are self-regulating, for if they are, then this becomes not so much a management tool but an argument for non-intervention in the heritage system. Either market mechanisms are effective in optimizing resource use, in which case intervention is unnecessary, or they are not, in which case the precise areas and causes of market failure must be identified so that intervention can be effective. Consider, for example, a heritage tourism site or city that receives more visitors than it can accommodate and, accordingly, delivers a quality of experience to the customer which is lower than that expected for the price charged. This then influences subsequent consumer decisions in favour of competing sites or cities or the same site at different times. Consequently, the argument has to be clearly made as to why a heritage product operating within a highly competitive market, which in general is more afflicted by over-supply of possibilities than any shortage, should not be allowed the automatic homeostatic adjustment of supply and demand through the market that applies to other free-market products. This is in fact the central question that stems from much of the preceding discussion of resources, outputs and capacities. Similarly, the answers will not merely indicate that intervention in general is needed, but more pointedly, will identify the precise intervention required at a specific point to correct a particular malfunction in the system.

Part of the argument may revolve around the consequences of the commodification of environmental resources. The operation of the system may be too sluggish or delayed to prevent irretrievable damage to the resource. Many heritage uses do not encourage rapid feedback from customers to producers of the sort experienced with other products. This is because a visit to a museum, historical site or town is a relatively rare event, perhaps even a once-in-a-lifetime occurrence for an individual site. The decision to purchase, especially in the case of heritage tourism, is generally made long before the product is consumed and on the basis of very imperfect knowledge of that product. For these reasons, the customer is not able to adjust behaviour according to the degree of satisfaction with the product – except, perhaps, over the very long term. In addition, because heritage users value resources in such different ways, they enjoy different utilities from the same densities of usage. In the extreme case, the visitor to Stonehenge, the Sistine Chapel or the Lascaux cave paintings may thus experience no diminution of the quality of their tourism experience, while simultaneously their feet, body warmth and breath respectively are causing such long-term damage to these sites that their use as preserved heritage is threatened. Furthermore, the absence of an efficiently operating pricing mechanism, as discussed above, leaves many heritage resources unpriced, as far as the individual customer is concerned, while many of the costs of the visit are external to the heritage facility. Therefore high costs may be incurred by the resource that are not reflected in the direct charges to users of the product who, in turn, are not deterred from purchase.

All these arguments support the view that the location of the resources largely outside the production accounting system leads to serious imbalances in costs and benefits, with the former being borne mostly by heritage resources and the latter accruing to heritage products. This has been highlighted as a specific problem of tourism (Berry 1996) but is merely a variant of the much more widespread so-called 'tragedy of the commons' problem (Hardin 1968). Here it is assumed that a number of farmers, operating as individual profit maximizers, have access to the grazing facilities of common land. Each individual farmer will incrementally increase his livestock as the addition of the marginal animal increases his return, up to and then beyond the point where the common land contributes diminishing returns: the collective resource is destroyed and all farmers presumably suffer. As Voogd (1998) has observed in relation to these sorts of social dilemmas in planning, what both appears to be, and from the community viewpoint certainly is, irrational conduct constitutes rational behaviour from the viewpoint of the individual, which, moreover, will be preferred to the alternative of individual restraint. This Voogd terms the 'sucker' option, which leads, not to conservation of the resource, but merely to the enhancement of another's profit.

Such imbalances are not rectified by a mechanism maintaining equilibrium. Therefore markets are not working in a way that secures the long-term existence of the heritage resource base because there is no effective automatic homeostatic adjustment. The creation of such a system would require many of the same measures currently being discussed in terms of the natural environment because the problem is in essence the same. Externalities must be internalized and costs borne by the user. The difficulties in applying this idea to heritage users lie in its detailed operationalization rather than its logic. While Krabbe and Heijman (1986) argue that the management of the environment in general needs to be based on the principle that agencies and individuals must respond to the entropy they create, there are practical difficulties in charging many users. Future generations are difficult to invoice for the costs of preserving their heritage but many option or existence demands can be costed. In the same way that the costs, including the opportunity costs, of the preservation of the tropical rain forest or the Indian tiger can be charged to those who value and are prepared to pay for them, so also can the continued existence of Mayan temples or Aboriginal rock paintings be charged, at least in part, to the inhabitants of richer countries who gain satisfaction from the knowledge of their preservation (*see* Chapter 9). The questions: 'who owns?' 'who uses?' 'who manages?' 'who benefits?' and 'who pays?' are all inextricably linked.

At a prosaic level, the heritage industries, most especially tourism, need to take more financial responsibility for the long-term maintenance of the heritage resources upon which they depend. This can take the form of substantial direct and voluntary subsidies to the agencies, usually in the public sector, which manage historic resources, or of compulsory taxation, which could be place- or user-specific. The main argument against this latter strategy is not, as the tourism operators usually argue, that it imposes a competitive disadvantage upon particular places or sites because this is, of course, one of the main objectives. Rather, the difficulty is that, as discussed earlier, the heritage tourism industry and heritage tourists are difficult to define and separate from other users and are therefore difficult to tax. In jurisdictions where add-on taxes are culturally accepted, especially North America, local hotel room taxes are frequently levied in an attempt to remedy the imbalance in costs and benefits: such taxes, however, do not discriminate between categories of user of the facility.

An important dimension of the mismatch between the costs and benefits of heritage can be related directly to spatial scale, and management strategies therefore need to redress imbalances in pursuit of what could be called 'inter-scalar equity'. In particular many of the most obvious external costs that provoke much of the opposition to heritage tourism development are borne by the specific site or locality, while many of the benefits are accrued at the national scale. For example, the costs that arise from the simple spatial co-existence of tourists and historic buildings, monuments and sites can lead to physical damage, whether intentional or not and, more subtly, the destruction of ambience. In addition the costs incurred may be less direct, in the form of additional public facility provision in historic places as a result of the presence of tourists. Compensation in the form of flows of revenues from heritage tourists to historic resources is likely to be indirect and delayed, as well as wholly inadequate to cover the costs incurred. The resource, to reiterate, is not activated by tourism. It already exists and will most probably continue to exist regardless of any payments from the tourism users, who are therefore in the curious position of being cross-subsidized by other local users. Even the various non-quantifiable benefits, such as increasing the consciousness of visitors of the value of preserving and enhancing aspects of the past and thereby gaining political support and legitimation from the visitor, are extremely indirect when tourists are drawn from distant political systems. Policies for redressing this mismatch of costs and benefits occur at a variety of scales, an issue to which we return in Part IV.

Conclusion

Almost all the issues discussed above in economic terms involve more general social attitudes. Sustainability is ultimately a normative idea, which involves the valuation of, and rights over, resources – in this case the past – and thus clearly over how such resources should be used now and in the future. Preservation and development are the two dominating strategic ideas in managing heritage, and sustainable heritage development is an attempt at reconciling them rather than choosing between them. Although all resources, whether natural or human, are only activated by the demand for them, heritage resources in particular, as we have argued, are especially capable of responding to demand and in that sense are particularly demand derived. If heritage cannot by definition be considered other than in terms of the demand for it, then heritage sustainability is both a development and a preservation issue. Management strategies for sustainable heritage development involve a complex set of choices about the relationships of a production system to a resource system, which is in simultaneous use for a variety of functions. Therefore, economic approaches can provide some guidance in the making of these choices, especially through their 'role in reconciling interdependent and conflictual objectives of development and conservation in relation to limited resources available in a given area' (Bizzaro and Nijkamp 1996b, p. 7). In the next chapter, we turn to the wider contexts of the role of heritage in economic development.

|7|

Heritage in economic development strategies

Introduction

In 1862, when the question of a public sector involvement in culture – in this case architectural preservation – was first tentatively discussed in The Netherlands, the then Prime Minister declared, to general agreement, that art is not the business of government nor is the government the arbiter of art or science. By 1992, however, a Ministry of Economic Affairs national policy document stated that Dutch cultural heritage could add greatly to the national and local economy and stimulate employment in the cultural sector (Ministerie van Economische Zaken 1992). This is but one example of a changing relationship through time between governments and culture, which has led to many cultural facilities and performances becoming dependent upon governments, to such an extent that many branches of culture are now a virtual state monopoly. Moreover, governments have become increasingly dependent upon culture as a constituent element within economic development strategies at many scales.

The traditional view of the relationship between culture and economics has two main dimensions. First, it is assumed that culture, including the preservation of heritage artefacts and sites, is a luxury consumer item purchased – whether by individuals or public bodies – from the surplus profits of economic growth. It is a 'merit good' deserving of economic support because of its non-economic benefits, usually expressed as the educational or social improvement of the individual or of society. Second, culture in general is thought to play a reactive or at best modifying role in economic development. In both perspectives, preservation and development are typically seen as opposites to be reconciled through compromise, while local cultures are merely modifying variables often acting as constraints. In neither case is culture viewed as an integral part of the local economy.

In the last few years, however, the relationship between culture and economics has shifted drastically. This is clearly demonstrated in The

Netherlands, for example, by comparing the 1985 and 1992 national policy guidelines of the ministry responsible for culture. The earlier document (Ministerie WVC 1985) is concerned principally with justifying the distribution of state subsidies between sectors and regions, the principle of social and spatial equity being paramount. The later policy, conversely (Ministerie WVC, 1992), focuses on ideas of efficiency and the place of cultural organizations and performances within other national political and economic objectives. Such a shift in approach is broadly reflected in many other western countries.

An instrumental role for culture has been discovered and is being practised. Heritage is an important element within both culture, broadly conceived, and, more narrowly, the arts. In most countries, what is discussed in this book as heritage, including the preservation of buildings, sites and districts, is the responsibility at the national level of Ministries of Culture and is treated as part of cultural policy at national and local scales. Again, such elements of heritage as past aesthetic productivity and the built environment as architecture overlap considerably with policies for the arts at most spatial scales of responsibility, these ranging in Europe from the Council of Europe and the European Commission to individual city administrations.

Three main economic dimensions can be identified to this development role of heritage. First, it is an economic sector in itself, using resources, producing products and generating returns in profits and jobs. Second, heritage is also one element in economic development alongside others, frequently exercising a catalytic or integrating role in development projects. Finally, it is used as an instrument in the management of economies at various spatial scales from the international to the local. The existence of a recognizable and important economic sector which can be labelled 'the heritage industry', the recognition that investment in heritage has strategic importance in national, regional and local economies, and, finally, that the public sector assumes a number of critical enabling and integrating heritage management functions, would all now be greeted as self-evident by governments and commercial enterprises in most parts of the world.

Admittedly some commentators have seen all these developments as less than advantageous for places, their citizens, cultures or even economies. The changes can be viewed as part of a shift, which many deplore, from an exclusive 'high culture' to a mass-produced commodified culture (Adorno 1991). This latter is assumed to be of a lower quality, thereby posing a threat to traditions of high quality cultural productivity. Indeed commodified culture can even be seen as a device whereby the pastimes of an élite become subsidized and supported by the taxes of the majority (Lewis 1990). Certainly attention to the development roles of culture does shift the focus from the intrinsic worth of the object or performance to its value in support of some other purpose. Similarly, it may be argued that the increasing importance of the economic roles of culture may result in little more than a privatization of what was previously a zero-priced public good (Hitters 1993). If heritage is held to be valuable in economic development, then its other values are likely to be discounted and their users may be dispossessed or priced out. Even an economist (Mossetto 1990) can argue that, although past economic activity may have produced art as a by-product through the use of surplus profit for conspicuous merit consumption, the cultural stock is unlikely to be replenished as a result of its current economic use. The relationship between economic development and culture is thus seen as parasitical.

If the protectors of culture are frequently fearful of economics, they may be reassured to learn that economists may be equally averse to using culture, and especially heritage, in development. Some see heritage as a symptom while others regard it as a cause of contemporary economic decline. For example, Moody (1996) argues that heritage is powered by nostalgia, which, in turn, is antagonistic to development. Historic periods of popular nostalgia correspond to depressions in the economic trade cycle, such as those which occurred in Britain during the 1880s, 1930s and 1970s. More generally, the postmodernist contention of a shift from an economic and social organization based on production to one based on consumption regards heritage as simply consumption of the past (Kneafsey 1994). Hewison (1987) goes further by concluding that the flourishing post-World War II British heritage industry is both a symptom of the existence of a 'climate of decline' and has also contributed to a backward-looking romanticism that has discouraged attempts to meet the challenges of development for the future, a factor which helps explain the country's comparatively mediocre economic performance over that period.

None of these counter-arguments are wholly convincing but they at least counsel caution. It is not necessarily contradictory to argue that heritage can both stimulate and retard economic development, while economic development may both support and destroy heritage resources. Rising heritage demands may result from economic prosperity and the search for wider leisure experiences or, conversely, represent a retreat from economic stagnation into a deceptively comfortable and dangerous complacency. The most pressing and imminent danger is the conventional wisdom, at least among decision makers, that investment in heritage – or culture in general – must inevitably be beneficial to both economic development and heritage resources by directly or indirectly producing a profitable return to each. Although this is rarely justified in detail, heritage investments are now loaded with multiple expectations of many quite different anticipated beneficial effects. Major investments of money and the energy of public agencies are occurring for no better reason than faith that something must happen as a result. The precise nature and effectiveness of all of these roles forms the principal content of this chapter.

Heritage as an economic activity

Of the many and diverse ways of viewing the relationship between heritage and economic activities, the three most prevalent in policy applications are considered here. First, heritage is an economic activity in itself, an industry commodifying past structures, associations and cultural productivity and trading these for an economic return that can be measured in jobs, profits or incomes. Second, heritage places can be treated as locations for economic activities and assessed according to their ability to attract, accommodate or repel economic functions. Third, and most indirectly, heritage in various manifestations can be used in the creation and promotion of place images for dominantly economic purposes.

Heritage as a culture industry

If an economy is classified according to its industrial sectors, then it is not difficult to envisage the existence of a group of 'culture industries' within which 'heritage industries' might appear as a sub-category, further subdivided into such sets as the 'building conservation', 'museum', or 'heritage theme park' industries. The obvious difficulty in pursuing such an approach is that these and similar classifications do not appear in conventional economic statistics, while the heritage industry is by its nature diffuse and difficult to disentangle from many other activities to which it is related, or within which it is often included.

At the national level, the Ministry of Canadian Heritage, for example, has responsibility, not only for historic buildings, national historic sites and nationally important artefact collections, but also for related fields such as national parks and wilderness areas, heritage rivers and even heritage fauna. Its remit extends to other diverse topics including sport provision, multicultural policy, relations with the monarchy and citizenship. Similarly, in addition to heritage, the UK Ministry responsible for culture also deals with the broadcasting media, national lottery and sport. At a local level in most European countries, responsibility for aspects of heritage, including building and area conservation, museums, archives, local history, arts and traditional crafts, is generally split fairly arbitrarily between a selection of political portfolios and administrative departments of planning and development control, culture, education, leisure and recreation, tourism and economic development, and marketing or promotion.

If government at all levels has failed to delimit a field of heritage for administrative purposes, this reflects the various ways in which heritage is related to so many other topics, while simultaneously fulfilling such a variety of roles that it is futile to attempt to assess its separate contribution to any one. This situation is replicated in the private sector where, for example, heritage centres and theme parks, 'stately homes' or historical pageants and commemorations are likely to be operated as part of a wider leisure, entertainment or media industry rather than a specific heritage or culture enterprise. Nevertheless, despite these difficulties, several attempts have been made to delimit either a 'heritage industry' (Hewison 1987, 1991) an 'arts industry' (Fischer *et al.* 1996) or more widely a 'culture industry' (Wynne

1992). The need to do this has usually been to generate comparative statistics to demonstrate either the growing importance of cultural industries compared with other activities, or the relative importance of this sector in one country compared with another. In both cases the motive has been to raise the awareness of governments and their citizens as to the economic importance of the sector.

Heritage as a tourism industry

It could be argued that heritage tourism is so important as an industry that it requires separate and extended treatment (see, for example: Boniface and Fowler 1993; Costa and van der Borg 1993; van der Berg *et al.* 1995; Robinson *et al.* 1996). However, it is so all-pervasive in most of the economic arguments raised so far that to treat it as a discrete industry serving a recognizable market segment, labelled heritage tourism, with targeted heritage tourism products, would be to miss most of the wider points discussed so far. It is argued here that in regarding heritage as a condition of place, heritage tourism, the heritage tourist, and tourism heritage do not exist, except perhaps as conceptual abstractions in the study of tourism as an activity. The question of spatial scale is also significant in that although tourism occurs locally, its economic impacts are much more widely diffused. Indeed, it has long been argued (see, for example, the comprehensive summary in Sinclair and Stabler 1997) that the economic benefits of tourism are most easily calculable at the national scale (as in balance of international payments, profits of national travel or accommodation corporations and the like), while the costs are more usually experienced locally.

It is easy to demonstrate that tourists make an important contribution to visitor numbers and ticket sales for many heritage facilities and exhibitions. Forty-four per cent of the visitors to London museums are tourists, the proportion being much higher for the ten largest institutions (Copley and Robson 1996). Well-sited and promoted themed heritage experiences such as Jorvik (York), 'Canterbury Tales' (Canterbury), 'Royalty and Empire' (Windsor) and the like are major tourist attractions, generating economic benefits for themselves and for ancillary services in the towns in which they are located. Very few heritage products, however, are produced for tourists alone; many, if not most, heritage buildings, museum collections and cultural festivals rarely encounter a tourist. Even those few that do are generally dependent for their appeal upon a much wider heritage setting, often the historic city as a whole for which tourism may be a marginal activity.

Similarly, when viewed from the consumer's perspective, the growth in heritage tourism is not explicable by isolating the behaviour and motivation of the tourist from a wider society. The situation is not, as is sometimes implied, that a completely exogenous demand for heritage leads to an influx of tourists who consume a foreign heritage and then return home to quite different consumption patterns. On the contrary, heritage tourism is merely one aspect of the increase in a much wider special-interest tourism in which pastimes, interests and attitudes practised at home are simply continued elsewhere. Heritage, and culture more widely, is increasingly a central part of the local life-styles of a new service class with new cultural consumption preferences. Thus the heritage tourist is more the resident on holiday than a special category of consumer whose motives and behaviour mysteriously change once an international frontier is crossed.

Indeed, the frequently deplored 'demonstration effect', whereby the tourist's consumption of heritage elsewhere influences behaviour and attitudes in the host society, is frequently reversed. In The Netherlands, as in most northern European countries, the holiday experience in Mediterranean countries has combined with wider social changes to promote the selective import of new consumer goods (especially food and drink), while perceived life-style attributes have influenced the introduction of urban phenomena including the boulevard café and, more broadly, the new uses of public space for public spectacle and spectator pastimes. These latter have themselves become major tourism attractions in cities such as Utrecht, Groningen or Maastricht (Duren 1993; Klerk and Vijgen 1993; Oosterman 1993; Ashworth 1997). Tourist and resident are now indistinguishable as well as being statistically inseparable. Tourists imitate residents who themselves are imitating their perceptions of the same tourists' home behaviour. The implications for policy of this integral functioning of tourism within local economies, and specifically the interplay of the internal and external markets for heritage, is that tourism plays a complex role in economic development strategies, interacting with many economic sectors at different spatial scales.

Heritage as a factor in the location of economic activities

One of the peculiarities of heritage is that it is both a particular type of activity and also a particular type of place. Here we consider the qualities of heritage places as locations for economic activities. Heritage buildings, sites and areas accommodate many diverse economic activities located there for numerous different reasons. This relationship between activity and site can be classified as:

- 'intentional', where the activity deliberately chooses a heritage site as conferring important advantages;
- 'ancillary', where the heritage attributes make some, but not a decisive, contribution to the locational choice;
- or 'coincidental', where the activity is indifferent to the historicity of the site and is located there for quite different reasons.

For three main reasons, however, this rational approach is in many cases quite spurious.

First, the history of the heritage conservation movement has proceeded more often on the basis of the initial motive to save buildings and only the subsequent and secondary need to occupy them, rather than as a response to the heritage requirements of economic activities. This is so even where, as in North America, the expectation of economic profit has typically been a *sine qua non* of conservation. Thus finding a function has often been a post-preservation exercise that has led to many activities using conserved premises without deriving any particular benefit from their historicity, or even having much control over the location decision. Local authorities or private charities, for example, finding themselves custodians of historic buildings, frequently use them for exhibitions, meetings, receptions and the like, only because such space is available and some use, however unprofitable in economic terms, is considered preferable to vacancy. Second, inertia plays a role in explaining most locational patterns but there are reasons to presume it is especially important in area conservation, where changes in the built environment may be reflected only slowly in changes in the spatial pattern of functions. Finally, a substantial proportion of occupiers of designated historic monuments, and even more so, designated heritage areas, are simply unconscious of the designations, or, even if aware, regard these as of no direct economic consequence to themselves.

Nevertheless, it is possible to review a checklist of the most relevant economic attributes of heritage locations and to compare these with the requirements of particular activities, making the assumption that different activities value the same attributes as either a cost or a benefit. In the long run, this determines the functional mix of heritage areas and also their ultimate success in attracting enough, suitable, financially viable occupiers of heritage space. Some distinction can be drawn between the characteristics of buildings and of the wider area in which they are set.

Leaving aside the question of whether land costs will be higher or not, location in a conserved building immediately imposes direct costs of higher maintenance, if only because it is likely to be more labour intensive and also, by virtue of its public monumental status, of a higher standard than elsewhere. Probably more important are the indirect costs upon an enterprise stemming from the restrictions upon change of the building. Constraints on expansion and adaptation will affect such matters as: facade decorations, the display of familiar company logos and external advertising; utility provision, including modern heating, lighting, ventilation and communication services necessary to meet contemporary codes of practice; and fenestration and related internal space divisions, which may not conform to current workshop or office practices and thus impose costs in efficient operations. To these can be added the costs of the conserved area in which the building is set, including restrictions on accessibility for motor vehicles, which have implications for the transport of materials, products, staff and customers.

Against this formidable list of costs must be set the benefits to be derived from heritage locations. These tend to be less obvious and less measurable.

The most important direct benefit relates to the ways the historicity of the building or area has a positive impact upon the enterprise located in it. These can be summarized as the related benefits of status, patronage, and address. Some qualities of the building and area are transferred by occupancy to the user who gains the status of tradition, continuity and reliability and, by inference, probity and trustworthiness as well as the good taste and public benefaction of artistic patronage. To these subjective qualities can be added the value of a recognizable address in a high-status neighbourhood, which may appear to confirm the quality or success of the enterprise in general. If the location is associated with other similar enterprises, this can lead to what in London could be recognized as the 'Harley Street' or even 'Saville Row' phenomenon, where the location confers customer recognition and ease of discovery, combined with immediate acceptability of higher customer charges. Traffic controls in conservation areas may restrict vehicular access but, conversely, may encourage pedestrian accessibility and associated opportunities for impulsive consumer behaviour.

The ways in which different enterprises weight these sometimes ambiguous costs and benefits largely determine the long-term functional pattern of heritage buildings and areas. Clearly those who are indifferent to, or can tolerate, the restrictions upon change, space arrangements and access, and who simultaneously can profit from the psychic or behavioural benefits listed above, will normally either remain in such locations after they are designated or move to them. Such enterprises fall into three main categories. First, there are activities that directly value historicity as part of their saleable product such as art, antiques, antiquarian and craft dealers. These may overlap with both the souvenir trade and second-hand and junk markets, as well as services such as some catering outlets (traditional restaurants), bars and even hotel accommodation (of the traditional 'Inn' variety), which are openly selling the past as an integral part of the product. Second, there are activities that are not directly doing this but which value the qualities that historicity may confer and which have modest space demands. These include medical, financial or legal consulting room services, in which the client's trust in the provider is critical. Finally, certain activities profit from the presence of people predisposed to be attracted to their products and services rather than from the historicity of the setting itself. One obvious manifestation of this is retailing where heritage may be deliberately sold by chains such as 'Past Times' in what Duffy (1994, p. 82) refers to as the 'Laura Ashleyisation' of the high street (after a British fashion store specializing in traditional designs).

Conversely, enterprises which derive little benefit from the qualities of historicity or the people it attracts, but do suffer from the restrictions on space, change and accessibility, will either avoid locations in historic buildings or areas, or seek new locations if trapped within them by the subsequent heritage designations of planners. Examples would include offices engaged in information storage and processing rather than public representation, and activities dependent upon an association with modernity rather than historicity.

Finally, there is a widespread incidence of what could be termed locational compromise whereby the costs of actual location in conserved areas are avoided by the choice of modern premises in a non-conserved district, while still reaping the wider benefits of location in an historic town or region. This is the use of heritage as an indirect amenity rather than as a direct locational consideration. Changes have occurred in the weighting of locational factors in the locational decisions of firms as the relative importance of transport costs of materials, products, energy and even labour have declined, leaving, if only by default, place amenity as an important locational variable (Dunning and Norman 1987). One study of a number of firms in Greater London (Evans 1993) found that a wide mix of recreational and decorative facilities with museums and old buildings was more important than sporting facilities and pubs to a majority of respondents. Such studies reveal little about the actual weight given to such variables in the decision to locate compared to other more easily quantifiable factors, but at the very least, other factors being more or less equal, firms will not locate in cultural or heritage 'deserts' (Whitt 1987). Heritage thus contributes to the vague but potentially decisive factor of access for employees to an attractive residential or recreational environment.

Heritage and the creation of economic place images

At first sight it may seem curious that heritage would have any role to play at all in the shaping of place images designed to encourage economic development. After all heritage is composed of aspects of the remembered, preserved and imagined past, while development is essentially planning and investment for a future that is different from, and presumably better than, any such past. It seems more logical for a place wishing to appear eager to change, and to this end shaping a local consensus favouring development, to actively disavow, or just passively forget, its past from which it wishes to escape into a brighter future. Thus in seeking a rapid transition from a rejected past to a desired future, many revolutions at least begin with a deliberate iconoclasm, or state-sponsored amnesia, that removes the cultural accoutrements of the past so that development into the future can proceed unfettered. Given this, why then does heritage assume such an active role in shaping contemporary place images, especially those deliberately designed to encourage development? Burgess's (1982) pioneering work into the promoted images of British local authorities identified four general qualities that dominated such images. These were: centrality; dynamism; identity; and quality of life. The latter two were formed principally from beauty, historicity and cultural facilities.

Two pieces of more detailed research from The Netherlands extend and exemplify these findings. The content of the promotional material of 16 medium-sized towns, all engaged in place marketing policies designed to attract external interest in development opportunities (not tourist visits) is summarized in Figures 7.1 and 7.2 (Voogd and van de Wijk 1989). Two main

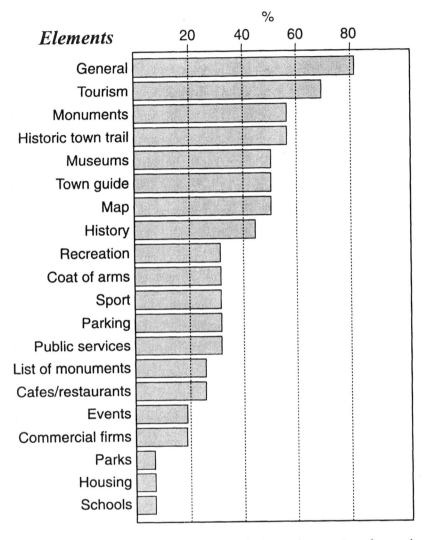

Figure 7.1   The role of heritage in the place marketing and promotion of a sample of Dutch towns
Source: adapted from Voogd and van de Wijk (1989)

conclusions can be drawn from Figure 7.1. First, in aggregate, heritage dominates the promotions: historic monuments, historic trails, museums, local historical narratives and even descriptions of coats of arms far outweighed what might have been thought more useful commercial information or descriptions of social facilities. Second, taken separately, while all the sample towns were making some use of historic elements, those with the most existing monuments and strongest existing heritage reputations used them least and vice-versa. Thus towns with the weakest heritage image, such as Schiedam (an industrial

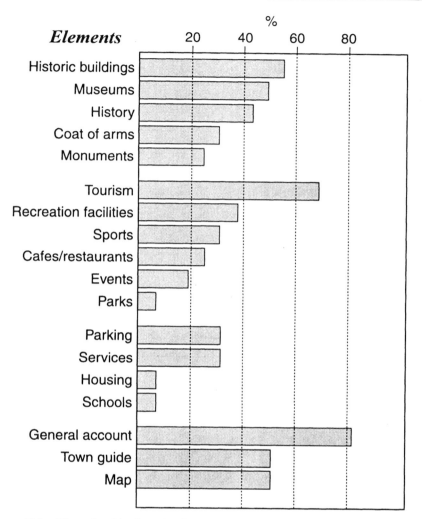

Figure 7.2   The role of heritage in the promotional literature of a sample of Dutch local authorities
Source: adapted from Voogd and van de Wijk (1989)

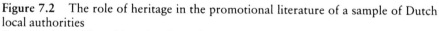

suburb of Rotterdam) or Amersfoort (a residential commuter town), felt most strongly the need to acquire one.

A second research project (van der Veen and Voogd 1989) was more specific in intent and took the form of an experiment in which a fictitious foreign company made enquiries about relocation possibilities among 78 local authorities in the northern Netherlands, a region where traditional economic activities are in decline and which is actively searching for new development possibilities. The content of the resulting promotional literature is shown in Figure 7.2 and again heritage was the dominant attribute stressed.

Accounting for these findings is more difficult than describing them, but explanations can be sought in both the decision-making processes of firms and the practical situation in which local authorities find themselves. Convincing potential investors that a place possesses what can be termed an 'entrepreneurial climate' involves more than merely relating statistics about, for example, the costs and availability of suitable land, the costs of transport or the availability of government subsidy or support. In much of Western Europe, these factors are of diminishing significance and, within most regions, do not significantly vary over space. Thus an individual local authority can safely assume that the value of such variables has already been assessed, and that the competitive choice is between specific locations within the region or country. In this process quite different variables are involved. If the promotion is related to models of the phases of consumer decision making, as in Figure 7.3, then the task of local authority promotion in the early phases is merely recognition and awareness. This is best served by presenting a distinctive identity, which, in turn, is most easily achieved by stressing a particular history and thus contemporary heritage. A place must put itself on the mental map of decision-makers and a distinctive heritage is the most obvious way of achieving this. Proceeding further through the process of choice, the preference for one place rather than another of similar general attributes and location is encouraged by what may seem commercially irrelevant but nevertheless colourful and memorable local details. Places in the Dutch experiment were exploiting past economic achievements as indications of future success, specifically using a romantic historicism and heritage that extolled the historically proven ethnic and even racial attributes of their populations to demonstrate local stability, probity and continuity.

More prosaically, it can be argued that local authorities have generally acquired two other promotional markets – the in-coming tourism market and their own citizens, the promotion of the place to itself. Each of these is an important market demanding attention in its own right, as well as influencing strategies and instruments for promoting incoming investment and entrepreneurial skills. Both tourism and 'self-marketing' are likely to favour the use of heritage elements in promotional images, albeit for different reasons. Heritage is used to create directly saleable tourism products while, in self-marketing, it is the most effective means by which individuals identify themselves with places and acquire a collective 'civic consciousness'. The practical point here is that if local authorities seek to extend the active promotion of these markets into external commercial marketing, they may not possess the skills to segment, separate and target the markets nor the financial resources to develop separate instruments of promotion. Quite simply, blunt multipurpose instruments are being used in promoting vaguely formulated multiple goals within dimly delineated consumer markets. Heritage is the safest and cheapest option in such an unknown environment.

Considering further actual cases of the role of heritage in place images, a fundamental distinction must be made between the deliberately projected

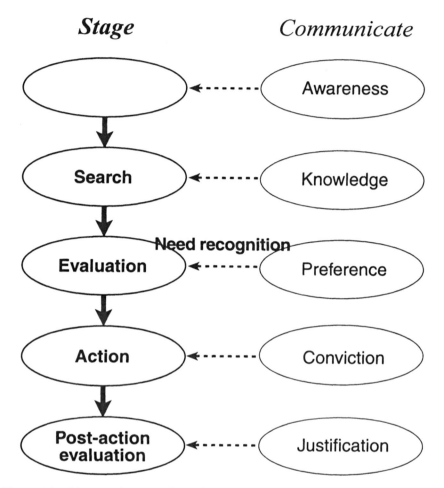

Figure 7.3 Place marketing and the phases of consumer decision making

images considered so far and those actually received by the potential users. These are unlikely to be the same, partly because enormous distortions occur in transmission, and also because the deliberately projected messages of place management authorities comprise only a small fraction of the total information being transmitted about a place. Numerous 'league tables', most usually at the city or national scale, summarize how people envisage places. 'Most liveable city' polls have long been popular in the United States and are seen by city managers as a judgement on the success, or otherwise, of their promotional programmes. Similarly, there are 'most workable' or 'investable city' leagues, which no doubt influence the locational decisions of people, enterprises and capital. While the specific role of heritage in such broad notions as 'liveability' is almost impossible to disentangle from many other, potentially related attributes, including the presence of cultural facilities, environmental quality, downtown liveliness and citizens' feelings of identity and belonging, equally it is clearly present. Thus the consistent top scorers in the United States tend to be older cities such as Seattle, Boston or San Francisco (Figure 7.4), with their historic associations and well-known conservation areas, although the most popular tourist-historic 'gems', such as Savannah or Charleston, are not always included. In Britain, too, top scorers like Edinburgh or Bristol have images with major heritage components but towns such as York or Cambridge with notable international reputations for heritage score badly. One possible explanation is that the very success of some cities in projecting a heritage image has led to intensive tourism development, which, in turn, creates economic or even physical features treated as negative factors in such a hypothetical residential decision. The most favoured cities tend to be those of sufficient size to offer a well-rounded collection of amenities, which may include heritage but is not dominated by it.

The general conclusion remains that however difficult – and indeed undesirable given its catalytic role – it may be to isolate the heritage component from other elements in the economic construction of representations of place, it is widely used in shaping place images intended to further the economic goals of place management authorities at all spatial scales. The arguments supporting this, as Weiler (1998) has pointed out, may depend more on anecdote than analysis and the objectives may be wide and vague, as in improving a city's 'imageability' or 'legibility' (Bianchini and Schwengat 1991). However, the decision of an enterprise, or more accurately of key individuals within an enterprise, to locate in one place rather than another may well be critically influenced, as with any other behavioural decision, by just such immeasurable variables and – even more significant – heritage may be the only competitive instrument available to places.

Local heritage in urban neighbourhood regeneration

If judged on the basis of the amount of literature or number of official studies, the neighbourhood or district, most usually within a city, is clearly the most important scale at which heritage is used to achieve more general planning objectives. To some, 'urban conservation is a sub-case of urban renewal' (Bizzarro and Nijkamp 1996b) and thus the conserved heritage of the built environment is just one of many planning policies applicable to local areas. If, as Bianchini and Schwengat (1991) have argued, urban regeneration in western cities in the past several decades has been largely 'property-led' and as so much local heritage is manifested in property, especially in the older areas of cities most subject to regeneration, then spatial coincidence alone would have involved heritage in much neighbourhood regeneration. More specifically, heritage has been seen as an instrument in general urban revitalization

Figure 7.4   A medley of heritage: a cable car climbs the hill from San Francisco's restored Fisherman's Wharf, with the former prison island of Alcatraz in the bay behind

(Wynne 1992), often as a strategy of last resort in specific problem areas that have proved largely immune to other policies (Lim 1993). As Stabler (1996, p. 431) admits, 'although conservation would appear to be significant in a number of successful regeneration schemes, it is certainly not a necessary condition for success' and, by implication, there are many urban regeneration programmes in which heritage plays only a minor enhancing role – or none at all. What conclusions can be drawn about the nature of the role played by heritage in local economic regeneration, if only so that these 'necessary conditions for success' can be determined?

Before considering this problem, it is necessary to re-visit some of the issues of prices, values, costs and benefits raised in Chapter 6. Some form of cost-benefit analysis is necessary to assess the wider monetary costs and benefits to an area of any major project of heritage conservation and local area regeneration. The difficulty of using conventional cost-benefit analysis, as a means of pricing the value of conservation in this way, is that heritage is only one of many investments in such multi-purpose projects in pursuit of a multiplicity of economic and non-economic goals. Lichfield's (1988) solution was to develop a 'community impact evaluation', which tries to assess cost and benefits directly and indirectly to the various main parties in the process. This indicates which sections of the community gain or lose through specific investments, or through the economic regeneration of the area as a whole. Although this, like any other form of multivariate analysis, has all the intrinsic problems of the measurement and allocation of particular effects to specific causes, variations on this approach have been used to assess the potential impacts of many individual projects.

Thus although there is some agreement that culture, including heritage, can be used as a catalyst in urban growth strategies (Whitt 1987), there is, nevertheless, a shortage of specific ideas of what this role or roles may be. In a field where optimistic declarations are more plentiful than analysis, there is some consensus that the conditions needed for culturally led local regeneration include policies that link form and function. Bianchini (1991) expresses this in more detail through his cultural planning paradigm, which argues for a holistic approach involving at least five elements of the city. These include: architecture; urban design more broadly; the local community; aspects of the infrastructure; and only fifth, the local economy, especially its responsiveness and flexibility. Thus the heritage of the conserved built environment, and of culture more widely, is called upon to play a number of different roles in neighbourhood regeneration. It can on occasion provide the main motive for such programmes and thus the central stimulus for local change: more usually its effects are catalytic, stimulating action in other fields, or just amplifying their effects. Three such roles are frequently specified – 'cachet', animation and externalities.

'Cachet' is a pervasive, but difficult to isolate (let alone quantify) reason for the inclusion of heritage elements in regeneration projects. Heritage buildings, locations and associations, together with the products, events and experiences produced from these, bring an aura of respectability, continuity and artistic patronage to a project that extends to other co-existent but more prosaic functions, which may in reality be providing most of the economic returns. If historicity and urban design is a critical component of that vague but essential characteristic of place identity, then the resulting local identification and civic consciousness plays an important if vaguely defined role in local economic revitalization. All investment is the result of a risk assessment in which confidence overcomes fear in an unpredictable future. The heritage elements provide a stage or background for other profit-seeking enterprises, while also facilitating the success of these undertakings. They are seen as contributing psychic stability and aesthetic satisfactions to the individual citizen but also, by extension, to the cohesion and sense of well-being of the communities in which they live. To this can be added the external promotional impacts of a recognizable 'signature restoration', a single building or site which symbolizes the whole project in the public imagination, as well as the psychic income gained by external investors who reap the status, not just of investing in a local economic venture, but of being associated in the sponsorship of a wider heritage project for the common good. It is this argument, however difficult to demonstrate statistically, that accounts in large part for the focal position of heritage in so many local revitalization schemes. The restored 'Faneuil Hall Marketplace', centrepiece of the Boston Waterfront

Figure 7.5   Boston, Mass.: Quincy Market in the Faneuil Hall Marketplace. Opened in the 1970s, this is a typical example of a 'heritage' shopping centre focused on food outlets and tourism-leisure shopping

(Figure 7.5), 'Piece Hall', symbolic of the newly confident nineteenth-century Yorkshire textile town of Halifax, restored historic ships in quayside developments, such as the *Great Britain* (Bristol) or *Bluenose* (Halifax, Nova Scotia), were not necessarily economic investments, if measured by the balance of the restoration costs and current returns, but their value to the wider economic regeneration of the areas in which they are set is incalculable.

Second, heritage can also contribute 'animation'. This encompasses bringing people onto the streets, especially when other urban facilities are closed, and also introducing a liveliness that becomes spectacle in itself. Visitors act as both performers and audience in public space and while this is not usually an important economic function, the process increases the 'footfall' of visitors, their length of stay and perhaps also their disposition to spend.

The third role is even more diffuse and largely impossible to quantify. Heritage facilities, perhaps not economically viable in themselves, are often included in multi-functional urban projects for the sake of a whole range of externalities, which they contribute to developments and districts (Snedcof 1986; Lim 1993). This may be little more than property improvement or art subsidy through the channelling of state funds from other non-local programmes. The case for the integration of local arts policies in local development has been aided, as Evans (1993, p. 26) has argued, by the move towards 'unitary development plans' in the United Kingdom and elsewhere and is motivated by a 'growing recognition of the value added potential of arts and a cultural input to urban and economic development'. The actual impacts, however, remain largely unresearched and the economic value of these externalities may well be weak (Lewis 1990). Public art, for example, may at best be little more than a visible symbol of reassurance to locals and investors that something is being done and that somebody cares about the public spaces in degraded areas. At worst, it may seem irrelevant or irritating to local residents who see their public spaces being colonized by an external cultural élite when investment in more pressing if mundane improvements is needed (Miles 1997). As Myerscough (1988, p. 109) argues:

> What seems to have happened is that an enthusiastic visual arts lobby appropriated the case for the arts in regeneration and applied it to public art in development.

Case studies of the use of heritage in local economic development strategies

In order to exemplify these points, four case studies are used to illustrate something of these complex interactions of a tourism use of heritage and other elements within an economic development strategy.

Heritage tourism as an agent of change: the case of Newfoundland

Many governments at various scales have eagerly grasped the promise of heritage as an economic resource in compensation for failure in other economic sectors. The not untypical case of Newfoundland combines the need for new economic stimuli in an island community where traditional economic activities are in steep decline, with the possibility of commodifying aspects of the natural, built and even social environment for sale to external markets as a heritage product. This policy of broadening the economic base has led, however, to largely unforeseen wider consequences for other aspects of Newfoundland's economy and society.

A combination of four centuries of fishing monoculture and few agricultural or other resources made an alternative or supplementary economic strategy seem attractive, while transport changes in the late nineteenth century apparently provided, if not an opportunity, at least a possibility seized upon then, and almost continuously since, by government (Overton 1996). A paradox is that tourism was seen as part of an economic and social modernization strategy, despite itself largely depending upon the creation of a self-conscious vision of a past. The Newfoundland government in particular thought that tourism would have both an internal and external catalytic effect upon the economy. The local population would become accustomed to a modern wage-earning and service provision economy, while the external promotion and experience of visitors would show the many other potential economic opportunities of the island to visitors who might also be investors, innovators or at least customers. A successful tourism industry, however, required saleable products. The first was derived from a natural environment, commodified into a variously interpreted, healthy, ecologically sound, or romantically inspiring 'wilderness'. Closely coupled with this was a product created from the existing economy, society and built environment, which involved turning the prosaic economic activity of fishing, its artefacts, structures, personnel and associated way of life, into heritage. Thus was created the representation of a simple but hardy fisherfolk, their 'historically genuine' boats, implements, clothes, wooden houses, fish-drying flakes and picturesque 'outport' settlements, as well as their 'authentic' culture of vernacular crafts, folk music, gastronomy and even jokes. A last outpost of pre-industrial civilization was put on sale for tourists (Mowat 1989).

The result was the growth of a heritage tourism industry, which has remained relatively modest in comparison with more market-accessible destinations. Successful commodification, however, has so branded the island and its people as 'traditional' that the contemporary identity of Newfoundlanders is now strongly dependent on the image of them created for external sale. Equally important, the successful selling of tradition as heritage tourism, with its less attractive concomitant of physical isolation, social backwardness, and slow-witted unadaptablilty, compromises the development of other economic activities.

Interactions of heritage and tourism: the case of Santa Fe, New Mexico

A similar case with different components is provided by Santa Fe, New Mexico, in the south-west United States. The interaction here is between economic and non-economic variables and objectives as well as between the three ethnicities from which heritage could be created, namely the native American, Hispanic/Mexican and Anglo-American. Economic change has interacted with political, social and cultural changes, sometimes as cause and sometimes as effect. The Spanish, later Mexican province, was conquered and occupied by US military force in 1846, a political change at least in part motivated by the earlier economic penetration along the Santa Fe trail from Kansas of 'Anglo' merchants, investors and even settlers. The second half of the nineteenth century was dominated by the political objective of US statehood, to be achieved though the economic re-orientation and integration of New Mexico with the American-Atlantic economy. The leading role in this process was played by the Anglo merchant class, their businesses, railways and projection of an economic boosterism. At the turn of the century, however, New Mexico was 'discovered' by artists and tourists. Largely indistinguishable, they brought a culture with them, a filter through which they sought to create a distinctive culture from the natural and ethnic components they discovered. Pioneer artists settled in the 1890s, especially in Taos and Santa Fe. They were attracted by the warm dry climate, low costs of living, perceived sympathetic local culture and increasingly the presence of other artists, would-be artists, and connoisseurs of '*la vie Boheme*'. The visitors, the artists and craftsmen they had come to experience and financially support, and the local promotion and tourism facilities were almost exclusively anglophone, but many of the cultural components they were using were either Hispanic or native American in origin. The important point is that a distinctive culture was created, ultimately labelled the 'Santa Fe style', which has become a highly successful heritage product. This is in part an adaptation from vernacular adobe architectural styles, gastronomy, textiles, pottery and a perceived relaxed 'Latin' way of life.

The success of this product is notable in two different respects. First, it has sponsored a substantial growth in tourism demand, which, in turn, has led to both a mass production and standardization of the heritage tourism product, as well as to a continuing broadening of the product range to include more yet 'undiscovered' aspects of the vernacular. Second, if tourism originally created the heritage and now heritage is creating the tourism, the process has gone further in that the tourist discovery of Hispanic and native American heritage architecture, design and even philosophies has prompted an increasing involvement of these ethnic groups in the manufacture and presentation of their heritage and its artefacts. Even more fundamental, they have evolved a greater self-awareness of their ethnic identities as these are reflected back to them by visitors. For example 'fiestas' and 'Indian' markets, originally created, or resurrected, by anglophone business interests for their tourism potential, are now increasingly run by Hispanic or native American groups and, even more significantly, for them.

A mix of endogenous and exogenous stimuli: the case of Dublin Temple Bar

Dublin, the European City of Culture for 1991, demonstrates, among many such possible cases, some of the interplay between international, national and local factors and particularly the potential catalytic role of international heritage designations in economic development. There is strong competition for the Council of Europe's annual accolade of 'European City of Culture', which can have a measurable influence upon the external image and local self-confidence of the city selected, resulting in increased public- and private-sector investment. There have also been unsuccessful examples, however, which for obvious reasons receive little publicity. In these instances economic gains may be small or even negative. In the worst scenarios, the designation may actually be counter-productive, acting as a public manifestation of existing deficiencies and local shortcomings which effectively deter subsequent investment. Either economic result is broadly comparable to those spectacular 'hallmark events', such as staging the Olympic Games.

In Dublin's case, the external stimulus reinforced, perhaps at a critical moment, existing agencies within the city and Ireland generally, which were struggling against what has been seen as the inherent anti-urban and anti-conservation biases of the highly centralized and commercially-led government apparatus. This had seriously damaged Dublin's built environmental heritage, especially its Georgian areas (Kearns 1983). The combination of an external valuation of the city's remaining historic architecture and design, together with the promotion of a national tourism product dependent upon a combination of the literary and theatrical arts and an urban/bohemian lifestyle, were powerful instruments in reversing existing urban policy during the 1980s.

Specifically the idea of conserving and developing the Temple Bar area as an artistic and heritage tourism district, a sort of 'left bank' on the right bank of the Liffey, can be traced back to the mid-1980s, but external support was needed to avoid its complete clearance and redevelopment as a bus station. Stabler (1996) uses the Temple Bar experience to demonstrate the long-term economic benefits of area conservation, even though the short-term costs of restoration and development forgone outweighed the immediate benefits. Within five years, the Temple Bar area was transformed into a semi-pedestrianized culture district, accommodating 225 businesses, employing 1600 people, serving both a tourism and local entertainment market as well as culture industries. Its subsequent beneficial effects on the city's cultural tourism income have been blighted, however, by the area's well-earned reputation for various forms of anti-social behaviour, not least on the part of tourists attracted by the very success of Temple Bar's heritage-based development.

Nevertheless, international designation can influence national and local policies and result in external promotion which may stimulate tourism and other economic activities that discover a new attractive location and also leave a lasting legacy in the urban fabric. In Dublin, above all, the conditions needed for such culturally-led regeneration required the coincidence in timing of an external stimulus, with long-term changes in local lifestyles and expectations of the roles of cities, and such areas and activities within them. If such a combination of conditions does not occur, external designation alone can be a 'dangerous honour' (Clohessy 1994), leading to a 'cultural overreach' by a provincial city unable to meet the expectations generated both internally and externally by that very designation. This creates disappointed consumers, a distorted public expenditure, a legacy of 'white elephant' facilities, and a damaged international image.

Heritage in multipurpose urban policy: the case of the Groningen Museum

The long-term structural economic problems of Groningen (population, 170 000), located in the province of Groningen in the north-eastern Netherlands, had proved largely impervious to three decades of national regional economic policy. They are now being approached through a local multipurpose cultural policy, the centrepiece of which is a new museum development. Groningen's difficulties are not unfamiliar to numerous other such places in Europe. The local economy was traditionally based upon now declining staple activities, including the processing of local and imported agricultural products (sugar refining, tobacco products, cardboard, potato starch, and associated engineering). These structural problems are reflected in – and compounded by – a poor national and non-existent international image of physical isolation, infrastructural inadequacy and social and cultural marginality (Meester and Pellenbarg 1997). The broad field of culture, the arts and urban design offered one albeit partial solution, in association with, rather than as an alternative to, more conventional policies of economic stimulation. The initiatives follow the reorientation of Dutch central government policy away from regional subsidies to peripheral regions towards strategies aimed at improving the European competitiveness of the national core in Ranstad Holland.

Policies for culture, art and heritage in Groningen are inextricably linked and include high-profile public festivals and events, urban design improvements, the extension of public art programmes, and the introduction of a number of standardized design features such as yellow brick roads in the city centre. The number of protected monuments has been more than doubled with extensive publicity given to historical associations, themes, trails and the like. The centrepiece, however, remains the new Groningen Museum, a city initiative financed by the Dutch national gas corporation and opened in 1994.

This was intended to have a number of different local impacts (Ennen 1997; Ennen and Ashworth 1998). First, as a new, distinctive 'signature building' for Groningen, it is intended to support a new self-image of a 'city of culture'. This encourages local civic consciousness and self-confidence in a city where incomes, employment and other socio-economic indicators lag far behind the national average (Pellenbarg 1994) and externally promotes the city on the national and even international stage. Second, the museum's location, on an artificial island on the ring canal between the railway and bus stations and the pedestrianized city centre, was intended to provide a visible symbol of urban entry (a monumental 'visiting card', historically echoing the city gates demolished in 1875). It also created a new pedestrian and bicycle routing system as the main axis of flows into and out of the city. In turn, this has altered the functional mix along the new routes into the city, encouraging the development of a cultural retailing strip, which has to some extent compensated for the decline in businesses along the previously used pedestrian route. Third, the contents of the museum's three major pavilions are probably less important than the structure itself. The uncompromisingly postmodern design is so visually intrusive as to provoke a response, whether positive or negative, and its location guarantees that many more people experience the exterior than the interior. It contains both traditional local historical artefacts (relating the story of the city) but also various modern arts which may or may not have any particular local associations. Fourth, the direct local economic impacts are difficult to measure. Visitor expenditure on entry fees, souvenir shop and cafeteria is much higher than expected, but this gives very little indication of the actual total economic impact of cultural tourists and excursionists attracted specifically by the museum, of other city users making incidental visits, or of its stimulation of other museums, galleries and cultural events in the city.

Finally, the local neighbourhood impacts are more easily estimated. There has been a considerable rise in property values in the area of the museum itself (despite the earlier misgivings of local residents' groups who opposed the development), partly as a result of new accessibility to and new consciousness of areas which were previously more isolated. In sum, Groningen's museum illustrates the various and complex roles played by heritage and, more broadly, culture, in the pursuit of diverse direct and indirect economic benefits. Among other similar cases is the Guggenheim Museum in Bilbao, a city with comparable structural and promotional problems to Groningen, and on a different scale and with different objectives, the complete 'museum island' of Frankfurt am Main.

Conclusion

This chapter has examined the various ways that heritage, either alone or in combination with the arts in general, is used as part of economic development policies. It should be stressed that although heritage is seen by many cities as a useful economic activity, generating windfall marginal gains, and even by some as the major support for their local economies, there are few cases where a town has deliberately made an aspect of its heritage the leading economic sector as a direct solution to economic failure in other sectors. Nevertheless, it is possible for specific heritage products to achieve such external fame that the local image and economy are completely dominated by it. Examples include Oberammergau's resuscitation and repetition of its historical 'passion play' and the Canadian logging town of Chemainus, BC, which compensated for the closure of its lumber mills by public mural paintings of its cultural and industrial past.

The conditions for success in these examples appear to be simply the small size of the places involved and a large amount of luck in that local enterprise seized an initial advantage ahead of potentially competitive imitators. Thus Stratford, Ontario, shows how a set of particular conditions prompted local initiative to grasp an unlikely chance circumstance in the 1950s, when the closure of the Canadian National railway locomotive workshops in what was effectively a one-company industrial town clearly provoked a desperate search for alternative economic activities. The solution was extremely unlikely in that the successful heritage element was not historic buildings or local events and personalities, but merely the town's name which linguistically associated it with the English town of Stratford-on-Avon, the birthplace of William Shakespeare. Notwithstanding that he had been dead some 200 years before Stratford, Ontario was even founded, the Stratford Shakespeare Festival was launched on the back of this unlikely coincidence, using local accommodation and labour and, eventually, external government subsidy. The result has been a major economic restructuring of the town from railway engineering for a national market to cultural tourism on a continental scale. This extends to a physical transformation of Stratford, including the introduction of swans on a re-landscaped River Avon.

The conditions for the success of Stratford can be listed as: an economic imperative with a severely limited range of options; a surplus capacity especially of land, labour and supporting services; a fortunate location relative to the market of the Metro Toronto suburbs; and also probably the timing of the initiative. All these factors contributed to the excess of economic benefits over costs. As in the preceding case studies, local enterprise was indispensable as was a considerable measure of good fortune. Thus heritage does have a relationship to economic development that is more than that of a passive resource which may be used in an economic activity. It is important to note, however, that most discussions of the economics of heritage have assumed precisely this and have been concerned with the cost-effectiveness, including opportunity cost, of heritage conservation and re-use. This continues to be the case since much that is written about heritage economics emanates from conservation interests seeking to justify resource retention (see Weiler 1998, who spells out the detailed arguments pertaining to well-being, equity of benefits and burdens, and use of public funds). On the contrary, however, if heritage is the contemporary use of the past, then it will always be a development option in itself, whether exercised or not, and will always, in that sense, be created by the uses for it. The issues and difficulties are not those of exploitation of a pre-existing endowment, the values of which are intrinsic to objects and sites, but those of co-operation and competition between consumers, economic sectors and spatial scales within which the economic considerations merge imperceptibly and inextricably into the cultural dimension discussed in Part II.

Heritage and scale

|8|

Heritage and scale I: the national

Introduction: heritage and scale

The idea of place was implicit throughout Parts II and III in their examination of the reasons why heritage has been created, and how it is being used for political, social and economic purposes. People, heritage and places have become linked together in a complicated and constantly mutating variety of ways. The cement binding these three elements together is a process of identification in which people identify with places because these places have a unique character or perceived identity. Heritage, the means by which people in a present associate themselves with people in a past, is a major instrument in the creation of identity. It is evident from the preceding discussion that only rarely is this association straightforward, when a homogeneous people associate with a homogeneous and unambiguous heritage, which is exclusively present only at a particular place. More usually, one of the two elements in the socio-political and economic dichotomy of heritage uses is discordant, either with the other or within itself. The potentially dissonant relationship between people and heritage has been the implicit theme of Parts II and III, whether explored through the political legitimation of governmental jurisdictions, the reflection of social identities, or the selling of heritage as a commodity on different markets.

Prior to addressing the national domain, some general comments regarding the relationship between heritage and scale are necessary. It is not sufficient to recognize that different scales exist and make distinctive contributions to the identification of individuals with place, because scale itself is a potent source of heritage dissonance. Heritage developed at different levels may not be complementary and harmonious, any one scale having the potential to undermine other levels (Figure 8.1). As we explored in Chapter 4, identities are multiply constructed, resulting in many, often overlapping, 'imagined communities', which may or may not coincide with identifiable spatial entities or with existing jurisdictional boundaries. As heritage is a major contributor to these identities, it is understandable that it is often differently defined, interpreted, claimed and even fought over. At a more prosaic level, institutions of governance at all spatial scales are engaged in the management of heritages that both give support to, but could also potentially subvert, their own legitimation.

It can even be argued that individuals identify with two kinds of heritage, or have two kinds of identification with the same heritage. One domain, which dominates the discussion here, is public in its expressions and implications. It is essentially place-bound and the subject of official public policies. The other is a private heritage of individuals and families composed of anecdotes and memories, photo albums and domestic customs. This exists in an ambiguous and complex relationship with individuals' feelings relating to identification with what is essentially place in the mind. Usually these two heritages are so separate that they rarely compete, although governments may try to aggregate private heritages into support for a public entity, particularly at times of crisis. An extension of the idea of identification with a private heritage of families, clans and tribes rather than cities, regions and countries may lead to the emergence of what Kearns (1998) has called 'diasporic cosmopolitanism' as a competitor to place-bound nationalism. Here, as in New World settler societies, the private heritage domain nurtures identification with individuals and families with a similar heritage regardless of their location or political jurisdiction, while conversely fostering a heritage distance from other social groups more spatially proximate.

Furthermore, because the meanings of identity spaces are undergoing continual renegotiation, disjunctions often occur in which, for example, these diasporic versions of allegiance may remain sited in past circumstances that pay little heed to the on-going evolution of identity in the metropolitan state. For example, the visions held of Ireland in North America (and Australia) by the descendants of emigrants often remain those of a nineteenth-century nationalist discourse framed as a narrative of English oppression. Although this perspective has long been heavily contested within both Ireland and North America itself, its malevolent and violent legacy is apparent in the substantial financial support from some Irish-Americans for the Provisional IRA (PIRA) and other Republican paramilitary organizations, whose claim to

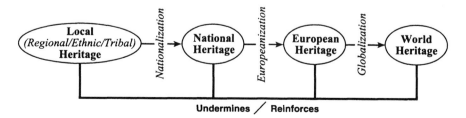

Figure 8.1 The interaction of heritage at different spatial scales from a European perspective

wage war in Ireland has been formulated in terms of that traditional national-ist rhetoric.

Other contemporary examples of 'diasporic cosmopolitanism' include the European Gypsies or Roma and, at least outside the states of Israel and Armenia, Jews and Armenians who are defined, both by themselves and others, through their religious or social observances. The spatial coexistence of public and private heritage identities is clearly yet another source of conflict. Place-defined jurisdictions may attempt to assimilate or eliminate the place-less non-conforming social groups. Similarly, and usually in defensive reaction, the latter may try to acquire places as homelands within which their heritages can be grounded.

Zionism is arguably the most successful of these attempts although by its nature it contains two intrinsic contradictions, both of which have serious heritage management implications. It does not provide a place for all those identifying with a Jewish heritage, nor physically include all places associated with Jewish heritage, many of which remain in other states. Second, it cannot claim the identification of all inhabitants of the place, Israel, which contains other heritages and heritage places. Other examples of a 'promised land' include the 'Return to Africa' movements which followed the nineteenth-century black slave diaspora and led to the foundation of the present states of Liberia and Sierra Leone, and even the West Indian Rastafarian association with a semi-mythical Ethiopia.

Heritage and the national scale

The creation of heritage and the creation of nations

To begin the discussion of heritage and scale at the meso-level of the nation might seem perverse but – as we explored in Chapters 2 and 3 – this scale has long been dominant in the history of the creation of heritage awareness and of its political uses. Indeed nationalism and national heritage developed synchronously in nineteenth-century Europe. The nation-state required national heritage to consolidate national identification, absorb or neutralize potentially competing heritages of social-cultural groups or regions, combat the claims of other nations upon its territory or people, while furthering claims upon nationals in territories elsewhere.

Small wonder then that the fostering of national heritage has long been a major responsibility of governments, while the provision of many aspects of heritage has become a near-monopoly of national governments in most countries. The dominance of the national is now so all-pervasive that it is difficult to imagine heritage without national museums, archives and theatres; without national monuments, historical narratives, heroes and villains; without national ministries, agencies, laws, policies and financial subsidies. Consequently, any discussion of sub-national heritages at the regional or local scale, or supra-national heritages at continental or global scales, must continually refer to the national scale which these complement or challenge. The clearest evidence that national political motives dominate in this field is that if the 'heritage industry' ceased to operate, the tourists stayed at home, and all non-national heritage organizations were dissolved, then most museums, monuments, and sites and their interpretations in most countries would remain largely intact.

To state that there is an intimate symbiotic relationship between national heritage and nation-states still leaves open the question of cause and effect. The discovery and propagation of a distinctive national heritage was a precondition for the creation of the nation-state but, conversely, the organizations and instruments capable of sponsoring and supporting a national heritage require the existence of a nation-state. The conception of a national heritage needs the prior creation of a national history in which the past is no more than 'a political resource whereby national identities are constructed and forms of power and privilege justified and celebrated' (Lumley 1988, p. 2). A national history is a narrative that 'postulates the existence of a collective subject – the nation' (Wright 1985, p. 146) and explains the shaping and maintenance of this distinctiveness through time. The narrative stresses the nation's long-standing and fundamentally different characteristics from other nations, most usually through a process of 'time collapse' which traces an unbroken evolution from as far back in the past as possible to the present. This story records past or continuing national conquests over space, nature, other peoples, collective triumphs and achievements but also past national injustices, claims and enmities. Thus the aim of the British Historical Association, founded in 1906, was, 'to provide a specific version of the national past as part of the struggle for national and imperial survival' (Centre for Contemporary History 1982, p. 7). The story-line must be clear. It requires 'nothing less than the abolition of all contradiction in the name of a national culture' and 'projects a unity that overrides social and political contradictions' (Bommes and Wright 1982, p. 264).

The construction of nineteenth-century Irish nationalism, for example, depended on a myth of 'Irish Ireland' in which time was foreshortened and an Irish past portrayed in which national consciousness dates to 'perhaps a millennium before the onset of modernity' (Bradshaw 1989, p. 345). Irish-Ireland was about the restoration of Irish society to 'pre-lapsarian state of harmony, wholeness and authenticity' (Ó Tuathaigh 1991, p. 57), one that predated the Viking, Anglo-Norman and English invasions and colonizations of the island which began *ca.* AD 800. However, as Brown (1985, p. 91) observes, 'those Irish writers, painters and polemicists ... who chose to identify and celebrate an ancient rural national tradition in Ireland were required to ignore much of contemporary Irish social reality', a general difficulty with national narratives and a further potent source of contestation (Graham 1994a and b).

History was not the only academic study used in this process of nation-creating and the rise of nationalism often coincided with an awakening of interest in national archaeology (Arnold 1990), geology, anthropology, regional geography and many aspects of cultural expression, all of which could contribute to the distinctive story of a nation. The founding of national amateur cultural and scientific associations, national learned societies – often under the patronage of the head of state – national universities and the pursuit of various 'national cultural revivals' all helped to create the national story and justify the establishment of national museums, galleries and artistic bodies, the establishment of state agencies for the protection and propagation of a national patrimony, and, ultimately, the framing of legislation and working methods that together constitute an institutionalized national heritage with a broadly based public education function.

The basic modernist themes of inevitability and progress were central to the creation of nationalist interpretations of heritage. The nation-state was depicted or imaged as the correct and normal means of relating people to territorial government and the result of some inevitable natural process, which policies could only accelerate or delay but not change. This process of national 'heritogenesis' is well illustrated by Central Europe (*see* Chapter 3). The redrawing of the European boundaries after World War I was viewed as the just fulfilment of national identity vested in the nation-state, a culmination of 'the evolutionary struggle that marked the rise of mankind from the primitive to the present' (Bowman 1924, p. 11). The nationalist movement that triumphed in the Versailles and related treaties was born of the national cultural heritage movements of the preceding century. However, plebiscites and meticulous cartography merely revealed that lines could not be drawn around identifiable self-conscious national cultural groups in such a way that each such nation formed a viable state, and each state consisted of only one such nation.

The resulting successor states of the dynastic empires were therefore either federations of nations needing to create a new Yugoslavian or Czechoslovakian identity, or states such as Poland and Romania where a numerically dominant core people were supplemented by the addition of, usually unwilling, sizeable minorities (Figure 8.2). Only Austria and Hungary, effectively pruned of non-German and non-Magyar speakers respectively, emerged without large national minorities. Their heritages became a matter of replacing the old imperial Hapsburg monuments and markers of the Austro-Hungarian empire with new contexts of national liberation and consciousness.

Policy towards minority heritage such as that of the Sudeten Germans, Hungarians, Ruthenes and Poles in Czechoslovakia, Ruthenes and Lithuanians in Poland, Poles in Lithuania, Germans in the Baltic States and Hungarians and Germans in Romania, was double-edged. Ethnic enclaves were seen as a threat to the national integrity and thus to be discouraged, often with some ruthlessness. Conversely, exclaves, that is members of a nation existing on the 'wrong' side of the newly drawn border, were to be encouraged and, if possible, protected as an object of ultimate irredentist

Figure 8.2 The fragility of national boundaries: the changing political geography of North-Central and North-Eastern Europe during the twentieth century
Source: adapted from Tunbridge (1998, p. 244)

reunion. A range of strategies of deliberate disinheritance evolved, including: the removal of minority language education and publishing rights; changes in place and personal names; monument removal or rededication; and even 're-conversion' to the appropriate national language, alphabet or religion. National minorities capable of creating a separate state, or uniting with neighbours in such a state, were generally treated more harshly than non-national minorities, such as Jews or Germans in Slovakia and Romania, who were too dispersed or distant from potential homelands to pose a comparable political threat.

Despite the strength of the historical evidence for the successful use of her-itage in creating nation-states, the process is neither inevitable nor stable.

Numerous examples exist of states failing to establish a deep-rooted and widely accepted national identity, despite attempts to create a national heritage through the control of public history. Many postcolonial states in South America and Africa lack a national identity, while Europe is littered with the monumental heritage of now largely defunct nationalisms. The former Yugoslavia during its 75 years of existence was unable to generate sufficient identity to withstand the separatist assaults of its component nationalisms. Belgium, created in 1830 as a fusion of French- and Dutch-speaking provinces, largely to satisfy the geopolitical considerations of the surrounding Great Powers, never generated a feeling of primary loyalty to the Belgian state to offset its two distinct ethnic identities (*see* Chapter 2). The usual nation-state panoply of national museums, monuments, national history and even a national monarchy proved insufficient in building a distinctive identity. The Belgian state has not catastrophically collapsed but has, in essence, slowly faded away in the face of pressures for separate institutions from each of the dominant Fleming and Walloon ethnic groups. When states have failed through external pressure, this has sometimes been aided by a failure to establish a broad-based national heritage and identity. Examples include the Confederate States of America and the former incarnations of states based upon minority identities, such as Rhodesia and South Africa.

The content of a nationalized heritage

Heritage plays three fundamental roles in shaping the content of nationalized, institutionalized public history. First, it is used to discover, delimit and thus name the basic entity, the nation. Second, it is the instrument by which the primacy of this nation within a territory is established historically. Third, it provides the means whereby variations from the national narrative can be managed.

Naming the nation

A fundamental first step in the process of nation creation through national heritage is the act of identifying and naming a distinctive group of people. No national heritage can be shaped until there is a named group of people with whom it can be associated. Thus the nomenclature itself acquires a deep political significance, being a claim on people and territory to be asserted or denied. The naming of many ethnic groups in Europe demonstrates the political consequences of terminology in conferring or denying legitimation, internally and externally, for the existence of separate states. The interests of existing states lies, of course, in denying competing legitimacies within their own borders, while extending their sovereignty by encouraging these externally.

To the Russians, the inhabitants of the Ukraine and Belarus were 'Little Russians' and 'White Russians' respectively, while the Ukrainian-speaking peoples of the sub-Carpatho-Ukraine and south-eastern Poland were called 'Ruthenes' by Poles and Magyars, thereby denying a potential irredentist

claim by neighbours, especially the Ukraine. Nineteenth-century Romanian
speakers claimed a Roman heritage through their nomenclature while, to the
governing Magyars of Transylvania, they were simply 'Vlachs', former inhabitants of the territory of Wallachia. To a Greek state expanding northwards,
they were merely wandering Thracian herdsmen with no legitimate territorial claim. The Slav speakers of the North Carpathian rim were 'discovered' by
two competing groups of scholars in the late eighteenth and early nineteenth
centuries. Czech intellectuals stressed the similarities between Czechs and
these Slovaks, thereby encouraging a legitimacy for a new state that ultimately stretched from the German to the Ukrainian borders (Wanklyn 1948).
At the same time, Magyar scholars denied the existence of any such cultural
link and stressed the separate distinctiveness of Slovak cultural expression,
thus legitimating the inclusion of this area in the traditional 'Lands of St
Stephen'.

Post-Cold War instability demonstrates that the process of nation discov-
ery and naming is by no means complete. The successor 'nations' of
Yugoslavia (*see* Figure 3.6) include the firmly established national ideas of
Slovenes, Croats and Serbs; conversely, 'Montenegrins' or 'Dalmatians'
(except for the Italian-speaking minority) are not recognized. The idea of
'Bosnians' seems to have been accepted only by Muslim inhabitants, while
'Hercegovinian' has been appropriated largely by Croats. 'Macedonians' are
defined as southern Serbs (by the Serbs), western Bulgars (by the Bulgarians)
and completely non-existent (by the Greeks), while the compromised state of
Macedonia includes some, but not all, of those defining themselves as
Macedonians, as well as many who do not. Finally, and very recently, a new
nationality has been discovered by the ethnic Albanian inhabitants of Kosovo.
Polities in search of national identities provide the converse of nations struggling to create states. Belarus, for example, is one example whose people have
so far shown little inclination to define themselves as a nation.

The idea of nationhood may be projected over more extensive territories. The claim, for example, to the existence of a racially, culturally or historically distinct 'Germania', 'Panslavia', or 'Panhellenic' region has usually
been a prelude to some form of conquest. For particular right-wing perspectives, even a discussion of the existence of regions such as 'Central
Europe', or *Mitteleuropa*, could entail accepting 'a central European confederation dominated by a greater Germany in which all German-speaking
peoples . . . would finally be united' (Heffernan 1998a, p. 74). In sum, these
and many more such cases emphasize the point that heritage is used, not
only to project the character and promote the claims of an existing ethnic
group, but is also the means by which such groups are made aware that they
exist at all.

Primacy of the nation

Once named, a nation needs to establish its primacy of occupation of the area
claimed. An obvious role of heritage is to justify a 'we were there first'

argument. For example, much inter-war German archaeology in Central Europe was a search for previous 'Aryan' occupation to justify concurrent claims to *Lebensraum* (Lemaire 1993). Again, archaeology in contemporary Palestine has been recruited to support the competing claims of Palestinian Arabs and Israeli Jewish settlers for territory through the justification of prior occupation. White settler societies in the Americas, Australasia and Southern Africa cannot other than concede historical primacy to Aboriginal groups, often naming themselves as 'First Nations'. Among the immigrant groups in North America, however, the claims of prior 'discovery' made on behalf of Champlain, Cabot, Columbus, Ericson, Brendan, Madog and many others assume a significance in justifying present or future assertions of particular ethnic groups. Indeed the ethnic identity of some of these figures (notably Columbus and Cabot) may itself be contested by competing groups.

A European example is provided by the 'Szeklers' of eastern Transylvania, who Hungarian scholars claim to be the descendants of the Magyar tribes left to guard the Transylvanian passes in the tenth century. Their settlement thus predated the arrival of Romanian-speaking peoples from the Danube Delta and therefore supports a Hungarian national claim to the area. Romanian scholars, however, argue that the Szeklers were originally Romanians who were forcibly 'Magyarized' in the course of the Middle Ages and that their presence therefore legitimates a Romanian claim to sovereignty. What might be viewed as an obtuse academic discussion takes on a contemporary political significance, which reduces history to 'a treasure hunt' (Paul 1993, p. 154) with very real prizes and penalties for winners and losers.

Variations on the national narrative

Having established the existence of the nation and its territorial primacy, heritage then has the task of accommodating differences, variations and dissonances. As we have seen in Chapter 5 in the discussion of multicultural societies, a national historical narrative need not be uniform and homogeneous. It can accommodate differences so long as the national heritage takes precedence over the differences between individuals and social groups, because as Wright (1985) argues, these acquiesce in a constituency of support. National heritage need not contradict the heritage of sub-national groups but it must subsume the micro-heritage of localities and social minorities within an over-arching macro-heritage of the nation, which can thus at least contain potential conflict. .

The modernist assumption of progressive linear narratives linking the past to a present which is seen as complete is usually but not always the dominant approach. Wright (1985) terms this the 'complacent bourgeois alignment'. It can be modified when heritage is seen by self-appointed custodians as an instrument for the defence of traditional national values, which are threatened by a society that has deviated from the past (Wright's 'anxious aristocrat alignment'). Less often, heritage may be treated in an 'anti-traditional technicist alignment', in which the past is treated as a discontinuity with the present, a swamp of reactionary tradition that must be rejected because of its threat to a future created as an antithesis to the past.

National heritages, however, are not necessarily homogeneous and may well grant varying levels of tolerance to political, ideological, socio-cultural and regional variations. The extent to which this occurs is dependent upon the attitudes adopted by governments towards their intervention role in cultural matters, including heritage. National comparisons demonstrate that crude distinctions in expenditure, and thus degree of direct government involvement, exist even among countries with quite similar political systems (Table 8.1). Such variations reflect many differences of national policy and circumstances but Mulcahy (1998) has argued that the degree and type of state involvement, including the approach to sub-national cultures, is basically dependent upon the political philosophy of states with respect to the arts, which he categorizes through the four cases in Table 8.2. Alongside the paradox of national heritage being largely place bound, and thus displayed locally, is the more fundamental paradox that the national governmental philosophy largely determines the degree of local autonomy. Thus a high degree of administrative decentralization to regions and cities, accompanied by local decision-making about the content and interpretation of heritage, may mean that heritage diversity and local distinctiveness exists because of – rather than in spite of – a national culture.

Table 8.1 Public expenditure on the arts

Country	UK pounds per head	Public expenditure (%)
United Kingdom	9.8	0.41
Netherlands	20.5	0.45
France	21.4	0.77
Germany	24.0	0.79

Source: (Evans 1993).

Table 8.2 An approach to sub-national cultures

	France	Norway	Canada	United States
Approach	Elitist	Popularist	Liberal	Libertarian
Government	Strong statist	Weak localist	Strong federal	Weak pluralist
Instrument	State subsidy	Local subsidy	State grants	Weak exemptions
Goal	Hegemony	Redistribution	Sovereignty	Privatism

Source: (Mulcahy 1998).

Managing the contending heritage

We now examine the extent to which a national heritage can tolerate, manage or assimilate contending alternatives, particularly at different spatial scales. This discussion centres on two questions concerning the management of heritage. First, how do, or did, non-national states manage heritage in order to prevent the development of a nationalism? Second, how is heritage managed in order to suppress or supplant existing national heritages?

The rise of the nation-state in Europe was preceded by polities based on personal feudal allegiance or adherence to a dynastic idea, which often had religious or ideological overtones (Graham 1998b). Even as late as World War I, official heritage was often harnessed to support ruling non-national dynasties, whether Hapsburg, Romanov, Hohenzollern or Ottoman. This relationship was most obviously manifested in the imperial showcase capitals. The heritage of the built environment in Vienna or Budapest are the archetypal statements of the alliance of government, church and military, which acted as the pillars of Hapsburg dynastic power until World War I. Heritage conflict was not between the imperial and local ethnic identities: indeed, the opposite prevailed, given an imperial strategy which recognized and encouraged myriad local cultures in order to divide and rule. The threat of nationalism emerged from the construction of nationalist narratives, which were principally the work of small intellectual élites. Languages previously spoken as varied local dialects were given standardized grammars, lexicons, dictionaries and literatures. Cultures were assigned names and histories so that people discovered that they were Romanians, Czechs, Slovaks, Poles or Latvians, each with their own pantheon of historical heroes and a distinguished heritage of resistance to the Turks, the Teutonic Knights, or the Russians. This self-identification increasingly came to compete with non-national identification, often encouraged by outside nations already 'free'.

The heritage ambiguities resulting from this nineteenth-century conflict between imperialism and nationalism are clearly seen in the city of Kraków, where the nationalization of heritage has always been incomplete. Paradoxically, the city fulfilled its role as the cradle of the nineteenth-century Polish national revival, largely as a result of its position within a multinational Empire. Its status, first as a 'free city' and later as the major urban centre (although not administrative capital) of the self-governing province of Galicia, allowed Polish language and literature to survive and shape the political aspirations of an educated middle class in a way that was not possible in the more culturally repressive regimes of Prussian or Russian-occupied Poland. Hapsburg policies of encouraging, or at least tolerating, local cultural expression within Austrian Galicia allowed a Polish intellectual and literary middle class to flourish and eventually create the resurrected national Poland of 1919. However, this new nation-state did not value much of the intrinsically Hapsburg heritage of Kraków that preceded it. The wonder of what remains in this city, which contains more UNESCO designated 'world heritage' buildings than any other, conceals the quantity that was lost (Purchla 1993), largely because of the change in political and ideological scale from the imperial to the national. It was not the 16 sieges and 28 major fires that damaged the nineteenth-century inner-ring developments and Austrian fortress complex, but changes in dominant tastes and values that led to their neglect and piecemeal demolition over the past 80 years.

One of the most obvious cases in which supranational ideology was super-imposed upon a pattern of nation-states occurred in Europe after World War II. The Cold War between the USSR and its allies and a United States-led NATO gave heritage an instrumental role on both sides as a vehicle of expression for competing ideologies and, more subtly, of ways of life that transcended the nation-state. Communist policy towards heritage was in practice somewhat ambiguous. On one hand, the intention was to create a new society quite different from a past now rejected as irrelevantly backward. Existing monuments and place nomenclature, as well as the preserved buildings, streetscapes and whole towns, were reminders of previous national or class identities now to be superseded. Alternatively, the preserved relics of the past were endowed with new and important educational roles. Even ideologically rejected structures could be used to demonstrate such themes as the triumph of people over adversity and, if possible, remind people of the stupidities or iniquities of previous regimes. More prosaically, the new regimes sought some association with the old if only to demonstrate continuity with a past, even if that were based upon the struggles leading ultimately but inevitably to present victory.

For example, in the Bulgarian city of Plovdiv, the long struggle of the Bulgars against the Turks was quite deliberately chosen as the central theme for the interpretation of this expensively conserved and reconstructed city. The 'reconstruction was a statement that the communist rulers saw them-selves as the legitimate heirs of the Second Bulgarian state and of the struggle against the Turkish yoke' (Newby 1994, p. 222), while an implicit parallel was also being drawn between the overthrow of Turkish rule and the over-throw of capitalism five centuries later.

Such generalizations about communist policy, however, require consider-able modification by time and place. Policies in Central Europe after 1945 were far more sympathetic towards heritage conservation, even when this could be viewed as specifically national, than was the case in the earlier years of the Russian revolution when there was a strong sentiment for sweeping away the past and beginning again at year zero. A number of Central European countries invested considerable effort in the conservation of the built environment after 1945. Poland, for example, developed what became known as the 'Polish School of conservation', which involved architectural reconstruction of almost totally destroyed cities, most notably Warsaw, and buildings in order to legitimate the Communist government as the natural heir of Polish history. Even in Germanic East Prussia, acquired by Poland after 1945, the demands of political legitimation in part motivated the painstaking reconstruction of Malbork or Marienburg Castle, a potent symbol of past oppression by the Teutonic Knights and, by inference, more recent Germans, but a site which also had Polish associations capable of suitable enhancement.

Policy towards heritage in the Soviet empire was quite different when – as in The Ukraine, Baltic, Caucasian and Central Asian Republics – national identity was perceived as a focus of opposition to, rather than a support for, the Communist regime. The three main policy options were: destroy; ignore; or reinterpret. The first was only practical for individual buildings or memorials and not for whole townscapes such as Riga, Vilnius or Bokhara, or for natural features such as Lithuania's sacred mountain. The second policy involved a neglect of the built environment, especially of the inner cities, many of which suffered disinvestment in favour of the development of socialist new towns elsewhere. The third approach was to accept the existence of the physical heritage, and even to maintain it, but to treat it as having aesthetic as distinct from contemporary political values. In focusing on the intrinsic qualities of the object rather than its relation to the people who created it, or the messages it was intended to convey, this policy of neutralization through 'museumification' was practised in the restoration and interpretation of many historic churches and monasteries and the mosques of Central Asia (Giese 1979).

The case of the former East Germany (GDR) was particularly complex if only because of the extraordinary artificiality of its geographical base for heritage interpretation (Tunbridge 1994; *see* Chapter 3). It shared Poland's problem of fitting a national heritage to an arbitrary territory, which had suffered comparable physical devastation but was also the front line – territorially and ideologically – in the Cold War. The GDR needed both to stress its difference from the larger and culturally identical people in West Germany through a new national heritage, as well as relate to the wider Soviet sphere. It had thus to distance itself from the immediate past as well as associate with a previous past heritage. In an attempt to reconcile these divergent objectives, the GDR was projected in heritage and tourism marketing as the true custodian of German national culture, in competition with West Germany, while also claiming revolutionary socialist credentials. The first stance was exemplified in the built environments of Central Berlin, Potsdam, Dresden and especially the German cultural capital of Weimar (Tunbridge 1998), while the second stressed the importance of popular revolt (as in 1848 or 1919), leaders of dissent (from Müntzer and Luther to Rosa Luxembourg and Liebknecht) and the heritage of towns such as Leipzig and Erfurt in these respects.

The British Empire (like others) made abundant use of heritage anchored by monumental iconography, to imprint a collective identity upon its unprecedented global domain. At its peak, from Queen Victoria's diamond jubilee (1897) through the Boer War to her death in 1901, the countless heritage expressions in the built environment culminated in the iconography of

Queen Victoria's statue inscribed *Regina et Imperatrix* and repeated in cities throughout the world. Subsequently, while ideas of one Imperial nationhood were stillborn, the bond of identity of a 'family of nations' was strongly expressed, both in Britain and the Dominions, through the metaphor of mother and growing children. This was symbolized by 'Empire Day', an annual heritage pageant on the former Queen's birthday, May 24th; by Empire-wide commemorative postage stamp series marking such events as coronations; and through British Empire Exhibitions, the first being held in

Figure 8.3   The road to nationhood through sacrifice in war: the Australian National Memorial in Villers-Bretenneux Military Cemetery, Somme, France

Figure 8.4 The South African memorial on the edge of Delville Wood, Somme, marks the site of horrific fighting and losses between 15 and 21 July 1916. Very consciously presented as an element in the patrimony of the South African state, this part of the memorial is a copy of the fortress overlooking Cape Town

Figure 8.5 The Caribou memorial to the dead and missing is at the centre of the ground fought over by the men of the Royal Newfoundland Regiment on the opening day of the battle of the Somme, 1 July 1916. Few survived unscathed. As Newfoundland joined with Canada in 1949, the Newfoundland Park site now has a distinctly Canadian ethos

London in 1924–5. Colonial involvement in the Sudan expedition (1898), South African War (1899–1902) and especially the sacrifice in the First World War ostensibly deepened the bond, expressed by war memorials and Imperial War Graves Commission cemeteries on countless battlefields in every corner of the Empire.

This iconography was, however, to provide a classic demonstration of the flexible, even paradoxical, heritage potential of the same resource through time. The bond of shared suffering was, particularly for the autonomous Dominions (Canada, Australia, New Zealand, South Africa and Newfoundland), also a national baptism of fire, which hastened the formal recognition of their independence in 1931, or – in Newfoundland's case – ultimate union with Canada in 1949 (Figures 8.3, 8.4 and 8.5). The countries heeded a further British call to arms in 1939 to emerge in 1945 as mature nations, their newly augmented war memorials now the badges of nation-hood. By the 1990s, monuments such as those to Canadian casualties of the disastrous raid on Dieppe in 1942, or to Australians or New Zealanders killed at Gallipoli in 1915, could even be recast as a symbol of rejection of a mother country that had wasted Dominion lives.

Conclusion

Clearly, the examples discussed here provide only a partial response to questions concerning the extent to which a national heritage can tolerate, manage or assimilate contending alternatives. These require also a consideration of the sub-national and supra-national scales of heritage because one of the most important issues concerns the extent to which these complement or compete with the national. Local challenges to the dominance of national heritage are more long-standing, while the supra-national is much more tentative and recent. Regional or local heritage may be treated as merely a variant of a wider national heritage complex and even as a source of strength as in 'unity in diversity'. Conversely, it may be viewed as a potentially dangerous competitor, leading ultimately to conflict, national disintegration, regional separatism and a new nationalism. Most countries can provide examples of local heritage existing at different points along a spectrum from complementarity to competition with the national scale. Federal states such as Canada are particularly vulnerable to separatism and heritage divergences in their constitutionally autonomous regions. Equally, international heritage can be merely an all-inclusive aggregate of national heritages which reinforces them. However, the putative continentalization of Europe and even more widespread globalization of heritage may shape an alternative heritage, which may oppose and even ultimately replace a heritage based upon the supremacy of the national scale.

|9|
Heritage and scale II:
the local

Introduction

The argument of this chapter is that heritage at the local scale is significantly different in content, function and thus management, from nation-state or supra-national heritage. The term 'local' covers a wide range of spatial possibilities, extending from a region within a nation-state, which can be an extensive area (for example, the US South) down to the precise locus of an event, which as a geometric point has, *sensu stricto*, no area at all but only location. In practice, almost all of the subsequent discussion concerns itself with three types of locality, the sub-national region, the city (whether defined as a whole or in terms of its component districts), and the site.

Similarly, 'local' in these contexts can be viewed as having meaning in a number of different ways, each of which has a different significance for our arguments here. We can even visualize a spectrum of local significance reflecting the type and importance of the degree of localization. The extent to which the local element is important ranges from the mere physical location of heritage in space, through its local management, to the contribution of heritage in defining the identity of localities. These three aspects of localization overlap with each other but can be considered separately under the headings of heritage and location, heritage as a function of local management, and heritage as a contributor to local identity.

Heritage and the local scale

Heritage and location

Much, but clearly not all, heritage is intrinsically linked to specific physical locations. Historical events, physical relics and surviving structures are located somewhere and that somewhere is, or can be made, a part of the

Figure 9.1   Part of the Ulster Folk Museum, Cultra, County Down: this open-air heritage facility comprises buildings brought to the site from all over Ulster and reconstructed in 'authentic' settings

heritage derived from these resources. People and objects can of course be highly mobile but, even so, they can be assembled at, or associated with, specific locations. Historical personalities can become place-bound in the sense of Robin Hood at Nottingham, Mozart at Salzburg and the 'Jolly Swagman' at Winton, Queensland. Museums, galleries, theme parks and interpretation centres all focus spatially, while localizing in one place heritage drawn from a wider area. For example, the 'Skansen' concept of the open-air folk museum (and its more recent imitators, the ecomuseum and regional theme park) deliberately assembles a microcosm of regional or national heritage into a single manageable and visitable site (Figures 9.1 and 9.2).

Even those aspects of heritage which are not necessarily specifically place related are often displayed or interpreted through specific sites, if only because it is easier for the consumer to identify with the physically and spatially concrete than with wider, more amorphous trends, ideas or situations. The familiar presentation that begins with 'on this spot . . .', or 'in this building . . .' is frequently using a location to enhance, or simply focus attention on, heritage whose significance is much wider than the site referred to. The heritage of slavery over three continents is demonstrated at Cape Coast Castle in Ghana, as is world-wide 'Monarchy and Empire' at Windsor in England. The continent-wide Jewish Holocaust is commemorated in Berlin and Prague among other sites in Europe and, more displaced from the occurrences, in Washington D.C. and Jerusalem. In these and countless other similar thematic

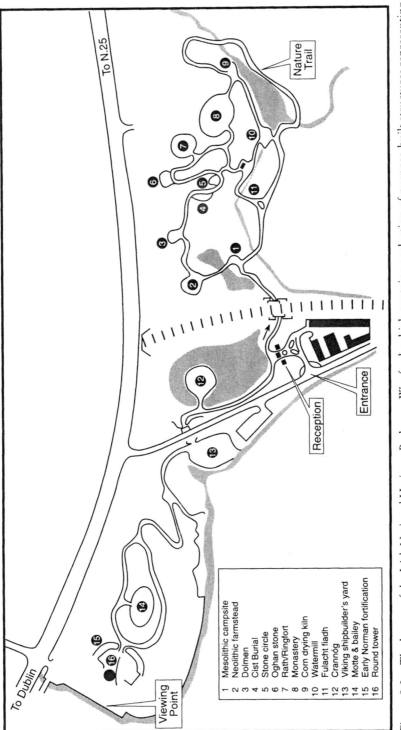

Figure 9.2 The layout of the Irish National Heritage Park near Wexford, which contains a selection of purpose-built structures representing typical Irish historic monuments
Source: adapted from Johnson (1999a, p. 257)

Legend for the map:

1 Mesolithic campsite
2 Neolithic farmstead
3 Dolmen
4 Cist Burial
5 Stone circle
6 Oghan stone
7 Rath/Ringfort
8 Monastery
9 Corn drying kiln
10 Watermill
11 Fulacht fiadh
12 Crannóg
13 Viking shipbuilder's yard
14 Motte & bailey
15 Early Norman fortification
16 Round tower

Map labels: To N.25, To Dublin, Nature Trail, Reception, Entrance, Viewing Point presentations, the local site is being used only as an instrument for the more effective communication of the wider heritage message.

The questions raised by this process concern the extent to which a specific location contributes to the heritage itself and what damage is inflicted upon the value of a heritage object if, for various reasons, it is separated from its locational context. Museums by their very nature break the link between object and site, removing the artefact from its surroundings and also placing it within a new taxonomic arrangement in association with other objects. It thus acquires a different value in an altered scheme of values, however conscientiously museums may attempt to repair the breach between object and site through the display of maps, reconstructions and the like. Buildings are even more linked to their sites if only because they are larger and thus possess a more obvious visual association with their surroundings. Despite this, however, they are frequently moved. The raising of the temple of Abu Simbel on the Nile is probably the best known example of saving structures from damage or destruction by natural or human environmental impacts, through the logically simple expedient of moving them to less threatened locations. Open-air folk museums often originated, less as deliberate collections, than as sanctuaries for buildings rescued from destruction.

Moving historic buildings has become an almost routine occurrence in North America when they impede redevelopment and relocation is a cheaper option than forgoing development gains. The argument against such relocation is that objects and buildings have a heritage value through what they are, but also through where they are. It could be argued, however, that in many cases where preserved monumental buildings or historical sites have become so engulfed in incongruous developments, moving them to a more appropriate and less visually incompatible site would add to their heritage value, or at least render this value more easily visited and appreciated. This is especially so in North American cities where 'development rights transfers' are used as a means of financing and encouraging building conservation. This instrument of development control and land management allows the owners of historic buildings to realize the development value of their sites by 'selling' their unused space to other, often neighbouring, sites. The public interest in the preservation of privately owned monuments is thus maintained, albeit at the cost of commensurately more development around the buildings. This can lead to historic buildings of comparatively modestly scale being buried within high-rise canyons to the extent where moving to a new location might be considered to be the lesser of evils.

Conversely, if surrounding development can reduce the heritage value of a building or object, a heritage structure can also be introduced deliberately into a new environmental context, expressly to confer a heritage status upon the new location. Old London Bridge, reconstructed at Lake Havasu in the Arizona desert, the liner *Queen Mary*, now moored at Long Beach, California (the best known among dozens of vintage ships adorning often alien revitalized urban waterfronts), and the Van Gogh collection assembled at the

Kröller Müller Museum at Otterlo, The Netherlands, had no previous associations with the places in which they are now located. The objects could have been located almost anywhere and the places concerned could have acquired almost any heritage object. By their very presence, however, even in such ostensibly incongruous sites, these heritage objects bestow a cachet upon the recreational resorts or sites of which they are now a part. The heritage structure has created a heritage location.

Heritage as a local management function

Even when heritage is created and maintained largely as a matter of national policy for the pursuit of national objectives, the execution of such policy will of necessity often be local, in much the same way as other aspects of national policy, including national education or health policies, are delivered through local schools and hospitals. The important question here is the extent to which this local management results in variations in the quantity, content or quality of the service delivered, an issue which invokes the simple question: who manages the heritage? In turn, this is related to the state's structure. Governance may be unitary and centralized, federal – with power and even sovereignty shared between federal and subordinate levels – or even more locally devolved to cities and districts. The legal structures of decision-making, however, may be less significant than the actual degree of toleration or encouragement accorded to local variation. A national unitary structure of governance may or may not reflect the existence of a unified culture and perceived common history. Thus some unitary states harbour considerable diversity. In the United Kingdom, for example, there remains a high degree of governmental centralization, despite recent political devolution to Scotland, Wales and Northern Ireland. But there is also a marked degree of local variation in the field of heritage selection and management, which relies on largely local initiatives and local implementation of national legislation. In contrast, The Netherlands has, at least in theory, a devolved governmental structure of provincial governments, but this is not reflected in marked economic, social or cultural differences between regions in what is broadly an economically, socially and culturally uniform national population. In almost all national jurisdictions, however, regardless of the type of devolution of sovereignty, responsibility for heritage management is divided between levels of governance.

The definition, recognition and listing of national heritage is the paramount national responsibility. This includes inventorization, the establishment of criteria for inclusion, the conferring of heritage designations and consequent legal protection. In France, the selection of conserved buildings and areas, and what can be termed 'stimulational leadership' (Kain 1975), was largely undertaken by a central Ministry of Culture as part of central government policy for the propagation of a national culture. The traditional role of the locality was one of implementation and exemplification of national heritage, rather than fostering any alternative – let alone competing – initiatives. Even in New World federal states, where there is no general framework of national legislation establishing a comprehensive and uniform system of monument preservation and urban conservation comparable to those developed in the countries of Western Europe, considerable residual powers nevertheless remain with the central government. In North America, national listing (The United States's 'Historic American Buildings Survey' and the Canadian 'Inventory of Historic Buildings'), the designation and management of key national historic sites, the national ownership and management of federal lands and properties, and numerous advisory, co-ordinating and stimulatory roles, are all important tasks of the federal authority. The US National Parks Service, in particular, is a pervasive presence in all these respects.

Sub-national jurisdictions usually participate in initiating or ratifying entries on national inventories and may even supplement the national level by creating additional regional or local lists of buildings and sites. In many federal states, however, heritage is controlled largely or in part by the lower levels, usually combined with other responsibilities such as culture, education and tourism. This may have occurred for the positive reason that heritage is seen as especially relevant to localities or, more negatively, because these topics were regarded as less important than defence or economic affairs, and can thus safely be left to subordinate levels for both legislation and implementation. In countries where sub-national jurisdictions correspond with and reflect major cultural and historical differences, then devolution both reproduces and fosters such regional identities. In Belgium almost all heritage concerns are the responsibility of the *Communité* or *Gemeenschap*, in Switzerland of the *canton* and in Spain of the autonomous region. Such devolution, however, also occurs in countries with far less marked regional linguistic and cultural differences. Second-tier administrations are responsible for most matters relating to public heritage in Germany, Austria and Poland.

In much of the New World, jurisdictional decentralization is constitutionally vested in inherited federal government structures, which usually originated more from the political history of colonial settlement and later federation than from marked cultural regional distinctiveness. In such political systems, land-use, planning and related issues are generally controlled by the second level of government – the states of the United States and Australia, or the provinces of Canada. Thus conservation legislation emanates primarily or substantially from the state/province level, admitting of considerable variation within each country. Canada typifies this division of responsibilities. Ontario is generally accepted as the most advanced province, the Ontario Heritage Act of 1974 remaining as the basic legislation (Ward 1986). This was incorporated into the Ontario Planning Act of 1983 and financially supported by the Ontario Heritage Foundation and the Ontario Community Heritage Fund prior to the impecunious 1990s. The application of the provisions of this legislation depends upon local initiative. The other provinces have generally intervened later and sometimes less effectively.

More generally, the lowest levels of government are concerned with at least some form of partnership with superior authorities in the selection, designation and financial subsidy of heritage, and with the local planning and management of heritage sites. One important consideration is that even in countries where most of the initiatives, legal structures and financial frameworks are nation-wide, such legislation is frequently permissive and thus dependent upon the reaction of local authorities to the available opportunities. The important variable then becomes less the existence of heritage possibilities than the rate of take-up of such potentials by local authorities. Given this propensity to respond locally, then considerable spatial variations will result. Consider, for example, the applications from local authorities for the designation of local heritage areas (*beschermde stads(dorps)gezichten*) in The Netherlands. In 1961, national legislation created the possibility of national area listing and subsidy but left the initiative to the local districts, which were required to submit detailed planning applications and commit some matching funds. Applications over time show a general trend of an initial pioneering period involving a small number of innovating authorities, followed much later by mass adoption. The innovating authorities tended to be the large and medium-sized cities, located especially in the three western metropolitan provinces. A clear distinction between a relatively heritage-rich core and a heritage-poor periphery developed, a pattern not explicable solely in terms of the spatial distribution of resources of old buildings and historical place associations. Some places were simply much more active in their responsiveness to possibilities than others, such heritage-mindedness being related to size, location in the political core, proximity to the national show-case cities, and the demonstration effect of neighbours. Over time, a process of diffusion took place from this pioneering core to other types of locality, and especially to the lagging peripheries, indicative of a continuous process of innovation and catch-up.

A final consideration in discussing heritage as a local management function is that there may well be a detectable propensity, most especially in the EU, towards a decentralization of heritage management and thus towards an increasing localization of heritage. In the first instance, this reflects the devolution of government functions and the idea of subsidiarity in decision-making, whereby competence – in this case over heritage – is exercised at the lowest level or as near to citizens as possible, thereby maximizing flexibility and local discretion. Secondly there are detectable changes in the nature of heritage itself, which is becoming more reflective of local priorities, goals and identities. The trend in governance clearly allows or even stimulates the heritage trend, which, to bring the argument full circle, requires or encourages local management of that resource.

In terms of its political administration, heritage management is as likely to be a result of the evolution of experience and working practice as of any considered ideology or principle. The seminal national legislation in almost all European countries occurred between 1960 and 1975. Local authorities have thus had a significant period to develop their expertise and experience in selecting, designating and managing heritage buildings and areas. This is the case both in countries such as the United Kingdom (Larkham 1996) and The Netherlands, where local initiatives were always important, and also those like France, Spain and Italy in which central governments once played a particularly dominant leading role but, more recently, have delegated powers to regional or local authorities.

The argument that the nature of heritage is changing depends on the assumption that the more successful the propagation of conservation, the more local it will become. In the earlier stages of monument identification and protection or the assembly of collections, preference was given to the rescue of the aesthetically spectacular and thus nationally unique. Thereafter, however, an increasing number of inevitably more modest, mundane and commonplace artefacts, buildings, sites and areas were included. Significance and uniqueness become matters of local rather than national context. This change in the content of heritage has been accompanied by a certain spatial diffusion from capital regions to more outlying provinces, and a movement down the spatial hierarchy from the nationally or internationally important to the regional and local, as the conservation movement finds greater acceptance at those scales. This trend is inevitably associated with rising costs, as more heritage is created to satisfy increasing local demands for it. Local benefits, choices and management imply local costs in market-oriented neo-liberal societies with their ethos of reducing the role and costs of central governments in favour of local and private initiatives.

Heritage and local identity

As identity is a major motive for the creation of heritage, then it is no surprise that heritage is the principal instrument for shaping distinctive local representations of place, which can be exploited for external promotion as well as in strengthening the identification of inhabitants with their localities. Two characteristics explain why heritage is one of the most important instruments in the shaping of such local identities. First, it is ubiquitous, all places on earth having a past and thus a potentially usable heritage. Second, it is infinite in its variety, every local past being inevitably different from the pasts of other places.

The social, political and economic uses of heritage are all apparent at the local scale. Local administrations have as great a need to justify their rule through the establishment of historic continuity and legitimacy as do the national governments discussed earlier. Indeed trends towards devolved management depend upon such identification of local people with their local governmental entities. The inclusiveness and representativeness of local heritage is a major factor in the cohesion of local societies, or at worst in minimizing conflict within them. Towns and regions also use heritage elements within local economic strategies in various competitive ways, not least in promotional place images designed to attract or retain economic activities (*see* Chapter 7).

All these arguments support the simple idea that the 'localization' of the past satisfies the various perceived needs of localities to discover, enhance and express their distinctiveness to themselves and to others. Heritage as a local phenomenon, however, cannot be considered in isolation from heritage at other spatial scales (*see* Chapter 4). In general, the contention here that there are compelling reasons for the increasing localization of heritage appears to contradict the ample evidence for the enduring importance of the national scale, and the equally important case for its internationalization. There are two different ways of thinking about this. The 'interscaler conflict model' regards the past as a potentially valuable resource to be competed for by different scales of governance. There are winners who capture the past by establishing their version of heritage, and thus their dominion, and losers whose heritage is suppressed or incorporated. This model thus encapsulates a continuous struggle for supremacy in which uniformity and fusion alternate with separatism and fragmentation: it is an unstable system for which there is no ultimate equilibrium condition.

In contrast, the 'hierarchical harmony model' sees identities at different scales interacting in a co-operative fashion. The local offers supportive and illustrative variations of wider aggregate national or international themes and reinforces a unity in diversity. 'Shadowing' may occur between different spatial scales when heritage identities communicated at one scale influence the image received at another. This can operate in either direction through the spatial hierarchy but is not inevitably dissonant, let alone leading automatically to conflict, as heritage, in common with many other place attributes, can exist simultaneously at multiple spatial scales.

For example, The Netherlands is a small and relatively culturally homogeneous country, where the conservation of the built environment developed in the nineteenth century in response to national concerns for a national patrimony, seen to be threatened by international trends of industrialization and urbanization. The operation of national legislation, financial subsidy systems and state agencies, even when applied locally through provincial and district authorities, has resulted in a fairly standardized style of building and historic area conservation throughout the nation-state. This style is now found in the historic centres of more or less all Dutch towns, almost regardless of local variations in physical, historical or cultural circumstances. In practice the 'Holland' town of the seventeenth-century 'Golden Age' – exemplified most famously in Vermeer's 'View of Delft' – has been ubiquitously replicated as the nation-state, centred on the western provinces, sought to legitimate itself and promote a national unity around the expression of an urban, mercantile, secular, bourgeois heritage.

More recently, this national model of urban conservation has been strongly challenged at the local scale. This assertion of local distinctiveness has a regional dimension, especially apparent in the cities of both the southern and northern provinces. Their historical experience and perceived way of life is seen as being more appropriately expressed through, respectively, a 'Burgundian' or 'Hanseatic' than a 'Holland' style. The challenge, however, is also a social and economic assertion of the distinctiveness of the individual city, regardless of its regional location. In what can be called 're-conservation', a new historical period or artistic style is being allocated to buildings and urban districts previously conserved, an act which asserts a local distinctiveness different from that of the western national core. Paradoxically, however, the more localities have asserted their independence of action from the national structures, the more open they have become to international influences, which are detectable also in their styles of heritage conservation and interpretation. Thus three simultaneously evident but essentially contradictory trends can be detected. Increasing internationalization is taking place as 'best practice' or, more cynically, 'currently most fashionable practice' cases from around the world are imitated. There is a re-regionalization with Groningen, Zwolle and Kampen, distancing themselves from the 'Holland' image of Delft, Leiden and Dordrecht, while coming to resemble Bremen, Rostock and Gdansk in a Baltic-Hanseatic heritage region. Meanwhile, in the south, Roermond, Venlo and Maastricht are incorporated into a Flemish-Burgundian region with Turnhout, Mechelen, and Leuven. Finally, an individualization of places is occurring, each seeking a distinctive branding and market positioning of the place-product.

As none of these trends is particularly unique to The Netherlands, this case could be replicated in cities everywhere. There may, however, be a sharper edge to the competition provided by the local scale to the national heritage identity, especially at a regional scale where separatist influences may flourish. This can occur even in small countries, as Belgium illustrates, but is more likely to arise in larger states and particularly in those in which regional autonomy provides a mechanism which can be turned as readily to centrifugal or centripetal ends. In Europe, this solvent is active in such cases as Scotland, Sardinia and Corsica, while one of the best examples is provided by Spain, a country which has rarely been a convincing nation-state.

Spanish regional identities have always been strong, not least in the Basque Country (Euskadi) and Catalonia. Even under the 40 years of Fascist control that followed the defeat of the Spanish Republic in the Civil War of 1936–9, the devolutionist instinct was apparent. Since Spain's return to democracy, it has appeared to be among the most convincing illustrations of the concept of 'Europe of the Regions'. In Catalonia, a broad nationalist consensus was established around a few – largely cultural – central themes, most notably the Catalan language, while, in Euskadi, internal cultural, ideological and political fragmentation led to radicals resorting to confrontation with the Spanish state, the repression of which was required – in turn – for violence to begin and spread (Conversi 1997). Euskadi has undergone a 'war of liberation' waged by ETA, which provides the closest parallel in Europe to PIRA.

Catalan nationalism has remained moderate and broadly united around its cultural platform, while clearly Catalans also continue to profess a distinct empathy with Spanish tropes of identity. Above all, their nationalism is not separatist, nor is it violent, the principal objective being to renegotiate the region's relationship with the Castilian centre in Madrid. In marked contrast, Conversi argues that the fragmentation of the Basque nationalist movement from its earliest origins made violence inevitable. In the absence of: a coherent and unifying nationalist ideology, sufficiently powerful in cultural terms to transcend the effects of urbanisation; the Castilianization of the Basque élite; and the effects of immigration; Euskadi's cultural space became plural and fragmented. Language is equally important to Basque nationalism but whereas Euskara – one of Europe's notably remote and enigmatic tongues – is in decline, Catalan is among the most dynamic regional languages in Europe, heady symbol of Catalonia's cultural regeneration. In that failure of the Basque nationalist movement to devise a similar programme of nationalist regeneration lies the propensity to violence expressed in ETA's action-repression-action theory, the Spanish state being provoked into the oppression and violence that helped cement a common identity out of chaos.

Among the large federal states, Canada's national heritage identity, focused in Ottawa, competes with regionalisms fostered by constitutional autonomy in Québec, Newfoundland and British Columbia. South Africa's new provincial autonomy, similarly designed to accommodate regional identity tensions, may likewise ultimately foster the secession of Kwazulu-Natal (Lemon 1995). Regional heritage dissonances usually climax in the major cities, where symbols of identity are concentrated. Barcelona represents Catalonia as Bilbao does Euskadi. Québec City is the classic Canadian illustration, its iconography resonant of Québecois aspirations for a separate republic (see Chapter 11). In sharp contrast, St. John's, Newfoundland, projects British imperial and monarchical symbolism as an assertion of both transatlantic links and also a certain distancing from Ottawa (Tunbridge and Ashworth 1996). Thus the heritage city may reflect regional dissonances with conflicting messages, a significant issue which we now explore from the perspective of its management.

The management of the heritage city

The concept of the tourist-historic city, first developed by Ashworth and Tunbridge (1990), has been applied and modified globally since (see, for example, de Bres 1994; Shaw et al. 1997). Its usefulness here is threefold. First, it focuses on the relationship between heritage and cities and, in particular, isolates the specifically urban attributes which contribute to heritage and can thus be managed by urban authorities. Second, by tracing the genesis of the heritage city, the model generalizes the processes which produce it but also allows variations from the norm to be classified into a geography of heritage cities. Third, the model provides a framework for understanding the detailed management of heritage at the local urban scale.

Heritage and cities

Much heritage has been created in cities, which are used in various ways as stages or showcases for its presentation. In addition, cities themselves may be heritage objects of major significance. Three basic urban attributes – size, spatial clustering and urban design – have a direct bearing upon cities as heritage centres. Each of these, but particularly the latter two, are susceptible to local management.

The argument concerning size merely postulates that all heritage results from past human interaction at specific places. Thus the larger the place, the more such interaction is likely to have occurred, thereby endowing that place with areas, buildings and sites to which heritage values can be ascribed. Furthermore, much heritage is mobile and larger places will tend to have accumulated, either by chance or design, more of it, whether or not the historic resources were originally created there.

The geographical clustering of heritage sites, associations and objects, both with each other and with ancillary supporting services, is necessary to produce a critical volume of heritage potential in a spatially restricted area. As with many other urban facilities, this process can be encouraged by considerations of the functional associations between heritage producers and consumers. The former provide different component elements in the total heritage product, which the latter then utilize although they require a spatial juxtaposition of the heritage products in order to consume them within their time-space constraints.

Finally, many design attributes of cities may contribute to the successful creation of heritage areas. Cities endeavouring to develop their heritage potential are dependent to a considerable degree upon the nature, quality and utility of their physical forms, especially in those areas being promoted as heritage districts. This is the case, not just for the heritage objects themselves, but a whole range of other contemporary urban features. Vehicular and pedestrian traffic management, public circulation spaces, obtrusive non-conforming elements, and details of street furniture, paving and lighting elements, all play critical roles in the shaping of heritage areas and, equally important, are within the powers of most local management authorities.

Consequently, it is clear that formally promoted heritage, as one type of urban form and urban function, cannot be separated from more general urban attributes. Therefore, local planning and management agencies commonly have the means to intervene effectively in designing urban heritage, which, in consequence, becomes an integral component of much broader urban planning. However, how, or even if, this occurs depends principally on the nature of the urban economy and the requirements of urban policy.

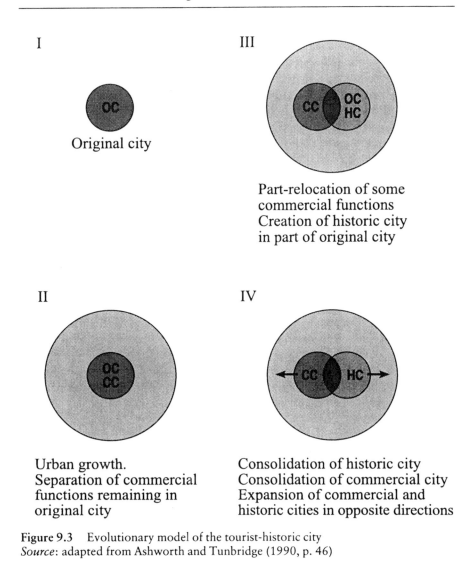

I

Original city

III

Part-relocation of some
commercial functions
Creation of historic city
in part of original city

II

Urban growth.
Separation of commercial
functions remaining in
original city

IV

Consolidation of historic city
Consolidation of commercial city
Expansion of commercial and
historic cities in opposite directions

Figure 9.3   Evolutionary model of the tourist-historic city
Source: adapted from Ashworth and Tunbridge (1990, p. 46)

The genesis of the heritage city

The heritage city, as distinct from just the old city or the historic city, comes
into being through a combination of social and economic processes operating
over time. The vicissitudes of history, the survival of a historic endowment
and deliberate policy all play crucial roles at specific moments. In a simple
evolutionary model (Figure 9.3), the 'original city' is assumed in the first
phase to include all urban functions, and subsequent growth is likely to occur
outwards in all directions. Consequently, in the second phase, there will be
an old centre and newer periphery. (Cases do exist where this did not happen

because of historical accident, peculiarity of site or complete city centre redevelopment; such examples, however, are far less likely to develop into heritage cities.) Two processes now take place which together lead to the
creation of the heritage city. First, the historic architectural forms in at least
part of the original city become valued and thus conserved. The extent to
which this occurs will reflect a combination of the extent and condition of the
architecture and design, the pressures for redevelopment on the area, and the
effectiveness of the local conservation lobby. Second, functional change will
take place. Some activities will experience pressures to migrate out of the heritage area, while others will be attracted to it. Conservation designations and
policies will impose costs upon occupiers of preserved buildings and conserved areas through higher maintenance costs, restrictions on the use and
adaptation of buildings, or constraints on some forms of accessibility.
Conversely, conserved areas or buildings offer increased benefits to users
through their enhanced historicity and the physical presence of people who
are attracted to them. Simply, some activities can profit from the historic city
despite the extra costs while others cannot. The result, with or without deliberate planning policies, is likely to be a partial physical separation of the heritage city and the central commercial city. We thus arrive at the fourth phase
in which a partially relocated commercial district overlaps with a heritage district in part of the original city. Subsequent growth of both the heritage and
commercial districts is then likely to occur in opposite directions. The former
extends into more of the original old city, while the latter expands outwards
while the area of overlap undergoes restructuring.

This model was derived mainly from the experience of European cities in
which the preservation of forms usually led, often with official encouragement, to the outmigration of functions. In North America, the sequence of
events has frequently been reversed in that it was typically the abandonment
of areas by commercial and residential functions which led to the creation of
'zones of discard' subsequently being conserved through either public or private initiatives (Ford 1979, 1994; Tunbridge 1987).

The mutually reinforcing relationship between the securing of the heritage
resource and the development of the tourist-historic city characteristically
involves a chain reaction between numerous agents. This is well illustrated by
the continuing reinforcement of Ottawa's heritage core (Ashworth and
Tunbridge 1990; Tunbridge and Ashworth 1996; Figure 9.4). Expropriation
and refurbishment of Sussex Drive, a key artery between government buildings, by the National Capital Commission (NCC) during the 1960s also revitalized the near-by Byward Market area – the former zone of discard – for
tourist-historic purposes. This involved the city as owner of the market facilities and many private entrepreneurs. By the 1980s, this outwardly expanding leisure-retailing core of the tourist-historic city was so successful in
attracting new museums and monuments, and both public and private sector
investment, that pressure grew for the creation of a Heritage Conservation
District to protect the heritage resource fuelling the tourist-historic economy

Figure 9.4 Part of Ottawa's heritage core: the Peacekeeping Monument – a symbol of reconciliation – on Sussex Drive, with an early heritage building, the Roman Catholic cathedral, behind

before exploitative development interests could destroy it. This was declared by the city in 1992 and while the 1990s recession has weakened the tourist-historic economy and muted the immediate significance of the designation, in the long run it is likely to further intensify and expand heritage creation and protection initiatives in Ottawa's tourist-historic city.

Geographical variants of the heritage city

Many possible variations from the hypothetical development model of the tourist-historic city can be identified.

Size

The model is derived from, and most easily applicable to, medium-sized examples where redevelopment and heritage conservation can occur in different areas. Much larger cities, in contrast, may have polycentric commercial and heritage areas and thus develop separate heritage 'islands' for their varied heritage resources, rather than a single contiguous centrally located heritage district. Again, smaller towns may lack this separation into 'old' and 'new' districts and, consequently, some will be preserved in their entirety. These are the so-called 'gem cities' in which modern functions are accommodated and tolerated only in so far as they conform to the paramount heritage function. Representative of a past 'golden age', these cities have passed through a stage of stagnation and neglect to be subsequently rediscovered as heritage. They occur world-wide and include European medieval walled towns such as Rothenburg (Bavaria) or Aigues Mortes (Languedoc), colonial towns like Savannah, Georgia, and even nineteenth-century 'New World' mining towns, as exemplified by Dawson (Yukon, Canada). Their preservation and management is often a matter of national heritage policy.

Physical site attributes

Pronounced physical barriers, whether natural (for example, a sharp difference in elevation) or historical (such as the survival of a now-preserved city wall) may lead to a complete rather than partial separation of the heritage and modern commercial districts. Many towns located in regions of chronic insecurity originally developed on defensible higher ground, expanding in more peaceful interludes beyond and below the original city. The functional migration of modern central commercial activities out of the historic city is thus reinforced and made physically more obvious by the distinction between the upper and lower towns. The former, the *acropolis*, often retained its architectural heritage through abandonment and possible later conservation rather than redevelopment. Examples are provided by many medium-sized and smaller towns around the Mediterranean coasts of Spain, Italy, Greece and Turkey. In extreme cases, such as Corinth, the modern city developed some distance away from the ancient settlement. Elsewhere, as at Bergamo, Urbino, Carcassonne or Gerona, there is more temporal and spatial continuity in the two contiguous 'cities', a heritage-dominated upper town and a modern commercial lower town. In other regions, the Mediterranean *acropolis* becomes variously the *burg, burcht, berg, borgo, borg, burgh* or *bourg*. In Europe, these terms generally define the fortified medieval military and ecclesiastical cores – often located on defensible high ground – which, as in Salzburg, Edinburgh or Bourges have now become the heritage cities.

Waterfronts

The most dramatic and widespread physical interruption of the urban pattern occurs in waterfront cities where the basic geometry of circular development is replaced by urban expansion inland and the creation of zones of discard along the waterfront. Port functions tend to migrate downstream in response to economic and technological change (Hoyle *et al.* 1988; Hoyle 1999), while the central commercial functions tend to move inland, maintaining their central position within the urban area. The heritage city can now evolve on or near the commercially discarded waterfront, using the surviving architectural heritage and historic associations, together with the added attractions of waterfront views and environments, linear promenades and leisure adaptations of water transport. Historic ships are almost *de rigeur*.

Figure 9.5 models this variant of the more general case (Tunbridge and Ashworth 1992; Tunbridge 1993). Since the 1970s, heritage waterfront development has become increasingly ubiquitous on a global basis

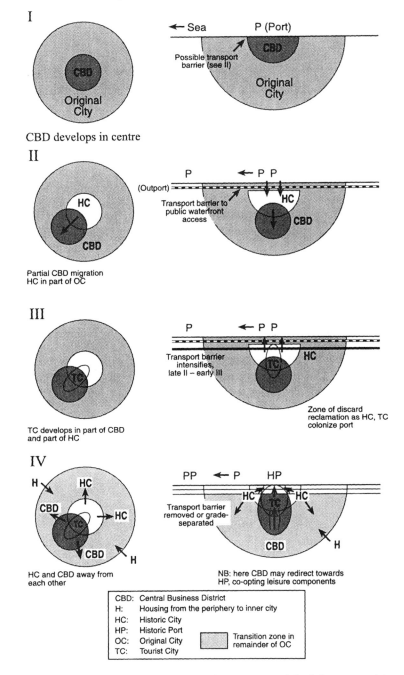

Figure 9.5   A waterfront variant on the evolutionary model of the tourist-historic city

(Bruttomesso 1993, 1997). Examples include Cape Town and the prominent US archetypes, particularly Baltimore, Boston or San Francisco. European examples include: major heritage tourism cities such as Lübeck or Venice; large multifunctional cities with extensive dockland redevelopments that include heritage components, such as London and, on a smaller scale, Rotterdam's 'Kop van Zuid' or Amsterdam's 'IJoevers'; and the special complications of heritage naval bases, such as Den Helder or Portsmouth. The sequence – port-industry migration, waterfront abandonment, and heritage waterfront creation – may even be repeated successively, as has occurred in Belgium with Bruges, Damme, Sluis and Zeebrugge.

Cultural/ national variants

Variations from any general model will also inevitably arise because of particular historical experiences and cultural particularities. The North American variant of the tourist-historic city has much in common with the European if only through the similarity and interactivity of their market economies, conservation philosophies and even tourism industries. There are, however, obvious differences in the quantity and antiquity of urban historic resources, which has led to differing valuations of historical artefacts and also to divergent methods of exploitation and presentation. In particular, North American tourist-historic cities tend to contain a larger proportion of contrived attractions. Further, the locations of many tourism facilities tend to be more widely distributed than in Western European cities, partly as a consequence of the early development of private transport. It is thus more difficult to define the heritage city in narrowly inner-city terms and so the concept of an urban-regional heritage system assumes a greater prominence. For example, Ford (1994) has identified both the existence of an 'old town' close to the traditional CBD core – very similar to the European-derived heritage city and shaped by the same processes of selective outmigration – but also many urban villages with heritage components, revitalized heritage waterfronts and festival market redevelopments.

Elsewhere, colonial cities including Zanzibar (McQuillan and Laurier 1984), Hong Kong or Nairobi often display a dualistic colonial-indigenous urban structure, which complicates their heritage presentation and commodification. One variant of the tourist-historic city model, developed in the context of Fremantle, Western Australia (Jones and Shaw 1992; Shaw *et al.* 1997), also appears applicable to other former British imperial cities, including Penang and Singapore, located around the Indian Ocean littoral. This involves the contentious transformation of declined colonial ports through a sequence of decay–restoration–pastiche, in which the final stage represents the complete commodification of heritage for tourism consumption (Figure 9.6). A Japanese variant (Satoh 1986, 1997) is based on the distinctive origin, subsequent evolution and planning problems of Japanese castle towns. Japanese historic buildings may be quite regularly completely rebuilt and even moved (Fitch 1995), reflecting the limited life-span of the

Figure 9.6 Fremantle, Western Australia: the complete commodification of heritage for tourism consumption

materials, and even incorporate modern materials and building structures without seemingly compromising the perceived authenticity of the site and structure.

A further particular variant of the tourist-historic city is found in much of the Middle East and North Africa, while resonances also occur in Iberia because of its medieval Moorish occupation. The Islamic city is organized on very different principles, its morphology dominated by a dense configuration of contiguous enclosures in which the buildings, served by cul-de-sac alleys, face inwards to central courtyards. These alleys open off marginally wider through routes – mostly roofed over to provide shade – that link the city gates to a centrally-located mosque. Such axes, often no wider than is necessary to admit pack-animals, are lined by the small individual shops of the *suqs*, the city's markets (Morris 1994). Architectural detailing is confined within the interior structures of the houses, little care being given to exterior appearances (Benevolo 1993). In the Andalucian city of Granada, for example, separated by the Rio Darro from the Alhambra Palace – indisputably one of the world's most evocative heritage sites – the old Moorish Albaicín quarter, with its low, courtyard houses and formless alleys, remains markedly distinct from the rectilinear morphology of the sixteenth- and seventeenth-century Spanish Renaissance town located around the cathedral (Figure 9.7).

Nowhere is the dualistic colonial/indigenous nature of the tourist-historic city better exemplified than in the Moroccan city of Fès (Figure 9.8).

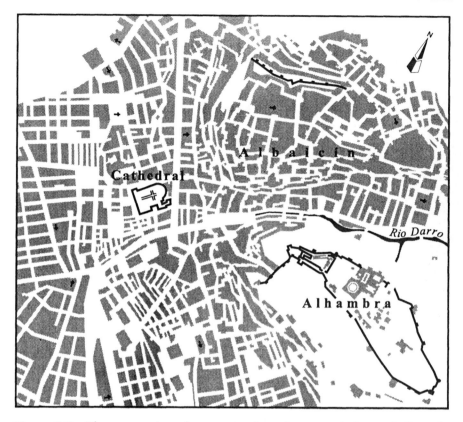

Figure 9.7 The contrasting elements in the urban morphology of Granada, Andalucia, Spain

Founded in 808, the *medina* of Fès El Bali comprises a number of separately fortified quarters and *suqs*, each dedicated to a distinct economic activity such as tanning, metal-working of various sorts or particular forms of retailing. Dominated by an incoherent maze of cul-de-sac alleys and straggling through routes, the city's plan lacks the discernible patterning and morphological aggrandisement of its European contemporaries. Even the great medieval Kairaouine Mosque – one of the holiest places in western Islam – is difficult to see, given the absence of any axial perspective in the street-plan, or a place of public assembly corresponding to the European cathedral square. In this context, the tourist-historic city is indistinguishable from the city as a whole, while a dramatic morphological contrast is provided by the linear street plan of the nineteenth- and twentieth-century French colonial *ville nouvelle*, located several kilometres to the south-west of the *medina* city.

Figure 9.8   The tortuous urban morphology of the *medina* of Fès El Bali, Morocco

Conclusion: from local to global and back again

All the above arguments for the localization of heritage would seem to suggest that there is an increasing distinctiveness of localities and thus divergence of identities. If heritage conservation at the local level is strongly linked to the idea of local identity and diversity, it may seem contrary to argue that heritage contributes towards a convergence of place identities. However, the practice of architectural and urban conservation may well tend towards a standardization of forms, a homogenization of places and thus a reduction in local diversity. There are three main reasons which explain why heritage intended to enhance local identity can, in reality, lead to its diminution.

First, there is a tendency towards a standardization of professional practice. Conservation architects, builders and planners are as fashion conscious as any other practitioners, while professional training and the transfer of technical and artistic practices establishes and transmits currently acceptable methods of working. So many heritage buildings or townscapes reflect the conservation style of the period of their restoration that they primarily convey messages about how pasts were viewed by practitioners at that time. These may have had little to do with the antiquity or symbolic meanings of the structures themselves. The result can be a national standardization of places restored during a particular period.

For example, large-scale restoration of urban areas in France originated with the Malraux Act of 1962, which designated areas for positive enhancement, the aim being to effect a renaissance of the historic quarters of French towns. These were protected as *secteurs sauvegardés*, designated and financed by the state in conjunction with local authorities, who were responsible for the conservation plans, land use and zoning. The model, echoed by many other *secteurs sauvegardés*, was Paris's Marais district (Kain 1981). Other examples include the painstaking reconstruction of the central areas of Polish cities after 1945, and the discovery and proliferation of a German neo-vernacular reconstruction style in the 1980s (Soane 1994). Such standardization may even have an international dimension as 'best practice' examples are propagated and skills and ideas diffused through intergovernmental and professional bodies such as UNESCO, ICOMOS (International Council on Monuments and Sites) and the Council of Europe. The proliferation of various European associations of cities such as 'The League of Car-free Cities', '*Quartiers en Crise*', 'The Walled Towns Friendship Circle' or 'The European League of Historic Towns' merely accentuates the trend to standard practice.

Second, urban development projects are increasingly executed and financed by globally active companies, which tend to minimize risk by repeating exemplars already successful elsewhere. Locally commissioned projects thus tend to resemble each other as archetypes are reproduced across countries and even continents. For example, the building renovation and functional revitalization of nineteenth-century decayed or abandoned inner-city industrial areas like Lowell, Massachusetts, Birmingham's jewellery quarter or Nottingham's Lace Market have a familiar similarity. Much urban waterfront regeneration, for example, has been labelled 'Rousification' after the pioneering developer, Rouse, as variants of San Francisco's Fisherman's Wharf and Ghiradelli Square have been reproduced across much of the rest of the world during the past 20 years (Tiesdell and Heath 1996).

Third, at the level of design detail, we can recognize what can be termed a 'catalogue heritagization' in which the same street furniture – whether lamp-standards, traffic bollards, litter bins, paving materials or even signage – is selected, presumably from the same suppliers, as being recognizably 'historic'. Even treating a new building in an attempt to render it more locally distinctive can result in a 'neo-vernacular historicist' embellishment, in itself so standardized that it ultimately reduces rather than increases the local character of the architecture. The result is that distinctive, original and admirable urban conservation and heritage enhancement projects, such as Louisbourg Square (Boston), Gastown (Vancouver), Elm Hill (Norwich), Petite Venice (Colmar), Bergkwartier (Deventer), or Botscherstrasse (Bremen), become quite literally the text-book examples, which are then reproduced around the globe by the next generation of urban heritage planners and managers. The historic districts of conserved cities thus become largely indistinguishable from each other, regardless of the local architectural characteristics or historic periods preserved. Each is merely marked as recognizably 'historic' through the use of such standardized heritage markers.

However, it is not merely non-local developmental processes that tend to reproduce standardized forms and patterns. Consumers of local heritage identities are also responsible. As places attempt to assert their distinctiveness by commodifying their local histories, cultures, and customs for non-local consumption, these attributes become selectively adapted. This provokes a new self-consciousness as that which was previously normal and unremarkable life-style and behaviour now becomes different, remarkable and marketable. It is the external international world that actually creates and consumes local ethnicities and cultures. This can be seen most clearly, albeit in an extreme form, in the departure lounges of that most placeless of facilities, the international airport, where local identity is expressed through icons, signs and souvenirs. This is just one manifestation of the postmodern globalization of locality. Food, music, folk customs and designs, confined until recently to a specific locality, are now universally available and consumed. In short, for the first time in world history, the difference between the vernacular and the international is becoming so blurred as to be indistinguishable.

Thus we can identify a number of paradoxes. The search for a distinctive local identity, expressed through local heritage, may lead to the loss of that identity through standardized reproducible forms. Meanwhile, an increasingly uniform and homogenous world constantly needs to reinvent localities along far more complex dimensions than in the past. We can thus argue either that the international scale has incorporated and annexed the local scale or, conversely, that localities have become global in their consumption and have thus appropriated the international scale. This facet of postmodernism regards the rediscovery of locality, including its design features, as an antidote to the homogeneous functionalism of international modernism. However, although eclectic postmodern design uses local heritages, ethnicities and identities, these local features are no longer tied to a specific locality. The vernacular is certainly stressed, but in a context far removed from that in which it was originally expressed, as well as in close juxtaposition to other quite different vernaculars. Localism has become divorced from locality. If modernism produced places that could be anywhere, postmodernism produces an almost infinite selection of somewheres capable of reproduction everywhere.

|10|

Heritage and scale III: from the national to the continental management of heritage

Introduction

In Chapters 10 and 11, we take the national scale as a frame of reference to discuss the concept of heritage at the supranational continental and global scales. Our focus thus becomes the ownership of heritage and the heritage dissonances which exist between nations as well as those arising from the idea that heritage can be the common property of communities of nations. The national scale of heritage identity remains enshrined in national museums, collections, histories, conservational legislative frameworks and practices. Conversely, international heritage organizations were generally created later, usually modelled on national institutions, financed by them and even subject to their veto. Such organizations tend, therefore, to balance national interests rather than override them in the pursuit of international concepts of heritage identity and meaning. Prior to examining the continental scale through the example of Europe, it is therefore necessary to discuss further the ownership of the past.

Who owns the past? Is there an international heritage?

Ownership and its rights can mean quite different things. A particular art work or monumental building may be owned by an individual, charitable organization, commercial corporation, or by the state on behalf of the collective people. None of these owners, however, have absolute rights over such property, nor does ownership in this sense define rights of enjoyment of the property by owners or others. Much of the history of the development of heritage planning over the past century revolved around attempts to define, and in practice limit, private property rights over heritage and thus to recognize the existence of much wider collective rights.

In most countries, for example, the ownership of historic buildings designated as monuments remains with the original individual or organizational owner. In Western Europe, but not usually in North America, property owners do not even have to agree to such a designation. Once designated by the public authority, however, the rights of the owner are restricted, with varying severity in different countries. At the very least, change or demolition must be notified and delayed; it is more usually regulated or prohibited, while in some countries the owner is legally required to maintain the property. Public subsidies are often linked to public rights so that, in accepting state help, owners relinquish some individual rights (for example of free subsequent disposal) or at least accept some collective rights (as of public access). Similarly, the normal individual right to sell, bequeath or otherwise dispose of heritage property is generally subject to various restrictions, these ranging between notification, the right of public purchase at market rates, and compulsory acquisition by the state.

Often the restriction applies less to the sale itself than to the buyer. The introduction of export licences for cultural property of a defined monetary or symbolic value is based on the idea that it is not private ownership but foreign private ownership that is the problem. A contemporary state, acting on behalf of a collective group, thus has a claim on an aspect of the past that overrides that of the individual. Similarly, the wider 'owners' of the heritage have both a moral right of access and a moral responsibility to contribute towards its support, whether through taxation or donation.

These arguments can become much more contentious and complicated. A particularly common and controversial aspect of this question is the attempt to link heritage objects with specific places, which are seen as the 'correct' location. The widespread nature of this problem stems both from the inherent mobility of both people and much of their heritage and also from the constantly mutating uses and claims placed on heritage. Artefacts can be bought and sold and thus tend to be located in the hands of rich individuals, museums or countries. They can be expropriated by governments and located in capital 'showcase' cities, or even simply seized or stolen. Empires in particular tended to collect the heritage of their far-flung domains, generating numerous contemporary demands by former subject peoples for the restitution of those artefacts. The distinctly peripatetic nature of much heritage can lead to quite bizarre cases of contested ownership. Human bodies are especially potent symbols and of course very movable. To show there is nothing new in such appropriation, Alexander the Great's body was kidnapped by his general, Ptolemy, and taken to Alexandria in Egypt to legitimate a new kingdom. The medieval wealth of the great Burgundian abbey of Vézelay was founded on pilgrimage to the shrine containing the purported bones of Mary Magdalene, which supposedly had been appropriated from the church of Saint-Maximin in Provence. The abbey went into decline, however, when in the thirteenth century it was admitted that the 'true' relics still remained at Saint-Maximin. The body of Columbus (or parts of it) are claimed by four different cities in two continents, while the body of a pre-historic 'Ice Man', recently discovered in an Alpine glacier, is claimed by both Austria and Italy.

The idea that 'wrongly' located heritage can be returned or 'repatriated' to the rightful owner in the correct location sounds like natural justice but depends upon determining moral as well as legal ownership. For example, the German archaeologist Schliemann took what he believed to be the 'treasures of Troy' unearthed in the 1873 excavation to his native Berlin, having first paid the Turkish government the money they required and having been refused permission by the Greek government to locate them in Athens. The artefacts were subsequently looted by the Soviets in 1945 and recently revealed to be in the possession of the Russian state. While Germany claims that its property should be returned, Russia argues that the artefacts 'belong' to humanity of which it is a representative. Meanwhile, both Turkey, in whose jurisdiction they were found, and Greece, which claims to represent the Homeric Greeks and Trojans, could make counter-claims. This case is typical of many where looting and re-looting leaves national governments arguing their respective rights over properties which were created long before any of these governments, or the states they represent, existed.

In spite of treaty commitments, numerous post-World War II heritage restitution issues remain outstanding, particularly between Germany and Russia. Some items have even yet to be located, the most famous being the legendary Amber Room panelling, originally made in Königsberg for Frederick I of Prussia and sent to St Petersburg in 1716 as a gift for that city's founder, Peter the Great. Although one fragment was apparently recovered in Bremen in 1997, its disappearance from Königsberg in 1945 remains one of the war's great heritage enigmas and a source of continuing tension between Germany and Russia.

The recurring claim by present possessors that they are acting as custodians for humanity, as Poland does in the case of Beethoven's manuscripts which are now in Kraków, links the present discussion of conflict over ownership to the notion of a common international heritage which we address later in this chapter. A rather more complex case is that of the 'Elgin Marbles', which is so widely known that the world-wide assembly of artefacts in imperial capitals has been called 'Elginism', and policies for its correction, 'de-Elginization' (*see* Chapter 6). The substantial facts of the case are not in dispute. The Parthenon frieze from the Acropolis in Athens was collected in an essentially discarded and ruinous state by Lord Elgin between 1803 and 1812 and brought from what was then Turkish territory to the British Museum in London in 1816, since when it has been conserved (arguably badly) and displayed. For more than a century, successive Greek governments have vociferously claimed the 'marbles' as 'Greek' heritage, a claim firmly rejected by Britain. The curious point here is that 'classical Greece' was largely an invention of nineteenth-century Western European Romantics and it was the countries of Western Europe, specifically Britain, Germany and France, which used that concept to legitimate their political ideologies, especially democracy and liberal humanism. Thus the artefacts of classical Greece constituted 'their' heritage while they supported the revolt of the Greeks from Turkey in the 1830s and the creation of the modern Greek state. Although modern Greek nationalism was rooted in medieval Christian Byzantium, rather than heathen Hellenism, the Greek state – once created – adopted the existing and largely western vision of Hellas to legitimate not only its sovereignty in mainland Greece but also its claims over large parts of the Aegean, Anatolia, Macedonia and Cyprus (Lowenthal 1988).

The 'Elgin' dispute is replicated throughout the world and is echoed in the doubtless well-meaning attempts of the UN agency, UNESCO, to establish some sort of international code of ethics on the national 'ownership' of 'misplaced' heritage and, where possible, its repatriation. Taken to its extreme, however, a focus on the national scale automatically excludes the international. For example, if we accept that the paintings of Rembrandt and Vermeer are Dutch national heritage because both artists lived in what is now the Kingdom of the Netherlands (albeit created only 200 years after their deaths), then all their work should be relocated from around the world to The Netherlands. In 1998, the Dutch government paid the highest recorded price for a painting so as to acquire 'for the nation' the last work of Mondriaan, an artist who lived and worked in New York. Presumably too, Dutch galleries should exhibit only Dutch painters, with the works of others being suitably repatriated. Pursuing this logic, the access of world citizens to their global heritage would be severely constrained. Conversely, to return to the Elgin dispute, if the Parthenon frieze like similar classical artworks in Paris's Louvre, Madrid's Prado and their equivalents, belongs to everyone, then its location in a free museum, in a highly accessible world city, is arguably better than being exposed on a hill-top in one of the world's most polluted cities. Whatever else, 'Elginism' was global and 'de-Elginization' would result in a global disinheritance in terms of both practical accessibility and psychic identification.

Finally, in terms of addressing the ownership of the past, and even more sensitive in many respects, is the growing concern and controversy over the ownership of heritage between groups within countries. This is especially the case when the cultural artefacts, and even human remains, of 'primitive' peoples were collected and displayed by others for their anthropological or cultural interest. For example, many native American or Inuit peoples argue that their cultures have been expropriated, often by museums, and not only 'stolen' but misused through misinterpretation or lack of suitable respect. Numerous museums now attempt to empower such groups by involving them in the presentation of their cultures. As with the controversies between countries, the question revolves around the ordering of claims upon heritage, its ownership, management and use. We now consider the implications of these points for a supranational heritage at the continental scale. This discussion focuses on Europe and builds on the argument in Chapter 4, where it was observed that some commentators hold that the EU represents the world's most significant supranational challenge to the enduring power of the nation-state.

Continentalism: a European heritage?

The need for a European heritage

As was argued in Part II, nationalism is but one form of identity and an individual can identify with imagined communities set in place at a variety of scales – local, regional, national, supranational, even global. The obvious question that arises from such reasoning is why should a European level of identity be required? Again, if contemporary Europe is defined by diversity and multiculturalism, resulting in an increasingly complex fragmentation of identity and allegiance, can a European identity really be created? At present a discordance exists between the political-economic integration and potential appeal of a unified Europe and the lack of legitimation accorded such a construct, perhaps because it lacks the validation of cultural consciousness vested in place. It is vital to remember, however, that the EU is far more than an economic union, a single market. Rather, it reflects an ideology, the central tenet of which lies in the creation of a social market economy, which combines market forces with a commitment to the values of internal social solidarity and mutual support. This involves, for example, an explicit commitment to reducing regional disparities in income and opportunity and to promote convergence and cohesion. It appears to be the case, however, that the wider ramifications of this agenda are not widely recognized or even appreciated, largely because of a lack of 'Europeanness' in the identity profiles of Europeans (Graham and Hart 1999).

Arguably, therefore, the successful integration of Europe might demand an iconography of identity that would complement, but not necessarily replace national, regional and local identities. Rose (1995) maintains that a sense of place does exist at the supranational level; the Renaissance, Enlightenment and Judeo-Christianity are seen as particularly European achievements. The construction of a European heritage identity would involve the manipulation of heritage, demanding the addition of new layers of meaning to built environments and landscapes that are already fundamental symbols within national or regional iconographies and narratives (Ashworth and Graham 1997).

The difficulties are profound. If we accept that Europe does require a heritage of identity and legitimation to complement – and indeed validate – its role in economic and political decision-making, this is not to suggest that the function of such an iconography rests in the imposition of some contrived and spurious rendition of unity. Rather, a European heritage must accommodate the centrifugal heterogeneity of place and a multicultural diversity of peoples and cultures. It follows that multiculturalism provides the only viable basis for a meaningful axis of European identity. Arguably, therefore, the successful integration of Europe requires an iconography of identity that would transcend national and regional identities. This involves the manipulation of heritage, demanding the addition of new layers of meaning to built environments and landscapes that are already fundamental symbols within national iconographies and narratives. In addition, these latter were generally imposed on a much more complex regional differentiation of place and its meaning that emanated from the territorial fragmentation of the Middle Ages.

As discussed in Chapter 8 (*see* Figure 8.1), regional icons, already re-designated as national symbols, might further be subsumed within a European heritage. In turn, however, such icons would derive a higher status from their allocated attributes of Europeanness, thereby enhancing their prestige as national symbols and ultimately inflating their potency as symbols of regional identity, consciousness and power. Arguably, therefore, a 'Europeanization' of heritage might ultimately emphasize the local and regional ferment that underlies the structure of nation-states created to contain that very diversity. It is this aspect of dissonance, in which the same objects carry an array of potentially conflicting meanings, that makes heritage – however necessary to constructs of legitimation – such a powerful and prolific source of political tension.

For example, the obscure early medieval Galician cult of *Sant'Iago* became a fundamental element of medieval European ecclesiastical politics, leading to Santiago de Compostela developing as the second most important pilgrimage centre in Europe after Rome (Figure 10.1). The cult was also central to the construction of an orthodox Spanish nationalism, forged through a narrative of the Christian reconquest of Iberia from the Moorish infidels (Graham and Murray 1997). In the iconography of the new Europe, however, the pilgrimage route to Santiago has been recreated physically and symbolically to signify the unification of the continent and its people, the 'Way' marked, not by medieval pilgrim shrines, but by the signposts of a 'European cultural itinerary' and the manifest efforts to develop northern Spain's tourism infrastructure (Murray and Graham 1997). In turn, unsurprisingly, the concept of the roads of Europe symbolically focusing on Santiago de Compostela has been adopted enthusiastically by the Galician government in its promotion of the region's identity and tourism industry (Figure 10.2). In this construct, the city, a European Capital of Culture for the Millennium, represents not Spain but the region.

However, such representations of regionalism may be largely symbolic, diagnostic of the fractured and fragmented nature of identity in Europe. As Agnew (1995) argues, regional identity in itself cannot be sufficient because the prospects for the local area are not decided at that scale. Ethno-

Figure 10.1   The medieval pilgrimage routes to Santiago de Compostela

nationalist movements such as those in Northern Italy, Catalonia and Euskadi are inevitably dragged into the political axis of the state as a whole and the greater EU; inevitably, the rhetoric of regionalism has wider connotations. What this suggests is that 'Europe of the regions' is no more valid a construct than 'Europe of the nation-states'. Instead, as we argued in Chapters 4 and 5, identity is becoming more diverse, no longer directly congruent with region or state. Each of these multiple layers of identity requires an intersecting and ultimately reconcilable heritage.

Consequently, if we accept that Europe does require a heritage of identity and legitimation to complement – and indeed validate – its role in economic and political decision-making, this is not to suggest that the function of such an iconography rests in the imposition of some contrived and spurious rendition of unity. Rather, a European heritage must accommodate a heterogeneity of place and a multicultural diversity of peoples and cultures. Indeed, it might even be located beyond the boundaries of the continent, an uncomfortable thought as the European Commission apparently seeks to construct

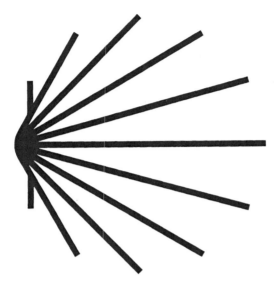

Figure 10.2   The contemporary *Camino de Santiago* route motif, symbolizing the roads of Europe focusing on the city and shrine of Santiago de Compostela

'Fortress Europe'. Preservable cases of a European heritage of architecture and urban design might include Boston as much as Bath, Santo Domingo as much as Seville and Québec City as much as Bordeaux. A European heritage has thus to recognize and reflect both this spatial dimension and also that the centrifugal mesh of nationalism and regionalism exists. It follows that multiculturalism provides the only viable basis for a cognate axis of European identity. However, it has also to be accepted that such diversity is not merely an issue of overlapping and competing layers of place and belonging but also includes the legacies of scattered minorities, misplaced peoples and misplaced heritages which, as we have discussed, contain the potential for conflict and atrocity. Thus, a European heritage should not exclude the 'non-European' located by historical circumstance within the continent, including the glories of the Arab legacy in Spain or Turkish heritage in Hungary. These are among the most important and interesting possibilities for shaping a multicultural heritage reflecting the heterogeneous societies of contemporary Europe.

What constitutes a European heritage?

In this context of multiple and overlapping sovereignties, in which the meaning of geographical space is becoming ever more contingent, the definition of Europe's heritage must embrace more than merely those built environments and human landscapes that occur within the continent's geographical limits.

It has to transcend the nation-state and region, yet respect their integrity, and it has to encompass diversity and multiculturalism within those states and across Europe. But what might constitute the content of such a heritage? There are two possible ways in which this might be defined.

The heritage of the idea of European unity

The origins, evolution and achievements of European economic and political union form a clearly definable and comprehensible narrative that directly meets the needs of popular identification of citizens as well as substantiating the legitimation of the existing institutions. It also directly confronts and subsumes the idea of national heritage, providing a clearly comprehensible goal and guide to the practical questions of content selection and interpretation. This narrative would culminate in the role of the EU and thus directly justifies its existence and pretension to power as almost historically inevitable.

There is, however, one practical but almost insurmountable difficulty. Very few resources, whether buildings, events or personalities from the European past, could be used to shape such a European heritage in competition with the resources available at the national level. The sacralized spaces of Brussel's decrepit Berlaymont complex, or the European Parliament in Strasbourg and the European pantheon – Monnet, Spaak, de Gasperi, Adenauer, Heath and the rest – would be the uninspiring raw materials available to shape a heritage in competition with the national and imperial capitals, collections, monuments and heroes. The summits and signings that mark critical moments, the politicians and administrators responsible for creating and fostering the European idea over the last 40 years, the buildings created to house them and the cities in which they are located, are unable to compete successfully in popular imaginations with the personalities, events and structures which underlie national – or even regional – heritage narratives.

The converse of the problem is that such a putative European heritage of integration would be further eclipsed by the quantitatively dominant heritage of atrocity, war and national consciousness in Europe that not only does not support interpretations of unity and a common Europeanness but actually flatly contradicts them. Even if the more amenable physical heritage artefacts of nation-state Europe were to be suborned to the European cause, having been re-equipped with suitably integrationist interpretations, an Orwellian rewriting of the nation-state past, the physical destruction or concealment of irreconcilable relics and the fostering of a 'collective amnesia' instead of collective memory – such as to some extent occurred in Eastern Europe after World War II – are beyond the powers of the European institutions, even if they were to envisage such an outcome. Policies of acceptance of national heritages, reinterpreted as either primitive precursors of the European idea or a warning against recidivist nationalism, rather than policies of conscious ignorance, would be easier but equally unlikely to succeed.

A unity of European ideas

A less drastic, more easily acceptable but equally less focused approach to heritage content would be to designate as European those ideas, aesthetic creations and activities that by their very nature were continental rather than national. Numerous architectural and artistic paradigms, political and economic movements, or scientific and technological developments suggest themselves as being intrinsically non-national and, although not necessarily specifically European either, could be visualized as common European creations or experiences. Many are safe (creating little dissonance), self-congratulatory (the consumer shares the achievement with the 'greats'), some are inclusive (disinheriting few excluded groups) and may even surmount the barriers of cultural and linguistic communication. In this respect conserved built environments and human landscapes – like music and dance – are in many ways ideal, being composed of internationally recognized forms, which are both an element in, and a stage for, wider cultural expressions, while acting as a primary resource for the major international heritage tourism industry.

Unfortunately, however, a definition of European heritage on these grounds is scarcely sufficiently rigorous or demanding to act as a means of empowerment for the European idea. First, the very embarrassment of riches provides little guidance for selection. Secondly, much of the interaction between Europeans that could form the basis for such themes is dissonant in some way or other to some Europeans. At its simplest the past is a contested resource and thus the recognition of any one claim upon it may disinherit others, sometimes with serious results. This is manifested in several serious ways in Europe. In the first instance, the nation-state is often perceived to be the outcome of a struggle for democratic freedom by a subordinated group demanding recognition. Such ideas are fundamental, for example, to Greek, Irish or Polish identity. Moreover, the region-states or even less overt expressions of separatist identity within the nation-states are equally defined by histories of subjugation and demands for freedom – Euskadi, Languedoc, Brittany, Scotland are but a few among many examples. Legacies of war and atrocity feature large in such identities – the Cathar repression in Languedoc, Cromwell in Ireland, Turkish atrocity in the Balkans, the destruction of Warsaw in 1944 – and in a wider sense, it has to be remembered that virtually all the states of Europe and their nationalist narratives were forged through war or in its outcome.

To return to the example of the medieval pilgrimage to Santiago de Compostela, medieval Europe's most popular saint (James) was characterized by an extraordinary duality of artistic iconography. On one hand, there was the humble *Sanctus Jacobus*, often depicted wearing the characteristic pilgrim garb of cloak and broad-brimmed hat, carrying a staff and adorned with the cockle-shell emblem of his pilgrimage. On the other, was the extraordinary representation of *Santiago Caballero* or *Santiago Matamoros* – St James the Moorslayer – riding a white charger through the skies above the *Reconquista* battlefields, wielding a bloody, dripping sword and surrounded by decapitated infidels, a potent iconography within a rendition of Spanish nationalism in which the state was forged in the gore of holy war and Castilian leadership (Graham and Murray 1997). To view several millennia of eventful European history as resulting only in High Gothic cathedrals, romantic castles, utopian Renaissance town planning, symphonic music and folk dancing is to raise modernist linear narratives of historic interpretation to new heights of complacent self-deception, which depict the steady progress of a perfectible humanity culminating in the best of all possible presents.

Instead, throughout Europe, evocatively dramatic memorializations of contested pasts are manifested in actual physical violence of battlefields, landscapes of death such as Verdun, Ieper, and the Somme, and in the landscapes of memory that cluster so thickly across the low-lying plains that extend through Belgium and eastern France towards Paris, in de Gaulle's words, 'the fatal avenue' in which 'we have just buried one-third of our youth'. But these do not necessarily negate the notion of Europeanness. Although few places on Earth have been fought over so continuously, one of the primary functions of European economic and political integration is to ensure that such carnage never again occurs. Thus the memorials, graves and battlefields of Picardy, the Chemin des Dames and Flanders – clearly national heritage – might also be construed as a heritage of European reconciliation, testimony to the unacceptable that must not be repeated.

However, the example of the battlefield at Waterloo (1815), ostensibly an ideal candidate for a heritage complex capable of European interpretation, demonstrates the practical limitations of reconciliation through the shared horrors of the past. In practical terms it was one of the last battles fought on a site small enough to be capable of being visually appreciated and understood on the ground: it involved troops from many countries and regions in what is now the EU: it was fought close to the present European 'capital' of Brussels: and the cause for which it was fought has now very little meaning for most visitors. It is thus a potentially ideal demonstration of the folly of warring nations and the wisdom of unity. In practice, however, this opportunity has so far been squandered. Official interpretation is military-technical, treating the battle as a strategic and tactical game, while most of the many museums and monuments are blatantly nationalist (commemorating for example the dashing élan of Marshal Ney and the 'Old Guard' or the steadfastness of the British infantry at Hougemont). The dominating mound and lion actually commemorates the somewhat undistinguished role of the Prince of Orange and was erected in an attempt to legitimate the short-lived Dutch annexation of Belgium. Most interpretation, however, is in the hands of private enterprises for whom the imperial glories of Napoleon or the military skills of Wellington make better marketable products for consumption by the large numbers of visitors than do casualty lists or sermons on the value of European political integration. Yet if Waterloo, its death and horror muted by time, cannot be used as quintessential European heritage, then what chance is there of exorcizing the more recent and bloody traumas of warring European nationalisms?

The question is, should the content of European heritage embrace the distasteful and the unacceptable? Do Srebrenica and Auschwitz qualify as well as Chartres cathedral, the Sistine Chapel or even the alien glories of the Alhambra Palace in Granada, albeit Europeanized by Falla's music and Lorca's poetry and plays? The memorable history of Europeans also embraces pogrom, persecution and prejudice, near continuous internecine war, oppression and genocide. Clearly, the Jewish Holocaust of 1933–45 remains pre-eminent, archetypically 'European' heritage and arguably the most serious heritage challenge facing contemporary European society in managing its past. European Jews – ironically the principal European people not nationally defined – were deported and murdered by Europeans in Europe in pursuit of a European ideology. The physical relics of *stetls* and camps remain throughout the continent, as do the memories of the victims, the perpetrators and the passive observers to haunt this and future generations of Europeans (Ashworth 1996). How would or even could a European heritage manage such a past? It is perhaps more comfortable to believe that a European heritage, which includes war and atrocity, commemorates only former divisions. But the past, no matter how awful, can still be seen as constructive if one of the functions of European unity is to prevent its re-occurrence. Thus, Europe's camps, graves, battlefields and memorials must constitute part of its heritage alongside the more acceptable and commodious icons that support our ethnocentric notions of European cultural hegemony and civilization.

Who can create and manage a European heritage?

At first glance, it might appear that many supra-national organizations might potentially be involved in European heritage: not only does much heritage obviously possess an international dimension, but despite the inhumanity of the continent's past, it is often seen as an easy and non-controversial manner of expressing internationalism, particularly if constructed as narratives of progressive perfectible humanity that gloss over – or absorb – the heritage of atrocity. Even then, however, closer examination does not suggest that this attention actually contributes over-much to a specifically European policy for a distinctively European heritage.

The European institution with the longest and deepest involvement in the heritage of the built environment in particular is not, as might be imagined, the EU but the Council of Europe. This continent-wide intergovernmental forum has long regarded culture in general, and the urban built environment in particular, as a major focus of its work. From the 1970s onwards, for example, it has publicized best-practice examples of planning historic cities in various countries with the implied intent, not so much of comparing European national practices, as using successful examples to stimulate the less active members. Equally promotional in its objective was the naming of years. 'European Conservation Year' (1970) was followed by arguably the most successful 'European Architectural Heritage Year' (1975), and subsequently by 'European Campaign for an Urban Renaissance' (1981) and 'European Year of the Environment (1989). These did provide national governments and agencies with an excuse and stimulant for increased heritage expenditure and raised the public profile of the topics. More recently the 'European City of Culture' designation has proved a similarly efficacious means of obtaining funds for cultural and tourism initiatives at the local city scale, although the meaning of the 'European' in the title remains vague and largely unexpressed (Boyle and Hughes 1991). In the latest initiative, to mark the Millennium, a number of cities (Avignon, Bergen, Bologna, Brussels, Kraków, Helsinki, Prague, Reykjavik and Santiago de Compostela) have been designated 'European Capitals of Culture'. Again, the European dimension is largely unexpressed as the various cities move to capitalize upon their self-promotion as cultural products. Although its activities have been predominantly urban, the Council of Europe has also been involved in other heritage initiatives, largely aimed at tourism promotion, albeit combined with truisms about European integration. In 1987, for example, it launched a cultural routes programme designed to celebrate the unity and diversity of European identity. The first of these itineraries was the pilgrim route – the *Camino* – to Santiago de Compostela, selected because its medieval predecessor has connected the remotest north-western corner of Galicia to all of Europe. On the strength of this, the Council was able to declare that the *Camino de Santiago*, lacking any apparent connotations of dissonance and contestation, symbolized attentiveness to others and a 'deeply felt commitment to the European experience' (Council of Europe 1989; Figures 10.1 and 10.3).

In some contrast, the EU (and, before Maastricht, the European Community) has taken only sporadic interest in the heritage of the built environment and even the few initiatives that can be discerned make no particular use of a distinctively European dimension. One difficulty is that the topic does not fit comfortably into the present structure of EU administration or decision-making. Responsibility for urban policy, for example, is split between DGXVI (Regional Policy) and DGXI (Environment); the former allocates subsidies supporting programmes that can be at the urban as well as regional scale, while the latter struggles to include the urban human environment within a natural environmental management brief. Other directorates, including DGXXIII (which is responsible for tourism), DGX (Culture) and DGXXII (Education), also cover various important uses of European heritage. Political responsibility is also divided between at least four of the 21 Commissioners' portfolios. This fragmented responsibility accounts in part, for example, for the failure of the arguments put forward by DGXI to have specific references to the historical role of European cities in nurturing a European civilization included in the Maastricht agreement (Williams 1996). In reality, European Commission concern with heritage amounts to no more than general exhortations that can be implemented only at the local scale through national conservation and physical planning systems. Thus, the

Figure 10.3   A Council of Europe route marker on the section of the *Camino de Santiago* west of Burgos

vision of European spatial patterns and policies published as *Europe 2000+* (CEC 1994) includes among its 11 focus topics, 'heritage preservation and conservation of historic areas'; such platitudes hardly amount to a distinctive European heritage policy in either content or method.

This discussion of the relative ineffectuality of official interventions into heritage at the European scale combines with two further important constraints on the development of a specifically European dimension to heritage. First, the dominant sphere of public sector intervention in the definition, preservation and presentation of heritage remains the national Member State governments and their agencies, operating in pursuit of notions of national heritage. Secondly, private commercial enterprises, which can loosely be bundled together as 'the heritage industry', play a major role in the presentation and use of the commodified past, including the use of heritage resources preserved and maintained by the public sector. Much of this heritage is part of a leisure industry that provides 'fun' experiences in response to a growing contemporary demand for the past as entertainment. Saleable products such as the 'the historic trail', pageant or *son et lumière* extend the highly marketable British 'Merrie England' approach to history to a 'Merrie Europe'. The point is not that this somehow constitutes a less valid (or worse less 'authentic') use of the past, these terms being quite meaningless when applied to heritage, but more simply that this is an alternative and competing economic use of the past to the political uses discussed here. Inescapably, however, what can be termed 'official public history' exists within this context of a history exploited as commercial entertainment.

Conclusion: towards a European heritage policy?

It is apparent that unavoidable dissonance exists between the various but simultaneously present scales, meanings and interpretations of heritage throughout Europe, and that within this heterogeneity of meaning and motivation the idea of a European heritage is poorly developed. But given the fragmentation of territoriality and sovereignty that is characteristic of the New Europe, it is important not to equate the creation of a European heritage with an all-encompassing, pervasive European identity. Rather, the function of a European heritage is to create a European dimension that can be added to already complex formulations and layerings of identity. It might embrace common principles such as the struggle for democratic and civil rights and the attendant sites of war and atrocity, common principles that can then be related to the specific differences of nation and region. Above all, therefore, a European heritage must be manipulated as a mosaic of similarity but also difference that reflects the political reality of overlapping layers of empowerment. It cannot comprise that which is common to all; as we have argued, this would result merely in an anaemic and sanitized heritage in which the hard questions posed by the past are obscured by superficial narratives of progression and European cultural hegemony.

The problem is that there is relatively little evidence of Europeans focusing on the meaning of Europe. One possible exception might be articulated through 'Europe of the cities' (the environment in which most Europeans live, work and recreate) but specifically the 'Europe of the historic cities'. If pressed to define the content of what is typically European as opposed to appertaining to some other continent, it is likely that images of Florence, Bath and Heidelberg, of *piazzas*, boulevards and buildings, would be evoked among many who do not live in these particular environments, cities or even countries. In these senses a European heritage already exists in the European imagination and is deliberately sought out and experienced by millions of tourists from this and other continents as well as willingly financed and defended from threat in well orchestrated campaigns to 'save our European heritage'.

More widely, however, Agnew (1996) argues that European places and states are defined through a process in which blocks of space become labelled with essential attributes derived from some 'Golden Age'. Europe, like the nation-states before it, needs to seize and define its own time–space block, which does not suborn national or regional heritage but complements these other scales in a postmodernistic diversity of plural identities and peoples which resist the political and commercial temptations that reduce heritage to insipid linear narratives. In other words, a European heritage has to portray dissonance and contestation as positive qualities, symbolic of the reality – to draw an analogy with Canada – that there is no one landscape or iconography that can encompass Europe's diversity. An ideal European heritage would thus not be symbolic of Europeanness subsuming national and regional identity but instead reflective of the complex dismantling of the synonymity of territoriality, sovereignty, nationalism and the state in the new Europe. It would embrace notions of multiculturalism and strive to be inclusive of all the continent's peoples, constructs ultimately necessary to validate and legitimate political and economic integration. It is unlikely that the only apparent present unifying principles, largely economic, will prove a sufficient cement. Nevertheless, as the study of multiculturalism in Chapter 5 indicated, the potential for dissonance is so great that the present *ad hoc* arrangements under which European heritage is organized and managed are unlikely to prove sufficient to this task. From this equivocal conclusion, we may approach the ultimate scale of heritage identity with considerable trepidation. The difficulties of establishing heritage identities above and below the incumbent national scales are clearly apparent.

|11|

Heritage and scale IV: towards a global heritage

Introduction

The concept of a common heritage of humanity has a universal appeal and seems to fit naturally with the development of global and other supranational institutions since World War II. The potential of such a common heritage lies primarily in its reinforcement of concepts of human equality, common destiny, shared stewardship of the earth, optimal use of scarce natural and cultural resources, and the consequent imperative of peaceful coexistence. It is an explicit challenge to chauvinistic extremism in the glorification of national heritages which have too often been harnessed to wider policies of national aggrandizement as an accessory to conflict and destruction. This continues to manifest itself (as in the former Yugoslavia) but its historical apogee was in Nazi Germany. It is thus appropriate that the global organization founded in the context of Nazi defeat, the United Nations – through its agency, UNESCO – should come to champion the concept of global heritage as an important adjunct to its development of other institutions fostering international security. This chapter begins with a discussion of the global management of heritage and examines the reasons why the continental heritage initiatives discussed in Chapter 10 should be consonant with and implicitly supportive of it. We analyse the case for a global heritage, before turning to a consideration of its limits and indeed its contestation. Finally, two case studies are used to discuss the problems and prospects of global heritage.

The assertion of the global claim

There is, as the preceding comments imply, a strongly felt need to believe in the existence of a world heritage as the common property of all peoples. Indeed the globalization of culture, economy and politics is an idea that is both more potent and has a longer history than many contemporary commentators allow. Moreover, it is notable that even when political or economic history has been portrayed in the context of the nation-state, culture has been described dominantly in terms of international movements, styles and trends (Graham and Nash 1999). Thus a widespread conviction exists that the wealth of millennia of human artistic productivity is the responsibility of the whole human community and should be freely available for the enrichment of all now and in perpetuity; equally, all should contribute to its protection and support. These global claims to heritage are reflected in the existence of international associations, pressure groups and intergovernmental organizations charged with designating, maintaining and promoting global heritage. UNESCO, for example, has extended its responsibilities to include both the preservation and stimulation of many aspects of culture, including conserved heritage, and also the means whereby such heritage is transmitted. Together with its subsidiary organizations such as ICO-MOS, it has produced ideal codes of practice, issued conventions on the protection of cultural property in times of war or disorder, and attempted to establish a body of international law about ownership of cultural properties and international trade in them. This global claim is sustained by three main arguments.

First, in terms of heritage production, political frontiers have been and remain highly permeable to aesthetic ideas and cultural movements. Even ethnic, social and linguistic divisions have offered fewer barriers to cultural than to most human activities. The nature of artistic expression itself, as well as the processes by which it is created, seem to favour a global approach. The hypothesis that artists, in whatever field, demonstrate a higher than average internationalism in their receptivity to ideas, functional networks and even personal migration behaviour, would be difficult to test statistically but seems to be supported by empirical evidence. Moreover, while the musical works of Tchaikovsky, Dvorak or Elgar, for example, may have originated in Russia, Bohemia and England, and certainly have been used in support of national or regional political identities, they are globally performed and appreciated both for their intrinsic worth and for the interest of their identity associations. Similarly, much of the conserved built environment is on free, permanent display, and needs no linguistic translation or expert interpretation. Thus it is directly intelligible to the consumer regardless of social or political allegiances (even though this may colour its meaning). Baroque architecture is fundamentally Baroque whether it is located in Kraków or Munich, Quito or Québec.

As explained in Chapter 9, conservationists have also tended to adopt standard approaches to heritage – the so-called 'heritagization' process, encouraged by the interchange of techniques, philosophies and 'best practice' examples. International financial and project development corporations use internationally trained personnel who interact through global networks. This reduces investment risks by reusing ideas and programmes that have proved successful elsewhere, and encourages the selection of the same design details such as materials, street furniture or signage, processes which both reflect an existing internationalism and also stimulate it further by producing – as with waterfront developments – a recognizable international heritage style.

Second, we can turn to the question of responsibility and action for heritage. The severe flooding in the Adriatic in 1966, which threatened the continued existence of the lagoon city of Venice, elicited a remarkable response (*see* Chapter 6). World concern about the future of 'its' heritage, even among people who themselves had not visited the city, was expressed in cash donations, offers of technical assistance and even volunteer labour. More than thirty years on, it can be concluded that this outpouring of global concern to 'Save Venice' had less direct impact than was then apparent. The protection of the heritage city would require such extensive control over the water in its surrounding lagoon that other functions of the region, especially navigation and industrial development, would suffer. Local economic concerns and political priorities were thus accorded primacy over international heritage priorities. In practice 'world heritage' is not protected by any world government but by sovereign national governments, and is managed by the local not the international community.

The particular example of Venice has been repeated both in that city itself and elsewhere, most notably in the simultaneous flooding of Florence by the River Arno, which destroyed or damaged a high proportion of the Renaissance art in the Uffizi Gallery. Even after the institution of the world heritage mechanisms discussed below, the Serb shelling of Dubrovnik in 1991 demonstrated that world concern over heritage is not readily translated into effective rescue action. This situation is manifested everywhere as international sentiment, and global financial and technical resources, may still prove all but powerless in the face of quite different local concerns. However, the world community continues to press its heritage claim, albeit sometimes quixotically given its jurisdictional weakness.

Finally, the global claim to heritage can be asserted from the perspective of the consumer. Visitors to museums, monuments, heritage sites and cities, and in addition the many more latent visitors who consume books and films about them, are demonstrating an active or optional claim upon them. If heritage is only definable (*see* Chapter 1) by and in the terms of the inheritor, then logically it is these consumers who are demonstrating the most compelling argument for inheritance. It can be argued that the inexorable growth of foreign tourism, and the importance of culture, heritage and art to that industry, is the most powerful expression of the existence of a common global heritage as the property of all peoples. Every international tourist is asserting the existence of a world heritage and the right of a global accessibility to it, as well as more mundanely selecting the content of that heritage and contributing to its support. This close symbiosis between heritage and tourism is not new. The desire to conserve and the desire to visit have always mutually stimulated the history of the heritage conservation movement in an inextricable relationship of cause and effect. Thus the eighteenth-century 'Grand Tour' of Northern

Europeans 'discovered' and consequently preserved the heritage of the classical Mediterranean world, which in turn became the main attraction for further visits.

The contestation of the global claim

Thus there is a strong case for asserting a global claim to heritage but it is not an uncontested one. Consideration of specific world heritage initiatives must be deferred until we have examined the several grounds for that contestation.

The problem of ownership

Any concept of a world heritage is challenged by the competition with other, more immediate, national and local scales of identity and meaning, which have been far more successful in colonizing the past than has the global. Faced with quite different national and local economic priorities, government procrastination and the sovereignty of the nation-state over 'its heritage', international sympathy, expertise and financial resources may be largely powerless to do more than renovate a few buildings. Moreover, in economic terms, heritage products can be regarded as 'superior goods', the consumption of which increases more than proportionately with income. Thus a concern for heritage does not develop unless other more pressing material needs have been met. A global heritage can only exist in a significant form when it is globally valued to the same extent, and that will not occur until the unlikely event of consumption priorities being similar throughout the world. Thus equality of valuation of heritage presupposes other more fundamental equities such as those of economic welfare. Consequently, given the extent of contemporary global inequalities, global heritage, including that located in regions in which heritage is not accorded a high priority, is in practice defined by the citizens of the wealthier regions rather than by indigenous peoples.

Apart from variations in economic well-being, the simple proposition that local inhabitants value heritage differently from outsiders means that fundamental distinctions exist between global and local claims on the past. Although conflict between these claims on heritage is by no means inevitable, the potential for such discord always exists. It is usually focused on the contestation of heritage between tourism and its role in the shaping of identities. Tourists are characteristically in search of 'their' heritage, those past associations in a particular place that they can recognize as relating to them, and which can be incorporated into their existing heritage constructs. They are not seeking the heritage of the indigenous population, defined as the pasts required by local identity needs. These are largely irrelevant to tourists and possibly even hostile – as, for example, in postcolonial contexts. Consequently, global heritage and its expression in global tourism conflicts with the views that the primacy of the local ownership of heritage is axiomatic, and that local authenticity and identity should take precedence over global recognition and identity. As in many museums, this localization of heritage elicits policies of local empowerment, which are seen as ripostes to the previous policies of the 'colonization' of local cultures (*see* Chapter 8). In this perspective, heritage is returned to local people and housed, cared for and interpreted by them. For example, the U'Mista Cultural Centre in Alert Bay, B.C., Canada, contains ceremonial 'potlatch' artefacts, which have been returned by national and provincial governments to the control of the local indigenous people. Ultimately, and this problem has arisen, such local communities could also dispose of heritage as being 'theirs to destroy', not 'ours to conserve'.

Consequently, it would seem that the globalization of heritage is to be resisted if heritage, and specifically that of the conserved built environment, is to be consciously used as an instrument for asserting the unique identities of places. We have noted, however, that global and local heritage perspectives are not inevitably in conflict. There may be consensus that the locally unique is of global stature and possesses a global market, the satisfaction of which confers significant economic advantages to the locality. Again, as in the case of some colonized local cultures – for example, that of the Australian Aborigines – a site or artefact may be interpreted as a specific occurrence of a world-wide revision of heritage meaning, which the global heritage claim may be persuaded to accept.

Nevertheless, a concept of *Mundus Nostra* as a global parallel to the idea of *Europa Nostra* (coined in 1963 in reference to a European conservation trust) will not just come into existence. Rather it must be created, and there should be no illusions about the difficulty of that task. As encapsulated in the concept of dissonance, all heritage by being someone's, must disinherit someone else. Thus a world heritage cannot be a mere summation of local and national heritages but becomes a denial of them, unless the other scales are adjusted to accept global values. If tourism is everywhere the enemy of authenticity and cultural identity (Turner and Ash 1976; Urry 1990), then it is part of a heritage problem and not a legitimate instrument for asserting the existence of a global heritage. Heritage is simply an assertion of ownership of the past and until that ownership can be collectivized on a world scale, rather than nationalized, localized or individualized, then heritage will more usually be a cause of national and local conflict than of global reconciliation.

The inherent limits of the global claim

Despite the potential of a common heritage in the harmonization of human and environmental relationships, and the steps taken internationally to promote it, further obstacles exist to its realization. Perhaps the most fundamental is the elastic nature and ever-expanding portfolio of heritage, characteristics often driven by economic priorities. These do not negate the possibility of a critical core of universally significant heritage, but certainly complicate its recognition. Furthermore, the innate dissonance of heritage between nations, produced by their rival interpretations of heritage, may actually be growing, given the resurgence of nationalist and ethnic identities and the continuation of mutual heritage destruction (Johnson 1995b). The Blue Shield initiative organized by ICOMOS is designed to deal with natural and human disasters to heritage sites and to ward off the particularly negative threat of war. In view, however, of the tempting military target presented by someone else's globally significant heritage, it is premature to envisage its success (Bumbaru 1992). Even the Member States of the EU have yet to harmonize discordant visions of, and education about, their inherited pasts.

The definition and recognition of global heritage poses a further set of difficulties. First, different cultures have divergent ideas as to how old, or how symbolic, the fabric of built heritage must be in order to be of world class. Second, the recognition of world heritage can lead, paradoxically, to its nationalistic appropriation by the possessor state for reasons both of political legitimation and economic gain. Third, the principle of respect for the sovereignty of nation-states endures. UNESCO is an intergovernmental forum and its instruments provide the world community with no independent means of intervention into the physical management, accessibility provision, political presentation or economic use of recognized global heritage. Nevertheless, especially where religion is involved, some states – as exemplified by Israel over the case of Jerusalem – have been reticent in according their heritage global stature in order to avoid world scrutiny or claim. National sovereignty can thus limit global heritage recognition, while division and transfers of sovereignty, both between and within federal states, create further difficulties.

The formal recognition of global heritage

Although few, if any, of the problems detailed above are insuperable, they do currently place serious limits on the rational development of global heritage. The genesis of international heritage action can be traced to the growing awareness of technological impacts on environment during the 1960s (Pocock 1997). UNESCO led three major and internationally publicized rescue initiatives: the relocation of the Nubian sculptures to escape the Nile waters rising behind Egypt's Aswan Dam – a national economic priority; restoration of Florence after the 1966 floods; and efforts to combat the recurrent winter flooding of Venice (UNESCO 1970). By the 1970s, growing environmental concern was expressed in the UN's Environment Programme, UNESCO's Man and Biosphere Programme and in a global discourse on national parks. These initiatives all favoured a world convention, leading to the 1972 UNESCO Convention for the Protection of the World's Cultural and Natural Heritage. This set up a non-governmental World Heritage Committee (WHC), charged with producing a World Heritage List of properties of 'outstanding universal value' from nominations brought forward by individual states, which had ratified the Convention and had, ostensibly at least, ensured the legal and management protection of the properties concerned. Cultural sites were to be assessed by ICOMOS (International Council on Monuments and Sites) and natural sites by IUCN (International Union for Conservation of Nature and Natural Resources). Pocock (1997) discusses the criteria for this dichotomy, the artificiality of which was quickly apparent and later more fully recognized. The WHC was also mandated: to produce a List of World Heritage in Danger in order to facilitate emergency assistance; to administer a World Heritage Fund in part to help needy signatory states protect their World Heritage Sites; and later to monitor the conservation of designated properties. The emergency role has recently been supplemented by World Monuments Watch, an annual list of the world's 100 most endangered cultural and historic sites, selected with respect to their wider significance (Heritage Canada 1996).

During their first twenty years, these mechanisms produced a steady growth of sites with a newly institutionalized global heritage profile and prestige. In 1994, however, a report to the WHC argued that designated world cultural heritage was biased in favour of Europe, historic towns, religious buildings and Christianity and against prehistory, the twentieth century, vernacular artefacts, and living traditional cultures. Pocock (1997) also notes that the material emphasis of recognized cultural heritage discriminated against essentially non-material societies. Thus sites in New Zealand and Australia such as Ayers Rock, hitherto designated as natural, have been reinterpreted to recognize their cultural landscape significance to, and actively involve, the Aboriginal peoples. Currently, a more general effort seeks to boost the World Heritage representation of relatively non-material cultures, most notably in Africa. Apart from these moves to redress imbalances, the numerical growth of sites has also prompted a shift of emphasis from uniqueness of heritage to its wider representativeness. Considering both global balance and numerical growth of sites, the WHC has requested the more advanced countries to slow down their rate of nomination (Pocock 1997).

Recent contention has focused upon the operational criteria of heritage artefacts and their authenticity, and the inconsistencies in interpretation, which have contributed to an imbalance problem. For example, rigid notions of the arbitrary concept of heritage authenticity (Ashworth and Tunbridge 1990) long precluded recognition of ancient Japanese temples subject to periodic rebuilding. Conversely, the central square of old Warsaw has been recognized despite its post-1945 reconstruction. Such inconsistencies have led the WHC to broaden its vision in keeping with evolving conservation theory and political reality, thereby accepting cultural relativism and decentralized regional decision-making. The management of cultural resources has expanded progressively beyond monuments alone to include industrial archaeology, modern architecture and much else. These trends are opposed, however, by (largely Eurocentric) critics, who argue that the equity of distribution between countries, continents and power blocks is overriding considerations of the 'intrinsic' value of a candidate World Heritage Site.

Contradictions persist in the application of the World Heritage Convention between state sovereignty and international interests, preservation and the increase of tourism and broadening the representation of the World Heritage List while maintaining its credibility. Nevertheless, the List continues to grow. This could undoubtedly be interpreted as an unseemly, even cynical, jockeying for comparative advantage in national prestige and tourism revenue, which often involves expedient political compromises. Given this, however, the World Heritage List has given a profile and a momentum to the idea of global heritage where none existed thirty years ago. Global declarations and mechanisms have provided standards to encourage best practice and access to a world reserve of technical and professional expertise. Furthermore, an ongoing debate is engaging with the meaning and potential achievements of world heritage.

As of 1997, 469 World Heritage Sites had been listed by UNESCO. These cover an immense diversity of natural and cultural phenomena. They range in scale and type from the Great Barrier Reef in Queensland, Australia, to the Giant's Causeway in Northern Ireland and Ironbridge Gorge, the hearth of early industry in Shropshire, England. San'a in Yemen and Fès El Bali in Morocco are among the first designated Third World cities, recognized for the integrity but vulnerability of their walled *medinas* (*see* Chapter 9). Canadian World Heritage Sites, which may fulfil a developmental role in remote locations, include: archaeological sites such as the Viking remains at L'Anse aux Meadows, Newfoundland; wilderness national parks including Gros Morne, Newfoundland and Banff in the Rocky Mountains; and urban examples ranging from Québec City (see below) to the much smaller Lunenburg in Nova Scotia.

World Heritage Sites: Robben Island and Québec City

Despite all the difficulties, contradictions and contestations, UNESCO's World Heritage Sites constitute the pinnacle of contemporary efforts to institutionalize the concept of a common global heritage for all the diverse manifestations of humanity and identity. This recognition endows the heritage artefact's home state with political and economic benefits without, however, an enforceable commensurate obligation to manage the Site in a manner consistent with the international interest. The designation can be withdrawn, but short of this politically very contentious step, it is effectively impossible to challenge development control, interpretation or obstacles to access to World Heritage Sites, be they physical or political. In order to explore these contradictions more fully, we use two case studies, Robben Island, South Africa and Québec City, Canada, both of which raise a set of significant questions concerning world heritage.

- What confers credible global significance on a heritage resource?
- Whose heritage, particularly how large a proportion of humanity, can it be considered to represent?
- How can it be conserved, managed and presented to sustain not only the resource itself, and any other scale interpretations placed upon it, but also its global significance?

Robben Island

As a contender for World Heritage Site status (1998), Robben Island, South Africa, illustrates the complexity of these questions. A windswept 474-hectare island in Table Bay, located 11 km off Cape Town, it has achieved world attention because of its use as a prison to incarcerate opponents of the former apartheid state (Figure 11.1). The particular signification, if not sacralization of Robben Island, derives from the eighteen-year imprisonment there of Nelson Mandela, leader of the African National Congress, first postapartheid South African president, and leading international statesman. His writings (Mandela 1994) and global stature as a champion of human rights have inevitably driven the agenda for consideration of the island's heritage significance.

The question 'what heritage?' is, however, very much more complex. The exploitation of the island's marine and other resources – notably seals and whales, previously lightly used by the Aboriginal Khoi population, began with Portuguese, English and Dutch explorers in the sixteenth century (Smith 1997). The subsequent Dutch settlement at the Cape (1652) led to quarrying on Robben Island for construction materials, and to its use as a 'pantry' for food supplies safe from depredation by the mainland native population. Centuries of further exploitation have transformed the natural environment, the present woodland consisting of exotic imports, which distort the original identity, but have provided a refuge for bird colonies. While this leads to dilemmas as to what constitutes 'natural' heritage, significant because the island includes a nature reserve and accommodates endangered species, it is the cultural heritage that is more important to the case for world heritage status. This latter is inseparable from European global imperial expansion. The early resource exploiters were followed mainly by the victims of banishment, who could be kept in conditions unseen by the outside world, and their keepers (Smith 1997). These victims included seventeenth-century rebels from the Dutch East Indies as well as Khosa chiefs imprisoned by the British following the Cape Colony frontier wars of the 1830s (Lester 1999a and b). To these early political prisoners were later added 'lunatics' and lepers. The most recent imperial heritage is provided by the remains of the World War II sea defences guarding the approaches to Cape Town. Since then, the maximum security prison, which held the opponents of apartheid, was constructed by 1964. The settlement structures of this history of banishment possess their own heritage attributes, colonial architecture, cemeteries and other elements

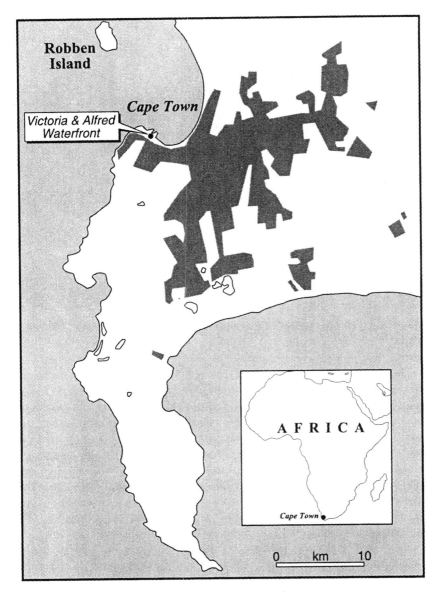

Figure 11.1　The location of Robben Island, South Africa

constituting a cohesive and intact resource undisturbed by Cape Town's redevelopment pressures (Figure 11.2).

The question, 'whose heritage?', is only partially implicit in the above. It is not difficult to show that Robben Island constitutes the heritage of all South Africans, whether directly implicated or not, and is centrally relevant to the present nation-building agenda. In substance and mythology, its historical

Figure 11.2 Robben Island: nineteenth-century colonial government buildings, restored in the 1990s

role both predates and meshes with the development of the Cape Colony through Dutch and British periods. It has since become the repository of apartheid and simultaneously symbolic of the whole country as a greater prison during that era. The presence on the island of a prominent Muslim shrine to an East Indian prince imprisoned there by the Dutch, also accords with South Africa's new multiculturalism. Indeed Robben Island is more clearly seen as a mirror of the larger state than as an adjunct of Cape Town, from which it was deliberately distanced. Beyond South Africa, it is also possible to link Robben Island with other countries, particularly Britain and The Netherlands, the Cape being an imperial provisioning stop en route to the east and thus a fulcrum in social, economic and environmental dealings between the 'mother countries' and their colonies. How far is its heritage theirs, and what does it say about them? The global identity of Robben Island is compounded by its strategic role in the defence of Cape Town during World War II, which left familiar heritage artefacts, albeit ones with sharply varying meaning among South Africans.

The question of how to conserve, manage and present Robben Island is problematical for South Africa. The debate is dominated by issues of physical maintenance and the ways in which the island is presented to South Africans and foreign visitors. There are three contending perspectives: environmental; tourist-commercial; and political. The first seeks restoration of a human–natural harmony from centuries of physical and symbolic abuse; the second to capitalize on an oceanfront heritage windfall; and the third to use the resource as flagship heritage in the forging of national identity and, beyond this, international recognition. Strong controls on disturbance and removal favour the environmental over the commercial, but do not guarantee a sometimes fragile resource against attrition by the rapid growth in the South African tourism industry. Even though access from Cape Town is controlled by limited sailings, the trip from the city's Victoria and Alfred Waterfront has become a high-profile attraction in what is already the prime regional tourist-historic magnet (Worden 1996, 1997). World Heritage Site status will inevitably increase tourism, an economic bonus which postapartheid South Africa cannot afford to discourage. Beyond resource conservation and management looms the problem of how to present the heritage both nationally and internationally, while serving national reconciliation but also promoting global significance. The potential dissonance can be moderated by management, although the demands of national reconciliation require a delicacy of inclusion and interpretation yet to be refined, if all South African stakeholders are to live with the meaning of Robben Island and, following centuries of division, accept its collective interpretation as a prime heritage stepping-stone towards a shared national identity. The critical and essentially non-negotiable heritage focus, which, it is hoped, will address both national and global scales, concerns human rights and democratic values.

Robben Island is now interpreted in the official publicity material as a place of historic victory of the human spirit over the denial of civil rights, a denial which must now be demonstrably corrected in pursuit of a new primacy of the democratic principles and values which were nurtured there and which became the sustaining myth in the liberation struggle. Attending Robben Island's proclamation as a National Monument and Museum, on South Africa's Heritage Day 1997, President Mandela summarized the new heritage imperative thus:

> . . . we will together find a way to combine the many dimensions of the island, and . . . we will do so in a manner that recognizes above all its pre-eminent character as a symbol of the victory of the human spirit over political oppression; and of reconciliation over enforced division. In this way we will help strengthen the ethos of heritage as a binding force . . .
>
> (Mandela 1997, pp. 4–5)

A pivotal contribution to reconciliation lies in the interpretation of the Afrikaner apartheid warders not as perpetrators of oppression but as co-victims, marginalized in a hardship posting and kept in ignorance of the true nature of the liberation struggle until taught by the prisoners themselves. This teaching role, as educated prisoners taught each other and their warders, means that the island is now interpreted as an 'open university' and no less than the cradle of South African democracy (Mandela 1994; Figure 11.3).

Figure 11.3 Robben Island: former prison courtyard, showing the windows of the cells which housed Nelson Mandela and his ANC colleagues

The concept of an ideal, such as human rights and democratic values, constituting the focus of a national (let alone world) heritage site may appear strange. To grasp the overriding political significance of such heritage in South Africa, it is necessary to understand the urgency and difficulty of nation-building in a multicultural society in which, uniquely, the former white rulers now constitute a proportion of fellow citizens equivalent to that of the black population in the United States (albeit generally much more economically powerful). It would be wrong, however, to regard this human rights heritage issue as a South African aberration. As the US analogy implies (*see* Chapter 5), many of the most advanced democracies are struggling with multicultural civic, as against ethnic, nation-building in which the protection of human rights has become critically important. The enshrinement of these values in heritage icons is a vital step in securing collective respect for them over time. The proposal to make Robben Island a World Heritage Site has thus significant resonances for the international community, increasingly so as more states grapple with the integration of exotic migrant minorities. In this regard it is highly significant that President Mandela's farewell visit to Canada (September 1998) gave priority to unveiling a plaque to the 1948 Universal Declaration of Human Rights, at the Canadian Tribute to Human Rights in Ottawa. This political use of heritage reflects a larger global imperative, which gives credibility to the projection of Robben Island as a World Heritage Site, primarily in terms of a global shrine to the triumph of the human spirit in enduring oppression and to the ultimate victory of human rights.

Québec City

Québec City, declared a World Heritage Site in 1984, is a fundamentally different example of the challenges imposed by this designation. As a city with a population in excess of 650 000 and a provincial capital in an advanced western democracy, Québec contrasts markedly with an isolated rural periphery such as Robben Island. Its management problems have.to do with urban development pressures and a potential divergence of official interpretation between its own provincial jurisdiction and the Canadian federal authority (Tunbridge and Ashworth 1996).

The basis for Québec's designation as a World Heritage Site lies in its status as the only remaining walled city in North America, the product of a synthesis between different cultures, and the hearth of French civilization on the continent (Figure 11.4). The designated area includes the environs of the walled city, founded in 1608, which now forms a small part of the metropolis. Within this area, the walled *haute ville* stands on a bluff above the St Lawrence River, with the original settlement, the *basse ville,* by the waterfront below (Figure 11.5). The former developed as the main centre of administration and urban life, while the latter fulfilled its mercantile role.

Notwithstanding this defensible site, Québec fell to the British following the Battle of the Plains of Abraham in 1759, an event which proved decisive to Canadian development in that it established British hegemony while absorbing a major francophone component in what became the province of Québec. As this population's linguistic and other cultural rights were later to be guaranteed, the pre-1759 French identity was not lost but rather increasingly modified by the British hegemony. This became more apparent in the *basse ville* as the mercantile function was reoriented to the needs of the British Empire and taken over by British entrepreneurs, while the waterfront and its structures were reshaped accordingly over time.

In the *haute ville,* the overlay of Britishness was more subtle as there was less displacement of function and identity. Moreover, the British minority often chose to redevelop in harmony with the existing French style. The most striking illustration of this is the Château Frontenac, built in the 1890s by railway interests of British origin as a tourism facility, but which has acquired a strategic, and ostensibly French, heritage identity dominating the skyline of the *haute ville.* The original city walls were reconstructed by the British with an eye to US aggression, and were furthermore preserved in the late nineteenth century at the behest of the British Governor-General of that time (Figure 11.6). Once anchored defensively by the Citadel fortress, their later aesthetic value was extended by the construction of Dufferin Terrace, above the St Lawrence, during the British period, when the port of Québec became a gateway of access for diverse immigrant populations, many of whom remained in the city. Following the Great Famine of the 1840s, they included a substantial Irish component who, for religious and class reasons, largely assimilated with the French population. Some cultural diversification

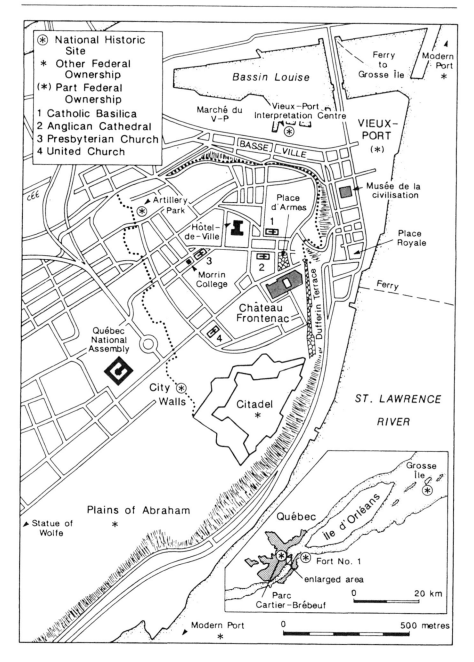

Figure 11.4   Québec City

Figure 11.5   Québec City: the *basse ville* with the *haute ville* above, showing the Citadel (left) and the Château Frontenac (right)

Figure 11.6   Québec City: the city wall with part of the *haute ville* to the left

continued in the twentieth century, although less so since Québec's gateway function has declined relative to Montréal, while the population of British descent fell sharply after 1950.

From this outline of the heritage resource, it is clear that the question of whose heritage must receive a composite answer. Unsurprisingly, the native American population is scarcely represented in the urban built environment, but has an underlying claim to heritage recognition. Recent immigrant minorities also have a modest claim. The essential dialogue, however, is between the French tradition, which has primacy in respect of most of the older buildings generally considered to be heritage landmarks (mostly religious and residential), and the British, which added much and repackaged the whole. This latter identity was often understated by continued reference to the pre-existing imagery. The battlefield of the Plains of Abraham is by definition shared, but highly susceptible to hypersensitive divergences of interpretation. In its finer detail, the streetscape iconography presents a confusion of contradictory heritage messages ranging primarily between high imperial British and recent French Québecois nationalist (Tunbridge and Ashworth 1996). That the population is now over 90 per cent francophone raises questions of the risk of disinheritance of the non-French in general and the British in particular.

The maintenance and presentation of Québec City's heritage is a very old issue, even by European standards. Concern for its conservation and tourism promotion was fostered during the Victorian period. The British role was inherited by the Canadian federal government in the late nineteenth century; in terms of major present-day heritage, this involved the military acquisition of the walls and the Citadel (which remains an official residence of the Canadian Governor-General) and the creation of a National Battlefields Commission to manage the Plains of Abraham. The national parks authority, now Parks Canada, acquired a major role in the late twentieth century as custodian of the federal presence and perspective in heritage issues, including direct control of several National Historic Sites (NHS). The federal perspective is a holistic interpretation of the city's heritage in keeping with its national, and now designated global, significance. This entails sustaining the British contribution along with that of smaller minorities, and the presentation of its message in both official languages, English and French. Recent initiatives have focused first upon the revitalization of the old port, in which an interpretation centre relates the diverse immigrant experiences of the British Imperial Period. Again, the Grosse Ile NHS in the St Lawrence chiefly commemorates the Irish immigrants who fled the Famine of the 1840s, but died of fever on the emigrant ships and were buried at this former quarantine centre.

The provincial perspective, however, potentially conflicts with this federal representation of heritage. The city is dependent on the provincial government of Québec, which has jurisdiction over the great majority of the land and thus the heritage resource. Provincial agencies protect heritage of different cultural origins and in practice much professional and considerable political co-operation exists between the levels of governance, which, together with the private sector, have a shared interest in the sustenance and integrated marketing of one of Canada's leading tourism attractions. However, French cultural hegemony within the province has created tensions of heritage identity and interpretation, which may ultimately compromise the city's world heritage status.

Since World War II, Québec has experienced a 'quiet revolution' in which its former dominantly rural Catholic introspection has been replaced by a secular, urbanizing society seeking a secure and distinct identity within or, if necessary, outside Canada. Federal efforts to accommodate this newly assertive nationalism have subsequently been compromised by nation-wide efforts to accommodate the wider multicultural diversity of Canada (*see* Chapter 5). Language is at the heart of Québecois *survivance*. Despite massive financial investment, the failure of the federal government's attempts to create national bilingualism led to a unilingual French policy in the province of Québec during the 1970s. This was applied to the streetscape, for example, in the form of signage control, meaning that a patina of French cultural identity was indiscriminately superimposed upon the built environment.

As the centre of provincial decision-making, Québec City has been at the heart of these processes, which have tended repeatedly to disadvantage non-French identities. In the 1960s, the battlefield statue of the ill-fated British victor of 1759, General James Wolfe, was blown up (although later rebuilt) and that of Queen Victoria became a museum piece. While no similar post-colonial identity removals have occurred, the province's restoration of Place Royale in the *basse ville* during the 1970s selectively recovered the early French identity from the British mercantile overlays, thereby reclaiming the first settlement nucleus at the cost of disinheritance of subsequent identities. The Québec Museum of Civilization, which was built nearby, fundamentally reinforced French associations through its initially unilingual presentation. These provincial initiatives have often been sharply discordant in architecture and message from the adjacent old port waterfront revitalization initiated by federal agencies. Meanwhile, the outmigration of the British population has rendered many of its institutions redundant, so that with no ill intent the heritage symbolism of Protestant churches, for example, has become diluted and marginalized. The election of expressly separatist provincial governments has given a sharper edge to French hegemonic tendencies, while the continuing threat of Québecois independence is destabilizing to any multi-scale reconciliation in heritage presentation, not least because this would remove all federal moderation. Should independence ever occur, it is difficult to see how Québec City could continue to be presented as a composite heritage, even given the will to do so, for this would challenge the fundamentally monocultural *raison d'être* of a sovereign Québecois state (Salée 1994). Furthermore, proponents of separation claim that it would produce a development boom for new embassies and other direct and indirect trappings of statehood. Fulfilment of that aspiration could well revive the development-control threat to world heritage status that was noted in the 1980s (Dalibard 1988).

In this line of reasoning, the unveiling in 1997 of a statue of General Charles de Gaulle, overlooking the Plains of Abraham, on the thirtieth anniversary of his nationalistic proclamation, '*Vive le Québec libre!*', casts a clear shadow on the city's world heritage designation. Conversely, the subsequent unveiling of a monument to the Québec Conferences, held during World War II, spoke directly to this scale. However, the historically correct exclusion of Canadian Prime Minister Mackenzie King from the depiction of Roosevelt and Churchill led to widespread accusations in Canada that the real purpose of the monument was to slight the nation, which perceives itself as having found its global identity in the trials of that time. The imperative of the tourism economy, however, often constrains the excesses of dissonant heritage interpretation and might arguably keep Québec City 'globally honest' in the interest of prosperity. Certainly the unilingual French policy has harmed heritage comprehension by a predominantly English-speaking (largely US) tourism market, so much so that tourism authorities have been at pains to produce literature and audio-visual material to compensate for the illegibility of the streetscape. On the other hand, the 'French' quaintness of the city is likely to be accentuated by this illegibility in the minds of tourists, most of whom have little idea that this was once a bicultural environment. It is by no means clear, therefore, that tourism can prevent a move or a drift into French hegemonic nationalist identity that would belie the city's status of World Heritage Site.

Conclusion: from despair to hope?

These two very different examples illustrate the complexity of decision and contention that is likely to surround the determination of heritage at the scale of global aspiration and designation. Moreover, the discussion has emphasized how the international dimensions of heritage reinforce the tension between the other heritage scales which emerged in the preceding chapters. In particular, higher scales, like lower, are often dissonant with respect to the dominant national scale of heritage identity. This tension, however, may also exist multilaterally. As we explored in Chapters 4 and 5, the regional may very well confront the continental as well as the national, although equally the regional and continental may dovetail in mutual dissonance from the national that divides them.

In terms of the international scales of heritage, the continental and global are not necessarily in mutual consonance. In Chapter 10 we suggested that Europe has both a responsibility and an opportunity to reconcile its own continentalism, evolving, albeit with difficulty, into global heritage identities. But it cannot be assumed that a Eurocentric continental-global rationalization of heritage would be acceptable in other continents, whether its overtones are imperialistic or the reverse imperialism of the 1990s *mea culpa* over Europe's historical global role. For example, it is not difficult to envisage African or even North American dissonance over continental–global harmonizations of the heritage of slavery, which might emanate from any potential European vision. Again, the lingering tensions over Eurocentric definitional criteria for World Heritage Sites demonstrate the risks of seeking a consonance of continental and global heritage scales in terms which conform to European perspectives.

The concept of world heritage is particularly appropriate for the recognition of themes regarded as significant to humanity as a whole. However, these inevitably invite dissonance in ideological as well as scale terms, in respect both to their legitimacy and to their geography of commemoration. The themes of genocidal atrocity, slavery and human rights, which clearly contain the potential for amalgamation into a multi-site global megatheme, are closely and controversially implicated in existing, proposed or potential World Heritage Site designations. Particular sites can offer locations which might prove universally credible – as Robben Island could for human rights, Auschwitz for genocidal atrocity and Goree in Senegal for slavery. None of these places, however, can provide interpretative unanimity or locational monopoly. The geographical problems of commemoration include the ultimate aspatiality of any such theme and the multiple and competitive locations of its key events. Often by design, these latter are remote from the main population centres now intended to associate with and consume the heritage. The problems are illustrated by UNESCO's diffidence over South Africa's attempt (for domestic political and tourist-economic reasons) to exploit its international African 'Slave Route' initiative. Slavery was certainly practised in South Africa but its connection with the pivotal transatlantic slave trade is more emotive and expedient than historically accurate (Worden 1996).

This chapter has argued that heritage is closely linked to places and is used as a means of identification of people with spatial entities. It may appear that the questions about the 'correct' spatial scale, or ownership, are either unanswerable, or at best susceptible to too many conflicting answers. Indeed this is often the case but it should be stressed that heritage is mobile, highly flexible, reproducible and malleable in that it can be interpreted in many different ways for numerous and even conflicting purposes, sequentially or even simultaneously. There is usually no difficulty about the same building, for example, fulfilling the identification needs of different people or different scales. Globalism, nationalism, ethnocentrism and localism can in many cases be reconciled once the problems are recognized and mutual claims respected. Moreover, the technologies of conservation, reproduction and interpretation can bring objects and artefacts closer to those who wish to experience them, so that the distinction between reality and virtual reality is becoming less discernible.

Conclusion: towards an integrated geography of heritage

The way in which heritage has been defined and analysed in this book places a premium upon meaning and its contestation. If heritage is the contemporary use of the past and is defined and constructed through present circumstances, then, because those are not agreed, heritage itself cannot be otherwise. It is the often conflicting meanings, combined with the multi-use and multi-consumption of heritage, which makes any attempt at synthesis so complex and prone to constant qualification. The simple circuit model outlined in the Introduction (Figure I.1) conceals a plethora of difficulties and complications in realizing a geography of heritage.

We make no claims that the book represents a definitive attempt at this goal. Rather it is an interim account, an initial attempt to bring together the many domains of heritage into a single coherent analysis centred ultimately on place. At the outset, we identified three dimensions along which heritage and geography intersect:

- heritage is inherently a spatial phenomenon, characterized by location, distribution and scale;
- it is a fundamental part of cultural geography's concern with signification, representation and identity;
- heritage is an economic instrument in policies of regional and urban development and regeneration.

The key point, which has emerged from our analysis, however, is that these dimensions are not in themselves mutually compatible, a conclusion which is central to any agenda of further research. We can summarize this issue through the medium of the book's three underlying themes.

The themes revisited

The plurality of use and consumption of heritage

To put it very simply, heritage remains a critical component in the construction of identity at a variety of scales and across a number of social axes, while, simultaneously, it is a ubiquitous economic good, sold without compunction by an increasingly globalized tourism industry that cares little for its socio-political role. Within both those broad realms of use, the production, use and consumption of heritage is segmented into a multiplicity of niches. It is this characteristic which produces the plethora of potentially contested, or at least irreconcilable, messages conveyed by any occurrence of heritage. As we have argued, dissonance is intrinsic to all heritage and while this does not necessarily spill over into actual conflict, it sometimes does. That dissonance is created both by the hybridity of heritage itself, and by the array of demands placed upon it.

In terms of the socio-political uses of heritage, we have argued for the continuing importance of representations of place in the construction of identity. Our analysis provides little evidence that the emergence of increasingly hybrid societies and 'time–space' compression has undermined the importance of place in determining the meaning of belonging. What it does show, however, is that the relationship between place and identity has become very much more complex, although we must be careful not to over-estimate its uniformity in the past. The analysis here also points to the limitations of multiculturalism, when it is operationalized in societies rather than treated as a theoretical discourse. The overt attempt to create multicultural representations of societies can itself be a potent source of dissonance as new patterns of disinheritance of heritage can emerge. Multiculturalism is not necessarily progressive, for, as Friedman (1997) argues, it can be seen to represent an abandonment of modernist ideas of assimilation. Meanwhile, existing identities resist such attempts at hybridization because these are interpreted as a threat to their continued existence. Clearly, these resistances constitute a research priority, particularly in deeply divided societies, which have little choice but to embrace a parity of esteem for all their component cultures if conflict is to be contained. In essence, multiculturalism seems more likely to be defined as a mutual respect for multiple cultures in any one society, rather than the integration of those identities into a new composite culture. There is little evidence of this occurring beyond the relatively superficial broadening, for example, of patterns of consumption.

The economic uses of heritage are often ignored in the literature, being regarded as somehow inferior to the cultural domain. This book represents one of the very few attempts to actually interpret heritage in strictly economic terms. As we have shown, there is an economics of heritage and heritage can also be located in economics. The key issues, which are less than transparent, include the effectiveness of heritage as a means of regional and urban development, particularly in terms of the often substantial capital costs involved. Again, a lack of clarity of purpose and understanding on the part of the heritage producers often means that exaggerated economic claims are made for the effectiveness of heritage as a means of development. In practice, the subsequent use of heritage is often insufficient to justify the initial capital investment.

It is pointless erecting value judgements concerning these processes. If heritage is the contemporary use of the past, then it is no less legitimate to use that resource for economic purposes than it is to exploit it for cultural reasons. The cultural values of heritage, both abstract and monetary, are also decided in the present. One critical aspect of the economic commodification of the past is that these processes help places retain their importance. Marketing of representations of place ensures that these are not defined by identity criteria alone, while, arguably, the absence of any economic dimension in most contemporary cultural arguments regarding the deconstruction of place significantly compromises their validity. Because place is a marketable commodity, this helps it retain an enduring cultural significance.

Conflicts and tensions – who decides?

It is inevitable that the multiple uses and functions of heritage create tensions. The answer to the question: 'who decides what is heritage?' is exceptionally difficult because so many actors are involved in the process. Thus any one expression of heritage has a multiplicity of answers to the question as it simultaneously carries an array of meanings. Clearly heritage can be part of processes of empowerment and the privileging of particular viewpoints. But equally, it contains a marked potential for the subversion of those viewpoints because it can carry alternative meanings. Thus, for example, there is often marked dissonance between official and unofficial representations of heritage, or – as we have seen – between cultural and economic uses. Heritage may represent the dominant ideological discourse, but that also ensures that it can become the focus of alternative meaning for those who dissent.

As we have shown, when taken to extremes, this reasoning leads to the destruction of a people's heritage. But even then, subversive meanings can be attached to the heritage of the victor, which is rich in connotations of oppression. In eighteenth-century Ireland, for example, a landed élite reconstructed the rural and urban environment to create a landscape triad of big houses, estates and improved towns characterized by formal town planning. A mere century later, this landscape had become a central emblem of oppression in the construction of Irish nationalism, which culturally rejected its modernist symbols in favour of the primordial wilderness of the Atlantic West; the big house became a literal target of nationalists as many of them were burned.

The complex ramifications of the issue, 'who decides?' mean that heritage is being loaded with more and more meanings derived from both its sociopolitical and economic uses. Clearly this process impairs the effectiveness of the messages being transmitted. These processes are little understood, there being remarkably little research on the ways in which people receive heritage messages and the meanings they derive from them. Because heritage is meaning, both producers and consumers – economic and cultural – can decide what it is. These lacunae in our knowledge also compromise the effectiveness of heritage as an economic development strategy. It would seem logical, however, that heritage must carry polyvocal messages in terms of its cultural meanings in hybrid societies. How effective these are remains a moot point. It might well be the case that because the cultural meanings of heritage are becoming ever more diverse, economically derived messages are more likely to dominate as they are arguably more focused on a particular audience, especially if the producer understands the segmentation of the particular market being targeted.

The question of scale – whose heritage is it?

Although our lengthy discussion of heritage and scale concluded on an optimistic note, it remains the case that the array of different scales, and the complex way in which these interact in both cultural and economic terms, significantly complicates the geography of heritage. It must always be remembered that because all heritage is someone's, it cannot be someone else's. As a result, we are observing more and more cases of the problems raised by the sacred and profane connotations of heritage in which someone's consecrated heritage is sold as someone else's entertainment. One of the most publicized examples of this concerns the return of heritage – that is, the prevailing meaning – to native peoples, as in Australia or North America. More widely, however, so much heritage is sacred as are so many heritage sites that this manifestation of dissonance is all-pervasive. How, for example, should the heritage of war and atrocity be packaged as an economic commodity?

The issue of scale, and the expanding access of consumers (at least those in wealthy societies) to heritage at those various scales through international tourism, compounds these difficulties. Nevertheless, we have argued throughout the book that the national remains predominant despite this increasing heterogeneity of scale. Not only is much heritage defined at the national scale, but the identity associations of nationalism remain immensely powerful. The nation-state may be under attack from other scales of belonging, but that does mean that nationalism is no longer relevant. Its supposed hegemony may have passed, but in a postmodern world of multiply constructed identities, nationalism remains as one of the most potent expressions of that diversity of belonging. In economic and governance terms, heritage may be operationalized at other scales, particularly the sub-national, but even if this helps subvert the national realm, regionalization, for example, shares precisely the same iconography of belonging to a territorially defined place that we find in the nation-state. In sum, the issue of scale means that even more messages are loaded onto heritage artefacts. Quite what consumers make of all this is unclear and the confusion of scale messages is again an area requiring extensive research.

The limitations of a geography of heritage

No matter how imperfect our knowledge of many significant aspects of heritage, the book represents the first significant attempt to place heritage in geography. As we have argued, heritage is central to contemporary conceptualizations of the discipline, while the very definition adopted here is clearly resonant of the polyvocality and hybridity of meaning and purpose in postmodern societies. Again, the all-pervasive idea of dissonance is congruent with the complex processes of contestation that characterize those societies. Heritage, however, also fulfils an important role in translating the theory of multiculturalism into the hard-edged world of actual politics for it is part of the processes by which space is produced and reproduced. It helps demonstrate that culture and its representation are inseparable from issues of equality, hegemony, social justice and resistances. But it shows too how difficult it is to transform representations of place defined by territoriality into more flexible and inclusive forms. Like other manifestations of culture, heritage is bound up in processes of social exclusion as well as inclusion. We have argued here for the enduring importance of the national, and observed that the articulation of the multicultural still often takes place within those confines. Again, the profound difficulties of creating other scales of heritage than the national have emerged from the analysis in Part IV. Dissonance, to reiterate, is intrinsic to all heritage at whatever scale.

Thus as more and more messages are piled on heritage, it may be that it is becoming less effective as a cultural medium. Conversely, this quintessential cultural good is emerging as an ever more important economic commodity, even if that process is not well understood. It is thus inevitable that the increasingly complex answers to questions concerning heritage definition and ownership are in themselves an enhanced source of dissonance and contestation. Hybridization, therefore, is not necessarily an antidote to nationalism, because it too can encourage processes of ethnification, ethnocentrism and racism (*see* Chapter 4). Above all, we need to understand resistances to hybridization. A geography of heritage shows that these remain profound. Meanwhile, the economic claim to heritage cannot be denied nor should we assume that it is subordinate to the cultural. The ensuing contestation of priority of meaning and ownership means that heritage in its complexity and hybridity models the endemic heterogeneity and diversity of contemporary societies. It also holds some potential to resolve conflict, although this must move beyond merely delineating sub-national and ethnic identities at the expense of the national. Nevertheless, the economic commodification of place through heritage will help ensure that it remains firmly fixed in representations of place, faithfully reflecting the enduring cultural and economic boundedness of societies.

References

Abu-Lughod, J. 1980: *Rabat: urban apartheid in Morocco.* Princeton, NJ: Princeton University Press.

Adorno, T. W. 1991: *The culture industry.* London: Routledge.

Agnew, J. A. 1995: The rhetoric of regionalism: the Northern League in Italian politics, 1983–1994. *Transactions Institute of British Geographers* 20, 156–72.

Agnew, J. A. 1996: Time into space: the myth of 'backward' Italy in modern Europe. *Time and Society* 5, 27–45.

Agnew, J. A. (ed.) 1997: *Political geography: a reader.* London: Arnold.

Agnew, J. A. 1998: European landscape and identity. In Graham, B. (ed.) *Modern Europe: place, culture and identity.* London: Arnold, 213–35.

Ahmad, A. (1995): The politics of literary postcoloniality. *Race and Class* 36, 1–20.

Alfrey, J. and Putnam, T. 1992: *The industrial heritage: managing resources and uses.* London: Routledge.

Anderson, B. 1991: *Imagined communities: reflections on the origins and spread of nationalism,* 2nd edn. London: Verso Books.

Anderson, J. 1988: Nationalist ideology and territory. In Johnston, R. J., Knight, D. B. and Kofman, E. (eds), *Nationalism, self-determination and political geography.* London: Croom Helm, 18–39.

Anderson, J. 1995: The exaggerated death of the nation-state. In Anderson, J., Brook, C. and Cochrane, A. (eds), *A global world? Reordering political space.* Oxford: Open University/Oxford University Press, 65–112.

Anderson, J. 1996: The shifting stage of politics: new medieval and postmodern territorialities. *Environment and Planning D: Society and Space* 14, 133–53.

Ardagh, J. 1999: *France in the new century: portrait of a changing society.* London: Viking.

Arnold, B. 1990: The past as propaganda: totalitarian archaeology through collaboration. *Antiquity* 64, 464–78.

Ashworth, G. J. 1991a: *War and the city.* London: Routledge.

Ashworth, G. J. 1991b: *Heritage planning: the management of urban change.* Groningen: Geopers.

Ashworth, G. J. 1993: *On tragedy and renaissance.* Groningen: Geopers.

Ashworth, G. J. 1994: From history to heritage – from heritage to history: in search of concepts and models. In Ashworth, G. J. and Larkham, P. J. (eds), *Building a new heritage: tourism, culture and identity in the New Europe.* London: Routledge, 13–30.

Ashworth, G. J. 1996: Jewish culture and Holocaust tourism: the case of Kraków-Kazimierz. In Robinson, M., Evans, N. and Callaghan, P. (eds), *Tourism and culture towards the 21st century*. Newcastle: University of Northumbria, 1–13.

Ashworth, G. J. 1997: Managing change in the city centre: the Groningen case. In Dingsdale, A. and Steen, P. J. M. van (eds), *The management of urban change in Europe*. Groningen: Groningen Studies 63, 123–44.

Ashworth, G. J. 1998: The conserved European city as cultural symbol: the meaning of the text. In Graham, B. (ed.), *Modern Europe: Place, Culture, Identity*. London: Arnold, 261–86.

Ashworth, G. J. and Ennen, E. 1998: De woonfunctie van binnensteden. In Seip, M. and Ashworth, G. J. (eds), *Binnensteden: analyse van gebruik en beheer*. Alphen aan den Rijn: Samson, 65–78.

Ashworth, G. J. and Graham, B. 1997: Heritage, identity and Europe. *Tijdschrift voor Economische en Sociale Geografie* 88, 381–88.

Ashworth, G. J. and Tunbridge, J. E. 1990: *The tourist-historic city*. London: Belhaven.

Ashworth G. J. and Voogd, H. 1990: *Selling the city: marketing approaches in public sector urban planning*. London: Belhaven.

Ashworth G. J. and Voogd, H. 1994a: The marketing of tourism places: what are we doing? *Journal of International Consumer Marketing* 6, 5–19.

Ashworth G. J. and Voogd, H. 1994b: Marketing and place promotion. In Gold, A. and Ward, S. (eds), *Promoting places*. London: John Wiley, 39–52.

Baker, A. R. H. 1984: Reflections on the relations of historical geography and the *Annales* school of history. In Baker, A. R. H. and Gregory, D. (eds), *Explorations in historical geography*. Cambridge: Cambridge University Press, 1–27.

Barnes, T. J . and Duncan, J. S. 1992: Introduction: writing worlds. In Barnes, T. J. and Duncan, J. S. *Writing worlds: discourse, text and metaphor in the representation of landscape*. London: Routledge, 1–17.

Bell, M. 1993: 'The pestilence that walketh in darkness': Imperial health, gender and images of South Africa c.1800–1910. *Transactions Institute of British Geographers* NS 18, 329–41.

Benevolo, L. 1993: *The European city*. Blackwell: Oxford.

Berg, L. van der, Borg, J. van der and Meer, J. van der 1995: *Urban tourism: performance and strategies in eight European cities*. London: Avebury.

Berning, G. and Dominy, G. 1992: The presentation of the industrial past in South African museums: a critique. *South African Museums Association Bulletin* 19, 1–14.

Berry, S. 1996: The changing economics of heritage tourism: who pays and who benefits? In Robinson, M., Evans, N. and Callaghan, P. (eds), *Tourism and culture towards the 21st century*. Newcastle: University of Northumbria, 39–52.

Best, S. 1995: *The politics of historical vision: Marx, Foucault, Habermas*. New York: Guilford Press.

Bhabha, H. K. 1994: *The location of culture*. London: Routledge.

Bianchini, F. 1991: *Urban cultural policy: national arts and media strategy discussion document*. London: Arts Council.

Bianchini, F. and Schwengat, H. 1991: Reimaging the city. In Corner, J. and Harvey, S. (eds), *Enterprise and heritage: crosscurrents of national culture*. London: Routledge, 212–34.

Bideleux, R. 1996: Introduction: European integration and disintegration. In Bideleux, R. and Taylor, R. (eds), *European integration and disintegration: East and West*. London: Routledge, 1–21.

Bizzaro, F. and Nijkamp, P. 1996a: *Integrated conservation of cultural built heritage*. Series Research Memoranda 12. Amsterdam: Vrijuniversiteit.

Bizzaro, F. and Nijkamp, P. 1996b: *Cultural heritage and urban revitalisation: a meta-analytic to urban sustainability*. Series Research Memoranda 30. Amsterdam: Vrijuniversiteit.

Bommes, M. and Wright, P. 1982: Charms of residence: the public and the past. In Centre for Contemporary Studies, *Making histories: studies in history writing and politics*. London: Hutchinson, 56–67.

Boniface, P. and Fowler, P. J. 1993: *Heritage and tourism in the global village*. London: Routledge.

Boorstin, D. 1964: *The image: a guide to pseudo-events in America*. New York: Harper Row.

Borg, J. van der 1990: *Tourism and urban development*. Rotterdam: Faculty of Economics, Erasmus University.

Borg, J. van der, Costa, P. and Gotti, G. 1996: Tourism in European heritage cities. *Annals of Tourism Research* 23, 306–21.

Bourdieu, P. 1977: *Outline of a theory of practice*. Cambridge: Cambridge University Press.

Bowman, I. 1924: *The new world: problems in political geography*. London: Harrap.

Boyle, M. and Hughes, G. C. 1991: The politics of the representation of the 'real': discourses from the left on Glasgow's role as European city of culture. *Area* 23, 217–28.

Bradshaw, B. 1989: Nationalism and historical scholarship in modern Ireland. *Irish Historical Studies* XXIV, 329–51.

Braudel, F. 1988: *The identity of France: vol. 1: history and environment*. London: Collins.

Braudel, F. 1990: *The identity of France: vol. 2: people and production*. London: Collins.

Brett, D. 1996: *The construction of heritage*. Cork: Cork University Press.

Brown, T. 1985: *Ireland: a social and cultural history, 1922–1985*, 2nd edn. London: Fontana Press.

Bruttomesso, R. (ed.) 1993: *Waterfronts: a new frontier for cities on water*. Venice: International Centre, Cities on Water.

Bruttomesso, R. (ed.) 1997: Venice. *Aquapolis* 2. Venice: International Centre, Cities on Water.

Bryson, L. and McCartney, C. 1994: *Clashing symbols*. Belfast: Institute of Irish Studies.

Buckner, P. A. 1994: *Multiculturalism in nineteenth century Canada: myths and realities*. St. John's: Institute of Economic and Social Research, Memorial University of Newfoundland.

Bull, H. 1977: *The anarchical society*. London: Macmillan.

Burgess, J. 1982: Selling places: environmental images for the executive. *Regional Studies* 16, 1–17.

Burtenshaw, D., Bateman, M. and Ashworth, G. J. 1991: *The European city: western perspectives*. London: Fulton.

CEC (Commission of the European Communities) 1994: *Europe 2000+*. Brussels: European Commission.

Centre for Contemporary History, 1982: *Making histories: studies in history writing and politics*. London: Hutchinson.

Cervellati, P. and Scannarini, R. 1973: *Bologna: politicae metodologia del restauro nei centri*. Bologna: Storichi.

Charlesworth, A. 1994: Contesting places of memory: the case of Auschwitz. *Environment and Planning D: Society and Space* 12, 579–93.

Christopher, A. J. 1994: *The atlas of apartheid*. London: Routledge.

Clohessy, L. 1994: Culture and urban tourism: Dublin 1991, European City of Culture. In Kockel, U. (ed.) *Culture, tourism and development: the case of Ireland*. Liverpool: Liverpool University Press, 189–95.

Cloke, P., Philo, C. and Sadler, D. 1991: *Approaching human geography: an introduction to contemporary theoretical debates*. London: Paul Chapman.

Colley, L. 1992: *Britons: forging the nation*. London: Yale University Press.

Connor, S. 1997: *Postmodernist culture*, 2nd edn. Oxford: Blackwell.

Conversi, D. 1997: *The Basques, the Catalans and Spain: alternative routes to nationalist mobilisation*. Reno: University of Nevada Press.

Copley, P. and Robson, I. 1996: Tourism, arts marketing and the modernist paradox. In Robinson, M., Evans, N. and Callaghan, P. (eds), *Tourism and culture towards the 21st century*. Newcastle: University of Northumbria, 98–110.

Cosgrove, D. E. 1984: *Social formation and symbolic landscape*. London: Croom Helm.

Cosgrove, D. E. 1993: *The Palladian landscape: geographical change and its cultural representations in sixteenth-century Italy*. Leicester: Leicester University Press.

Costa, P. and Borg, J. van der 1993: *The management of tourism in cities of art*. CIEST 2. Venice: University of Venice.

Council of Europe 1989: *The Santiago de Compostela pilgrimage route*. Architectural Reports and Studies 16. Strasbourg: Council of Europe.

Cuming, D. and Weiler, J. 1997: Progress and perils of preserving heritage districts: Ontario's experience in perspective. *Heritage Canada* 5, 6–11.

Dalibard, J. 1988: Can tourist towns be liveable? *Canadian Heritage* 14, 3–4.

Dalrymple, W. 1997: *From the holy mountain*. London: HarperCollins.

Daniels, S. 1993: *Fields of vision: landscape imagery and national identity in England and the United States*. Cambridge: Polity Press.

Davies, N. 1996: *Europe: a history*. Oxford: Oxford University Press.

Dear, M. 1997: Identity, authenticity and memory in place-time. In Pile, S. and Keith, M. (eds), *Geographies of resistance*. London: Routledge, 219–35.

de Bres, K. (1994), Cowtowns or cathedral precincts? Two models for contemporary urban tourism. *Area* 26, 57–67.

Donald, J. and Rattansi, A. (eds) 1992: *'Race', culture and difference*. London: Sage/Open University.

Douglas, N. 1997: Political structures, social interaction and identity changes in Northern Ireland. In Graham, B. (ed.), *In search of Ireland: a cultural geography*. London: Routledge, 151–73.

Driver, F. and Samuel, R. 1995: Rethinking the idea of place. *History Workshop Journal* 39, vi–vii.

Duffy, P. 1994: Conflicts in heritage and tourism. In Kockel, U. (ed.) *Culture, tourism and development: the case of Ireland.* Liverpool: Liverpool University Press, 77–86.

Duffy, P. J. 1997: Writing Ireland: literature and art in the representation of Irish place. In Graham, B. (ed.), *In search of Ireland: a cultural geography.* London: Routledge, 64–83.

Du Gay, P., Hall, S., Mackay, H. and Negus, K. 1997: *Doing cultural studies: the story of the Sony Walkman.* London: Sage.

Duncan, J. S. 1990: *The city as text: the politics of landscape interpretation in the Kandyan kingdom.* Cambridge: Cambridge University Press.

Dunning, J. H. and Norman, G. 1987: Location choices of offices of international companies. *Environment and Planning A* 19, 613–31.

Duren A. J. 1993: Change in the attraction of Amsterdam city centre. *Built Environment* 18, 123–36.

Dwyer, J. C. and Hodge, I. D. 1996: *Countryside in trust: land management by conservation, recreation and amenity organisations.* Chichester: John Wiley.

Dyer, G. 1998: How the 'new' francophones will save Canada. *Globe & Mail,* Toronto, March 28.

Edensor, T. and Kothari, U. 1994: The masculisation of Sterling's heritage. In Kinnaird, V. and Hall, D. (eds), *Tourism: a gender analysis.* London: John Wiley, 115–34.

English Heritage 1999: *Register of buildings at risk.* London: English Heritage.

Ennen, E. 1997: The Groningen Museum: urban heritage in fragments. *International Journal of Heritage Studies* 3, 144–56.

Ennen, E. and Ashworth, G. J. 1998: City centre management: Dutch and British experience of a new form of planning. *European Spatial Research and Policy* 5, 5–15.

Evans, E. E. 1981: *The personality of Ireland: habitat, heritage and history,* 2nd edn. Belfast: Blackstaff Press.

Evans, G. 1993: *An urban renaissance? The role of the arts in urban regeneration: a survey of local authorities in Greater London.* Papers in Leisure and Tourism Studies 4. London: University of North London Press.

Evans, K. 1998: Competition for heritage space: Cairo's resident/tourist conflict. In Tyler, D., Guernier, Y. and Robertson, M. (eds), *Managing tourism in cities.* Chichester: John Wiley, 179–92.

Fay, S. and Knightly, P. 1976: *The death of Venice.* London: Deutsch.

Felski, R. 1994: The gender of modernity. In Ledger, S., MacDonagh, J. and Spencer, J. (eds), *Political gender: texts and contexts.* New York: Harvester Wheatsheaf, 144–55.

Ferguson, B. 1991: Places with a past: new site specific art in Charleston. *Canadian Art* Winter, 69–70.

Fischer, M., Rauhe, H. and Wiesand, A. J. (eds) 1996: *Arts administration in Europe.* Bonn: ARcult Media.

Fitch, J. M. 1995: *Historic preservation: curatorial management of the built world.* Charlottesville, VA: University Press of Virginia.

Ford, L. R. 1979: Urban preservation and the geography of the city in the U.S.A. *Progress in Human Geography* 4, 211–38.

Ford, L. 1994: *Cities and buildings: skyscrapers, skid rows and suburbs.* Baltimore, MD: Johns Hopkins University Press.

Friedman, J. 1997: Global crises, the struggle for cultural identity and intellectual porkbarrelling: cosmopolitans versus locals, ethnics and nationals in an era of de-hegemonisation. In Werbener, P. and Modood, T. (eds), *Debating cultural hybridity: multicultural identities and the politics of anti-racism*. London: Zed Books, 70–89.

Gellner, E. 1997. *Nationalism*. London: Weidenfeld and Nicholson.

Giese, E. 1979. Transformation of Islamic cities in Soviet Middle Asia into Socialist cities. In French, R. A. and Hamilton, F. E. I. (eds), *The Soviet City*. London: John Wiley, 145–65.

Gilbert, M. 1997: *Holocaust journey: travelling in search of the past*. London: Weidenfeld and Nicholson.

Gillis, J. R. 1994: Memory and identity: the history of a relationship. In Gillis, J. R. (ed.), *Commemorations: the politics of national identity*. Princeton, NJ: Princeton University Press, 3–24.

Gilroy, P. 1987: *There ain't no black in the Union Jack: the cultural politics of race and nation*. London: Hutchinson.

Gilroy, P. 1993: *The Black Atlantic: modernity and double consciousness*. London: Verso.

Goodall, B. 1993: Industrial heritage and tourism. *Built Environment* 19, 93–104.

Graefe, A. R., Vaske, J. J. and Kuss, F. R. 1984: Social carrying capacity: an integration and synthesis of 20 years research. *Leisure Sciences* 6, 31–45.

Graham, B. 1994a: No place of the mind: contested Protestant representations of Ulster. *Ecumene* 1, 257–81.

Graham, B. 1994b: Heritage conservation and revisionist nationalism in Ireland. In Ashworth, G. J. and Larkham, P. J. (eds), *Building a new heritage: tourism, culture and identity in the New Europe*. London: Routledge, 135–58.

Graham, B. 1994c: The search for the common ground: Estyn Evans's Ireland. *Transactions Institute of British Geographers* NS 19, 183–201.

Graham, B. 1996: The contested interpretation of heritage landscapes in Northern Ireland. *International Journal of Heritage Studies* 2, 10–22.

Graham, B. (ed.) 1997: *In search of Ireland: a cultural geography*. London: Routledge.

Graham, B. 1998a: Contested images of place among Protestants in Northern Ireland. *Political Geography* 17, 129–44.

Graham, B. 1998b: The past in Europe's present: diversity, identity and the construction of place. In Graham, B. (ed.), *Modern Europe: place, culture and identity*. London: Arnold, 19–49.

Graham, B. 1999: The past in place: historical geographies of identity. In Graham, B. and Nash, C. (eds), *Modern historical geographies*. Harlow: Prentice Hall, 70–99.

Graham, B. and Hart. M. 1999: Cohesion and diversity in the European Union: irreconcilable forces? *Regional Studies* 33, 259–68.

Graham, B. and Murray, M. 1997: The spiritual and the profane: the pilgrimage to Santiago de Compostela. *Ecumene* 4, 389–409.

Graham, B. and Nash, C. (eds) 1999: *Modern historical geographies*. Harlow: Prentice Hall.

Graham, B. and Shirlow, P. 1998: An elusive agenda: the development of a middle ground in Northern Ireland. *Area* 30, 245–54.

Gregory, D. 1994: *Geographical imaginations*. Oxford: Blackwell.

Gruber, R. G. 1992: *Jewish heritage travel: a guide to Central and Eastern Europe*. New York: John Wiley.

Gruffudd, P. 1995: Remaking Wales: nation-building and the geographical imagination, 1925–50. *Political Geography* 14, 219–39.

Guibernau, M. 1996: *Nationalisms: the nation state and nationalism in the twentieth century*. Oxford: Polity Press.

Habermas, J. 1996: The European nation-state: its achievements and its limits. In Balakrishnan, G. and Anderson, B. (eds), *Mapping the nation*. London: Verso, 281–94.

Hall, S. 1995: New cultures for old. In Massey, D. and Jess, P. (eds), *A place in the world? Place, cultures and globalization*. Oxford: Open University/Oxford University Press, 175–214.

Hall, S. 1996: Introduction: who needs identity? In Hall, S. and Du Gay, P. (eds), *Questions of cultural identity*. London: Sage, 1–17.

Hall, S. (ed.) 1997: *Representation: cultural representations and signifying practices*. London: Sage/Open University.

Handler, R. 1994: Is 'identity' a useful cross-cultural concept? In Gillis, J. R. (ed.), *Commemorations: the politics of national identity*. Princeton, NJ: Princeton University Press, 27–40.

Hardin, G. R. 1968: The tragedy of the commons. *Science* 162, 1243–48.

Hardy, D. 1988: Historical geography and heritage studies. *Area* 20, 333–38.

Harvey, D. 1989: *The condition of postmodernity*. Oxford: Blackwell.

Harvey, D. 1996: *Justice, nature and the geography of difference*. Oxford: Blackwell.

Hastings, A. 1997: *The construction of nationhood: ethnicity, religion and nationalism*. Cambridge: Cambridge University Press.

Haswell, R. F. 1990: The making and remaking of Pietermaritzburg: the past, present and future morphology of a South African city. In Slater, T. R. (ed.), *The built form of western cities*. Leicester: Leicester University Press, 171–85.

Head, L. 1993: Unearthing prehistoric cultural landscapes: a view from Australia. *Transactions Institute of British Geographers* NS 18, 481–99.

Heffernan, M. 1995: For ever England: the Western Front and the politics of remembrance in Britain. *Ecumene* 2, 293–324.

Heffernan, M. 1997: Editorial: the future of historical geography. *Journal of Historical Geography* 23, 1–2.

Heffernan, M. 1998a: *The meaning of Europe: geography and geopolitics*. London: Arnold.

Heffernan, M. 1998b: War and the shaping of Europe. In Graham, B. (ed.) *Modern Europe: place, culture and identity*. London: Arnold, 89–120.

Henry, W. A. 1994: Pride and prejudice. *Time* 27 June, 32–35.

Hensel, W. 1969–70: The origins of western and eastern Slav towns. *World Archaeology* 1, 51–60.

Heritage Canada 1996: Monuments at risk. *Heritage Canada* 3, 21.

Hewison, R. 1987: *The heritage industry: Britain in a climate of decline*. London: Methuen.

Hewison, R. 1991: Commerce and culture. In Corner, J. and Harvey, S. (eds), *Enterprise and heritage: crosscurrents of national culture*. London: Routledge, 162–77.

Hitters, E. 1993: Culture and capital in the 1990s. *Built Environment* 18, 111–22.

Hobsbawm, E. J. 1990: *Nations and nationalism since 1780: programme, myth, reality*. Cambridge: Cambridge University Press.

Hobsbawm, E. J. and Ranger, T. (eds) 1983: *The invention of tradition*. Cambridge: Cambridge University Press.

Horne, A. 1977: *A savage war of peace*. London: Macmillan.

Hoyle, B. S. 1999: Scale and sustainability: the role of community groups in Canadian port-city waterfront change. *Journal of Transport Geography* 7, 65–78.

Hoyle, B. S., Pinder, D. A. and Husain, M. S. (eds) 1988: *Revitalising the waterfront: international dimensions of dockland redevelopment*. London: Belhaven.

Jackson, P. and Penrose, J. (eds) 1993: *Constructions of race, place and nation*. London: UCL Press.

James, H. 1884, Penguin edition 1983: *A little tour in France*. Harmondsworth: Penguin.

Jarman, N. 1992: Troubled images. *Critique of Anthropology* 12, 179–91.

Jess, P. and Massey, D. 1995: The contestation of place. In Massey, D. and Jess, P. (eds), *A place in the world? Place, cultures and globalization*. Oxford: Open University/Oxford University Press, 133–74.

Johnson, N. C. 1993: Building a nation: an examination of the Irish Gaeltacht Commission Report of 1926. *Journal of Historical Geography* 19, 157–68.

Johnson, N. C. 1995a: Cast in stone: monuments, geography and nationalism. *Environment and Planning D: Society and Space* 13, 51–65.

Johnson, N. C. 1995b: The renaissance of nationalism. In Johnston, R. J., Taylor, P. J. and Watts, M. J. (eds), *Geographies of global change*. Oxford: Blackwell, 97–110.

Johnson, N. C. 1999a: Historical geographies of the present. In Graham, B. and Nash, C. (eds), *Modern historical geographies*. Harlow: Prentice Hall, 251–72.

Johnson, N. C. 1999b: Framing the past: time, space and the politics of heritage tourism in Ireland. *Political Geography* 18, 187–207.

Jones, R. 1997: Sacred sites or profane buildings? Reflections on the Old Swan Brewery conflict in Perth, Western Australia. In Shaw, B. J. and Jones, R. (eds), *Contested urban heritage: voices from the periphery*. Aldershot: Ashgate, 132–55.

Jones, R. and Shaw, B. 1992: *Historic port cities of the Indian Ocean littoral: the resolution of planning conflicts and the development of a tourism resource potential*. Occasional Paper 22, Indian Ocean Centre for Peace Studies. Perth: University of Western Australia.

Kain, R. 1975: Urban conservation in France, *Town and Country Planning Review* 43, 428–33.

Kain, R. 1981: *Planning for conservation: an international perspective*. London: Mansell.

Kallen, E. 1995: *Ethnicity and human rights in Canada*. Don Mills: Oxford University Press.

Kearns, K. C. (1983): *Georgian Dublin: Ireland's imperilled architectural heritage*. Newton Abbot: David and Charles.

Kearns, G. 1998: Historical geography as the basis of identity: nationalism, diaspora and cosmopolitanism. Paper read to the 10th International Conference of Historical Geographers, Coleraine.

Keith, M. and Pile, S. (eds) 1993: *Place and the politics of identity*. London: Routledge.

Keneally, T. 1982: *Schindler's ark*. London: Hodder and Stoughton.

Kesteloot, C. and Mistiaen, P. 1997: From ethnic minority niche to assimilation: Turkish restaurants in Brussels. *Area* 29, 325–34.

King, R. 1995: Migrations, globalization and place. In Massey, D. and Jess, P. (eds), *A place in the world? Place, cultures and globalization.* Oxford: Open University/ Oxford University Press, 6–44.

Kinsman, P. 1995: Landscape, race and national identity: the photography of Ingrid Pollard. *Area* 27, 300–310.

Klerk, L. and Vijgen, J. 1993: Inner cities as a cultural and public arena. *Built Environment* 18, 100–110.

Kneafsey, M. 1994: The cultural tourist: patron saint of Ireland. In Kockel, U. (ed.), *Culture, tourism and development: the case of Ireland.* Liverpool: Liverpool University Press, 101–16.

Kong, L. 1993: Negotiating conceptions of sacred space: a case study of religious buildings in Singapore. *Transactions Institute of British Geographers*, NS 18, 342–58.

Kong, L. 1995: Music and cultural politics: ideology and resistance in Singapore. *Transactions Institute of British Geographers* NS 20, 447–59.

Kong, L. and Tay, L. 1998: Exalting the past: nostalgia and the construction of heritage in children's literature. *Area* 30, 133–43.

Kong, L. and Yeoh, B. S. A. 1994: Urban conservation in Singapore: a survey of state policies and popular attitudes. *Urban Studies* 31, 247–65.

Koonz, C. 1994: Between memory and oblivion: concentration camps in German memory. In Gillis, J. R. (ed.), *Commemorations: the politics of national identity.* Princeton, NJ: Princeton University Press, 258–80.

Krabbe, J. and Heijman, W. J. M. 1986: *Economische theorieen van het milieu.* Assen: Van Gorcum.

Larkham, P. J. 1996: *Conservation and cities.* London: Routledge.

Larkham, P. J. and Barrett, H. 1998: Conservation of the built environment under the Conservatives. In Allmendinger, P. and Thomas, H. (eds), *Urban planning and the British New Right.* London: Routledge, 68–82.

Leciejewicz, L. 1976: Medieval archaeology in Poland: current problems and research methods. *Medieval Archaeology* 20, 1–15.

Lefebvre, H. 1991: The *production of space.* Trans. Donald Nicholson-Smith. Oxford: Basil Blackwell.

Lemaire, T. 1993: Archaeologie en ideologie. *Archaelogisch Informatie Cahiers* 5, 46–9.

Lemon, A. (ed.) 1995: *The geography of change in South Africa.* Chichester: John Wiley.

Leonard, J. 1996: The twinge of memory: Armistice day and Remembrance Sunday in Dublin since 1919. In English, R. and Walker, G. (eds), *Unionism in modern Ireland.* Dublin: Gill and Macmillan, 99–114.

Lester, A. 1999a: Historical geographies of imperialism. In Graham, B. and Nash, C. (eds), *Modern historical geographies.* Harlow: Prentice Hall, 100–120.

Lester, A. 1999b: *Colonial discourse and the colonisation of Queen Adelaide province, South Africa.* London: RGS-IBG Historical Geography Research Group, Historical Geography Research Series 34.

Lewis, J. 1990: *Art, culture and enterprise: the politics of art and the cultural industries.* London: Routledge.

Ley, D. 1996: *The new middle class and the remaking of the central city.* Oxford: Oxford University Press.

Leyshon, A., Matless, D. and Revill, G. (eds) 1998: *The place of music.* New York: Guilford Press.

Lichfield, N. 1988: *Economics in urban conservation*. Cambridge: Cambridge University Press.

Lichfield, N. 1997: Achieving the benefits of conservation. *Built Environment* 22, 103–110.

Lim, H. 1993: Cultural strategies for revitalising the city: a review and evaluation. *Regional Studies* 27, 589–95.

Livingstone, D. N. 1992: *The geographical tradition*. Oxford: Blackwell.

Longley, E. 1991: The rising, the Somme and Irish memory. In Ni Dhonnchadha, M. and Dorgan, T. (eds), *Revising the Rising*. Derry: Field Day, 91–105.

Lowenthal, D. 1985: *The past is a foreign country*. Cambridge: Cambridge University Press.

Lowenthal, D. 1988: Classical antiquities as national or global heritage. *Antiquity* 62, 726–35.

Lowenthal, D. 1991: British national identity and the English landscape. *Rural History* 2, 205–30.

Lowenthal, D. 1994: European and English landscapes as national symbols. In Hooson, D. (ed.), *Geography and national identity*. Oxford: Blackwell, 15–38.

Lowenthal, D. 1996: *The heritage crusade and the spoils of history*. Cambridge: Cambridge University Press.

Lumley, R. (ed.) 1988: *The museum time machine*. London: Routledge.

McKay, I. 1994: *The quest of the folk: antimodernism and cultural selection in twentieth century Nova Scotia*. Montreal/Kingston: McGill/Queen's University Press.

McLean, F. 1998: Museums and the construction of national identity: a review. *International Journal of Heritage Studies* 3, 244–52.

McQuillan, D. A. and Laurier, R. 1984: Urban upgrading and historic presentation: an integrated development plan for Zanizibar's old stone town. *Habitat International* 8, 43–59.

Mallet, G. (1997), Has diversity gone too far? *Globe & Mail*, Toronto, March 15.

Mancuso, F. 1993: The Venice waterfronts. In Bruttomesso, R. (ed.) *Waterfronts: a new frontier for cities on water*. Venice: International Centre, Cities on Water, 58–74.

Mandela, N. 1994: *Long walk to freedom*. London: Little, Brown and Co.

Mandela, N. 1997: Proclamation speech, Robben Island National Monument and National Museum, Heritage Day (September 24). *Rainbow* 4, 4–5.

Massey, D. 1994: *Space, place and gender*. Minneapolis: University of Minnesota Press.

Massey, D. 1995: The conceptualization of place. In Massey, D. and Jess, P. (eds), *A place in the world? Place, cultures and globalization*. Oxford: Open University/Oxford University Press, 45–86.

Mathieson, A. and Wall, G. 1982: *Tourism: economic, physical and social impacts*. London: Longman.

Matless, D. 1992: An occasion for geography: landscape, representation and Foucault's corpus. *Environment and Planning D: Society and Space* 10, 41–56.

May, J. 1996: Globalisation and the politics of place. *Transactions Institute of British Geographers* NS 21, 194–215.

Meester, W. J. and Pellenbarg, P. H. 1997: Measuring the effects of regional marketing campaigns: the case of Groningen. In Dingsdale, A. and Steen, P. J. M. van (eds), *The management of urban change in Europe*. Groningen: Groningen Studies 63, 103–22.

Melosh, B. 1994: Introduction. *Gender and History* 6, 315–19 (special issue on public history).

Mercer, D. 1993: 'Terra nullius': aboriginal sovereignty and land rights in Australia. *Political Geography* 12, 299–318.

Merriman, N. 1991: *Beyond the glass case.* Leicester: Leicester University Press.

Miles, M. (ed.) 1997: *Art, space and the city.* London: Routledge.

Ministerie van Economische Zaken 1992: *Nota ondernemen in toerisme.* Den Haag: Staatsuitgeverij.

Ministry of Housing and Physical Planning, 1989: *National environmental policy plan: to choose or to lose.* Den Haag: SDU.

Ministerie WVC 1985: *Notitie cultuurbeleid.* Den Haag: Staatsuitgeverij.

Ministerie WVC, 1992: *Investeren in cultuur: note cultuurbeleid 1993–6.* Den Haag: SDU.

Mitchell, D. 1998: Writing the western: new western history's encounter with landscape. *Ecumene* 5, 7–29.

Moody, N. 1996: Treasure hunts: Lovejoy, the antiques road show and the pleasures of tourism. In Robinson, M., Evans, N. and Callaghan, P. (eds), *Tourism and culture towards the 21st century.* Newcastle: University of Northumbria, 210–23.

Morris, A. E. J. 1994: *History of urban form before the industrial revolutions*, 3rd edn. London: Longman.

Morton, D. and Granatstein, J. L. 1995: *Victory 1945: Canadians from war to peace.* Toronto: HarperCollins.

Mossetto, G. 1990: *A cultural good called Venice.* Nota di Lavoro 90.14. Venice: University of Venice.

Mossetto, G. 1993: Culture and environmental waste: an economic approach. In Konsola, D. (ed.), *Culture, environment and regional development.* Athens: Regional Development Insitute: University of Athens, 115–24.

Mowat, F. 1989: *The new founde land: a personal voyage of discovery.* Toronto: McClelland and Stewart.

Mulcahy, K. V. 1998: Public culture and political culture: a comparative analysis in France, Norway, Canada and the United States. In Snickars, F. (ed.), *Culture and economic development.* Stockholm: Royal Institute.

Murray, M. and Graham, B. 1997: Exploring the dialectics of route-based tourism: the *Camino de Santiago. Tourism Management* 18, 513–24.

Myerscough, J. 1988: *Economic importance of the arts in Britain.* London: Policy Studies Institute.

Nash, C. 1996: Geo-centric education and anti-imperialism: theosophy, geography and citizenship in the writing of J. H. Cousins. *Journal of Historical Geography* 22, 399–411.

Nash, C. 1999: Historical geographies of modernity. In Graham, B. and Nash, C. (eds), *Modern historical geographies.* Harlow: Prentice Hall, 13–40.

Nash, C. and Graham, B. 1999: The making of modern historical geographies. In Graham, B. and Nash, C. (eds), *Modern historical geographies.* Harlow: Prentice Hall, 1–9.

Newby, P. T. 1994: Tourism: support or threat to heritage. In Ashworth, G. J. and Larkham, P. J. (eds), *Building a new heritage: tourism, culture and identity in the New Europe.* London: Routledge, 206–28.

Nijkamp, P. (ed.) 1990: *Sustainability of urban systems: a cross-national evolutionary analysis of urban innovation.* Aldershot: Avebury.

Nora, P. 1989: Between memory and history: *les lieux de memoire*. *Representations* 26, 10–18.

Ogborn, M. 1998: *Spaces of modernity: London's geographies, 1680–1780*. New York: Guilford Press.

Ogborn, M. 1999: Historical geographies of globalisation. In Graham, B. and Nash, C. (eds), *Modern historical geographies*. Harlow: Prentice Hall, 43–69.

Oosterman, J. 1993: Welcome to the pleasure dome: play and entertainment in urban public space: the example of the sidewalk cafe. *Built Environment* 18, 155–63.

O'Riordan, N. 1975: The Venetian ideal. *Geographical Magazine* 47, 416–26.

Osborne, B. S. 1998: Constructing landscapes of power: the George Etienne Cartier monument, Montreal. *Journal of Historical Geography* 24, 431–58.

Ó Tuathaigh, G. 1991: The Irish-Ireland idea: rationale and relevance. In Longley, E. (ed.), *Culture in Ireland: division or diversity*. Belfast: Institute of Irish Studies, 54–71.

Ó Tuathail, G. 1996: *Critical geopolitics*. London: Routledge.

Overton, J. 1996: *Making a world of difference: essays on tourism, culture and development in Newfoundland*. St. John's: Institute of Economic and Social Research, Memorial University of Newfoundland.

Parker, A., Russo, M., Sommer, D. and Yaeger, P. (1992) Introduction. In Parker, A., Russo, M., Sommer, D. and Yaeger, P. (eds), *Nationalism and sexualities*. London: Routledge, 1–18.

Paul, L. 1993: The stolen revolution: minorities in Romania after Ceaucescu. In O'Laughlin, J. and Wusten, H. van der (eds), *The new political geography of Eastern Europe*. London: Belhaven.

Pearson, D. G. 1994: *Canada compared: multiculturalism and biculturalism in settler societies*. St. John's: Institute of Economic and Social Research, Memorial University of Newfoundland.

Peet, R. 1998: *Modern geographical thought*. Oxford: Blackwell.

Pellenbarg, P. H. 1994: Groningen: regional capital of the Northern Netherlands. In Pellenbarg, P. H. and Kooij, P. (eds), *Regional capitals*. Assen: Van Gorcum, 63–84.

Philo, C. 1992: Foucault's geography. *Environment and Planning D: Society and Space* 10, 137–61.

Pile, S. and Keith, M. (eds) 1997: *Geographies of resistance*. London: Routledge.

Pilkington, H. 1998: *Migration, displacement and identity in post-Soviet Russia*. London: Routledge.

Ploszajska, T. 1999: Historiographies of geography and empire. In Graham, B. and Nash, C. (eds), *Modern historical geographies*. Harlow: Prentice Hall, 121–45.

Pocock, D. 1997: Some reflections on world heritage. *Area* 29, 260–68.

Poole, M. A. 1997: In search of ethnicity in Ireland. In Graham, B. (ed.), *In search of Ireland: a cultural geography*. London: Routledge, 151–73.

Powell, R. 1997: Erasing memory, inventing tradition, rewriting history: planning as a tool of ideology. In Shaw, B. J. and Jones, R. (eds), *Contested urban heritage: voices from the periphery*. Aldershot: Ashgate, 85–100.

Pratt, M. L. 1994: Women, literature and national brotherhood. *Nineteenth-Century Contexts: An Interdisciplinary Journal* 18, 29–45.

Purchla, J. 1993: Kraków from the monument preservation perspective. In Zuziak, Z. (ed.), *Managing historic cities*. Kraków: International Cultural Centre, 189–99.

Radford, J. P. 1992: Identity and tradition in the post-civil war south. *Journal of Historical Geography* 18, 91–103.

Robinson, M., Evans, N. and Callaghan, P. (eds), 1996: *Tourism and culture towards the 21st century*. Newcastle: University of Northumbria.

Rose, G. 1993: *Feminism and geography: the limits of geographical knowledge.* Minneapolis: University of Minnesota Press.

Rose, G. 1994: The cultural politics of place: local representation and oppositional discourse in two films. *Transactions Institute of British Geographers* NS 19, 46–60.

Rose, G. 1995: Place and identity: a sense of place. In Massey, D. and Jess, P. (eds), *A place in the world? Place, cultures and globalization*. Oxford: Open University/Oxford University Press, 87–132.

Sack, R. D. 1992: *Place, modernity and the consumer's world*. Baltimore, MD: Johns Hopkins University Press.

Said, E. 1978: *Orientalism*. New York: Columbia University Press.

Salée, D. 1994: Identity politics and multiculturalism in Québec. *Cultural Survival Quarterly* 18, 89–94.

Samuel, R. 1994: *Theatres of memory; vol. 1; past and present in contemporary culture*. London: Verso.

Satoh, S. 1986: Innovations in town planning policies and methods in old Japanese castle towns since the Meiji restoration. Adelaide: Proceedings Adelaide World Planning and Housing Conference.

Satoh, S. 1997: The morphological transformation of Japanese castle-town cities. *Urban Morphology* 1, 1–18.

Schama, S. 1987: *The embarrassment of riches: an interpretation of Dutch culture in the Golden Age*. London: William Collins.

Schama, S. 1995: *Landscape and memory*. London: HarperCollins.

Seymour, S. 1999: Historical geographies of landscape. In Graham, B. and Nash, C. (eds), *Modern historical geographies*. Harlow: Prentice Hall, 193–217.

Sharp, C. A. 1986: *Heritage conservation and development control in a speculative environment: the case of St. Johns*. St. John's: Institute of Economic and Social Research, Memorial University of Newfoundland.

Sharp, C. A. 1993: *Preserving inner city residential areas: the planning process in St. John's, Newfoundland, 1983–91*. St. John's: Institute of Economic and Social Research, Memorial University of Newfoundland.

Shaw, B. J., Jones, R. and Ling, O. G. 1997: Urban heritage development and tourism in South East Asian cities: a contestational continuum. In Shaw, B. J. and Jones, R. (eds), *Contested urban heritage: voices from the periphery*. Aldershot: Ashgate, 169–96.

Shaw, D. J. B. 1998: 'The chickens of Versailles': the new Central and Eastern Europe. In Graham, B. (ed.) *Modern Europe: place, culture and identity*. London: Arnold, 121–42.

Shurmer-Smith, P. and Hannam, K. 1994: *Worlds of desire, realms of power: a cultural geography*. London: Arnold.

Sillitoe, K. and White, P. H. 1992: Ethnic group and the British census: the search for a question. *Journal of the Royal Statistical Society A* 155, 141–63.

Sinclair, T. and Stabler, M. 1997: *The economics of tourism*. London: Routledge.

Singh, R. P. B. 1997: Sacredscape and urban heritage in India: contestation and perspective. In Shaw, B. J. and Jones, R. (eds), *Contested urban heritage: voices from the periphery*. Aldershot: Ashgate, 101–31.

Smith, A. D. 1991: *National identity*. Harmondsworth: Penguin.

Smith, C. 1997: *Robben Island*. Cape Town: Struik.

Snedcof, H. 1986: *Cultural facilities in mixed use developments*. Washington, D.C.: Urban Land Institute.

Soane, J. 1994: The renaissance of cultural vernacularism in Germany. In Ashworth, G. J. and Larkham, P. J. (eds), *Building a new heritage: tourism, culture and identity in the new Europe*. London: Routledge, 159–77.

Soja, E. 1989: *Postmodern geographies: the reassertion of space in social theory*. London: Verso.

Soja, E. 1996: *Thirdspace: journeys to Los Angeles and other real-and-imagined places*. Oxford: Blackwell.

Soja, E. and Hooper, B. 1993: The spaces that difference makes: some notes on the geographical margins of the new cultural politics. In Keith, M. and Pile, S. (eds), *Place and the politics of identity*. London: Routledge, 183–205.

Squire, S. 1994: The cultural values of literary tourism. *Annals of Tourism Research* 21, 103–20.

Stabler, M. 1996: Are heritage conservation and tourism compatible? An economic evaluation of their role in urban regeneration. In Robinson, M. (ed.), *Tourism and culture*. Newcastle: Centre for Travel and Tourism, University of Northumbria, 417–46.

Taylor, M. 1997: Conservation in a multicultural environment. *Journal of Architectural Conservation*, 3, 72–79.

Tiesdell, S. and Heath, T. 1996: *Revitalising historic urban quarters*. Oxford: Architectural Press.

Tunbridge, J. E. 1981: Conservation trusts as geographic agents: their impact upon landscape, townscape and land use. *Transactions Institute of British Geographers* NS 6, 103–25.

Tunbridge, J. E. 1987: *Of heritage and many other things: merchants' location decisions in Ottawa's Lower Town West*. Ottawa: Carleton University, Department of Geography Discussion Paper 5.

Tunbridge, J. E. 1993: The tourist-leisure dimension: North American waterfronts in comparative perspective. In Bruttomesso, R. (ed.), *Waterfronts: a new frontier for cities on water*. Venice: International Centre, Cities on Water, 290–96.

Tunbridge, J. E. 1994: Whose heritage? Global problem, European nightmare. In Ashworth, G. J. and Larkham, P. J. (eds), *Building a new heritage: tourism, culture and identity in the New Europe*. London: Routledge, 123–34.

Tunbridge, J. E. 1998: The question of heritage in European cultural conflict. In Graham, B. (ed.), *Modern Europe: place, culture, identity*. London: Arnold, 236–60.

Tunbridge, J. E. 1999: Pietermaritzburg, South Africa: trials and traumas of conservation. *Built Environment*, in press.

Tunbridge, J. E. and Ashworth, G. J. 1992: Leisure resource development in city-port revitalisation: the tourist-historic dimension. In Hoyle, B. S. and Pinder, D. A. (eds), *European port cities in transition*. London: Belhaven, 176–200.

Tunbridge, J. E. and Ashworth, G. J. 1996: *Dissonant heritage: the management of the past as a resource in conflict*. Chichester: John Wiley.

UNESCO (1970), *Protection of mankind's cultural heritage*. Paris: UNESCO.

Urry, J. 1990: *The tourist gaze: leisure and travel in contemporary societies*. London: Sage.

Urry, J. 1995: *Consuming places*. London: Routledge.

Veen, W. van der and Voogd, H. 1989: *Gemeentepromotie en bedrijfsacquisitie*. Groningen: Geopers.

Voogd, H. 1998: Social dilemmas and the communicative planning paradox. Paper read to Planning Theory Conference, Oxford Brookes University.

Voogd, H. and van de Wijk, W. 1989: Recreatieve imagos en gemeentelijk voorlichting. In Voogd, H. (ed.), *Stedelijk planning in perspectief*. Groningen: Geopers, 61–74.

Waitt, G. and McGuirk, P. M. 1996: Marking time: tourism and heritage representation at Millers Point, Sydney. *Australian Geographer* 27, 11–29.

Wall, G. 1983: Tourism cycles and capacity. *Annals of Tourism Research* 10, 268–70.

Walsh, K. 1992: *The representation of the past: museums and heritage in the postmodern world*. London: Routledge.

Wanklyn, H. G. 1948: *The eastern marshlands of Europe*. London: George Phillips.

Ward, E. N. 1986: *Heritage conservation: the built environment*. Ottawa: Lands Directorate, Environment Canada.

Warner, M. 1981: *Joan of Arc: the image of female heroism*. London: Weidenfeld and Nicholson.

Weiler, J. 1998: Dollars and sense: the economics of conserving built heritage. *Heritage* 1, 17–20.

Werbener, P. 1997: Introduction: the dialectics of cultural hybridity. In Werbener, P. and Modood, T. (eds), *Debating cultural hybridity: multicultural identities and the politics of anti-racism*. London: Zed Books, 1–28.

Werbener, P. and Modood, T. (eds) 1997: *Debating cultural hybridity: multicultural identities and the politics of anti-racism*. London: Zed Books.

Western, J. 1985: Undoing the colonial city. *Geographical Review* 75, 335–57.

Western, J. 1996: *Outcast Cape Town*. Berkeley and Los Angeles: University of California Press.

Westover, J. and Collins, G. 1987: Perceived crowding in recreation settings. *Leisure Sciences* 9, 113–127.

Whitt, J. A. 1987: Mozart in the metropolis. *Urban Affairs Quarterly* 12, 15–36.

Williams, C. H. 1998: Room to talk in a house of faith: on language and religion. In Graham, B. (ed.), *Modern Europe: place, culture, identity*. London: Arnold, 186–209.

Williams, R. H. 1996: *European Union spatial policy and planning*. London: PCP.

Winchester, H. P. M., McGuirk, P. M. and Dunn, K. M. 1996: Constructing places for the market: the case of Newcastle, NSW. *International Journal of Heritage Studies* 2, 41–58.

Withers, C. W. J. 1995: How Scotland came to know itself: geography, national identity and the making of a nation, 1680–1790. *Journal of Historical Geography* 21, 371–97.

Woolf, S. 1996: Introduction. In Woolf, S. (ed.), *Nationalism in Europe, 1815 to the present: a reader*. London: Routledge, 1–39.

Worden, N. 1996: Contested heritage at the Cape Town waterfront. *International Journal of Heritage Studies* 2, 59–75.

Worden, N. (1997): Contesting heritage in a South African City: Cape Town. In Shaw, B. J. and Jones, R. (eds), *Contested urban heritage: voices from the periphery*. Aldershot: Ashgate, 31–61.

Wright, P. 1985: *On living in an old country: the national pasts in contemporary Britain*. London: Verso.

Wynne, D. 1992: *The culture industry: the arts in urban regeneration.* Aldershot: Avebury.

Yeoh, B. S. A. 1996: Street-naming and nation-building: toponymic inscriptions of nationhood in Singapore. *Area* 28, 298–307.

Yeoh, B. S. A. 1999: Historical geographies of the colonised world. In Graham, B. and Nash, C. (eds), *Modern historical geographies.* Harlow: Prentice Hall, 146–66.

Zetterholm, S. 1994: *National cultures and European integration.* Oxford: Oxford University Press.

Index

Printed in the United States
135591LV00002B/57/A